Collected Poems R. N. Currey

Collected Poems R. N. Currey

David Philip   CAPE TOWN
James Currey   OXFORD

James Currey Ltd
73 Botley Road
Oxford
OX2 0BS

David Philip Publishers (Pty) Ltd
PO Box 23408
Claremont 7735
Cape Town

British Library Cataloguing in Publication Data applied for

ISBN 0-85255-573-3

Typeset by Katherine Kirkwood at Long House, Cumbria
in 10/12 Poliphilus and Blado Italic
the typeface used by Lynton Lamb,
typographer and friend of R.N. Currey
in the Oxford University Press edition of *Formal Spring*.
Printed and bound in Great Britain
by Antony Rowe Ltd, Chippenham, Wiltshire

Contents

Contents

Contents

VI *Christmas & Family Verses*   149

Contents

Contents

Acknowledgements

During this last decade, since the death of my wife Stella and my severe impairment of sight, I have had so much help from so many people, that I hope I may be excused for mentioning only a few of those who have been able to help me most.

My thanks go to Jane Hadcock, who has helped me as an editor with a close understanding of my writing that has added enormously to the pleasure I have had in working on this book. Her husband Jerry Hadcock arranged for two Colchester Royal Grammar School pupils, Nicholas Alexander and Matthew Sparrow, to come in and help me sort out my papers.

I owe special thanks to my long-standing friends Tony Locke and George Young who have given me valuable help with the revision of verse translations. Joy Harman has been a regular consultant on my South African poems and Marguerite Wood has been a constant support over the years, recently giving me substantial help with the accuracy and arrangement of the American verses. Gwenneth Jeffries, an old friend, helped especially with difficult typing.

I am particularly indebted to Ronald Blythe for taking so much trouble to write such a generous Introduction. I have had a happy literary association with him for some fifty years.

I am grateful to Mike Kirkwood for the series of discussions we had over several days leading to his perceptive study of my South African and war verse. And I thank his wife Katherine who showed great skill and patience in typesetting a manuscript which presented special difficulties in arrangement and rearrangement.

J. F. Elam, when headmaster of the Colchester Royal Grammar School, made it possible for me to do regular broadcasting for the BBC and to pay visits to South Africa and the United States. Jack and Joan Elam remained life-time friends.

Without the generous support of friends, neighbours and the medical profession, I would not have been able to get on with this project at all. I feel particularly grateful to the following and know that I must have forgotten names of people important to me: Jill and Simon Blaxill, Fab and Natasha Casale, Guido Casale, Dorothy Churchill, Geoffrey and Jennifer Churchman, Michael and Michelle Connell, Dr Nicholas Dixon, Marion Eadie, the Edwards brothers, Lorraine Evans, Jonathan and Alison Ewebank, Stuart and Valentine Francis, Jan Goodger, Pam Howatt, Dr Richard Hudson, Robert and Penny Jacklin, Dr Peter and Doreen Kennedy, Alison Koziarski, Peter and Margaret North, Susan Olaf, Sister Rosemary Stone, Lorraine Tucker, Dr Kim Wilbraham and Paul Wright.

My son James and his wife Clare stand out as those without whom this project would not have begun or been carried through, while Andrew and his wife Elspeth have given me constant help and support over the years.

Introduction
Ronald Blythe

In 'In Memoriam: Roy Campbell' (p. 3), a poem which R. N. Currey later came to see as an important part of his entrance as a South African poet, he speaks of this friend as a surfer on turbulent waters who is able to retain his faith and true identity whilst being thrown this way and that by powerful forces. Currey himself has lived through nearly the whole of the twentieth century and has witnessed upheaval in three continents but has kept an unshaken voice. This complete opus of his poetry shows how distinctively he has held his own. Although there are echoes of an empire voice and a commonwealth voice, it is a quintessentially English voice which predominates. The voice speaks with a Iyrical clarity through and across great swathes of recent history. It needed this collected edition to reveal its range and its consistency. The work of many writers falls into periods and phases, and tellingly so, but Ralph Currey's falls into countries, South Africa, India and Britain, though with no or little alteration or abandonment of his earliest ideals. He reminds one of William Hazlitt sitting above the pass in Wales on his twenty-first birthday and promising himself that he would never give up what he at that moment held dear. In his case it meant all kinds of ethical and political battles ahead. In Ralph Currey's case it was simply that he could never be other than he was, and thus we have him, a long-lived and yet youthful poet who has held on to his early candour all his days.

At the beginning an Oxford friend, Francis House, thought that Currey wrote like Thomas Hardy, seeing perhaps a similar fertility and observation. The huge difference between Currey and so many of his contemporaries, of course, was his lack of strict boundaries. He was born in Mafeking in 1907 during the heyday of empire, was stationed in India in the forties just before – and no one at that moment would have thought it possible – the end of empire, and also worked quietly as a schoolmaster for forty years at Colchester. One would have expected his life and poetry to be heavily marked out by these times and places, and so to some extent they are. Yet they remain all one. Those close to him know that the house he has lived in since the thirties is only two Victorian streets away from that in which Wavell was born in the 1870s, and that Roman soldiers lie buried under his garden wall; this romantic juxtaposition could be a metaphor of Currey's own existence. But all that he unselfconsciously says is that he was once a gunner, though one who recorded what happens to men in war. Or to men in love. Or to men and women anywhere.

These *Collected Poems* are astonishing in their coverage of private and public experience, in their ability to reveal the secret self present at certain events in history, in their amusement and delight and forgiveness, and in their skill. A revelation is explained in the dictionary as 'a striking disclosure of something previously unknown or not realised', and although Ralph Currey's work has been widely read and often anthologized for half a century, its full import has certainly not been realized. In this it is no different from the work of other poets who are known chiefly by the same pieces in a score of anthologies. How everything alters with the complete text! A useful way to read Currey would be alongside twentieth-century English history. The right way is to read him as a unique witness to his own existence wherever it happened to be. So many writers from his background and years would have shown signs of once being swayed or repelled by passing doctrines, from fascism to apartheid, but what Currey shows is a kind of sanity of the imagination. Language enchants him.

Currey's father was a Wesleyan Methodist minister who left England to serve as a chaplain during the Boer War. His mother's family had been in South Africa since 1849. A Devon ancestor had built church organs. Currey was to collect and publish the argumentative letters and journalism of his great-grandfather Thomas Phipson who became Sheriff of Natal and who scanned the southern skies for the transit of Venus. His grandfather, the hero of *Vinnicombe's Trek*, had built churches for Dutch Reformed congregations in the Transvaal. Currey himself was to benefit from the Methodist practice of making their ministers move on every three years. Thus he journeyed from Mafeking to Johannesburg and then to Boksburg and Ermelo before, at thirteen, being sent away to Kingswood School, Bath, carrying with him invaluable sights and sounds. The latter may not have been thought at the time an asset where conventional English education was concerned, but his background played a large part in the making of the poet. He carried around with him a kind of bright coinage from his peripatetic South African childhood whose value was both incalculable and disturbing. Boksburg, full of Cornish miners and young men riding around wearing bandoliers. Ermelo, where they taught him history from the Dutch angle, where he had his first ride in a car, where every boy went to school bare-foot. And then to Jamaica, where his father was appointed Methodist synod representative to oversee the whole Caribbean, where some of his white clergy colleagues were wed to black wives – and where Currey was taught to be a good horseman.

It was during these formative years that landscape after landscape was offered to Currey to make what he could of them in time to come. From the veld to the Jamaican mountains, from Somerset to Carlisle. Writers receive dual educations which run alongside each other, that given conventionally and that given to themselves. There was Kingswood School and Wadham College. There was lying in a darkened room at school with pink-eye, reconstructing Shelley's 'To a Skylark' from memory. There was discovering his first literary friends at Oxford. In 1943, staring from a troopship at Durban, whatever feeling of displacement he may have experienced, vanished. He distantly recognised what 'used to be/My childhood, now it's my maturity' ('Durban Revisited 1943', p. 3). At that moment on the crowded deck he saw that as a poet he stood both within and without Britain and its empire, a position which not only gave him moral authority but an unusual clarity, both of which were served with the kind of unclouded language used by later poets such as Derek Walcott. This was the first poem by Currey to be recognised in an anthology by the South African writer Roy Macnab. In *The Africa We Knew* (pp. 1–29) Currey has to deal with epic matters, with huge journeys and great courage, but also with the wonderfully remembered minutiae of mainly rural life. Many of these poems contain the simple purity of domestic interiors by Dutch painters. Perhaps his entire experience and understanding of South Africa is epitomised in 'Lost World', written to his mother on her death in 1959. She was an artist in the making:

> At seventeen she put up her hair
> And trippled down in her riding-habit
> To pass the barbed-wire picket of the new
> Camp for burger families – innocent still
> Of every overtone but improvisation. ('Lost World', p. 6)

The girl of English roots in one of the first of the twentieth century's concentration camps, Edith Vinnicombe stares out challengingly from this tribute as those who cannot take sides always do.

The poems which make up *Tiresias* (pp. 31–65), the collection which Currey published in 1940, although including the oracular 'Now That the War is Here' (p. 64), were celebrations of the present. In 1932 he had married Stella Martin, the daughter of J. P. Martin whose 'Uncle' stories would become a popular addition to the children's book-list in the 1960s. Stella herself wrote plays and novels. She and Ralph had met as children at Johannesburg. He thought that *Tiresias* was about 'my learning to write' but what this book reveals is the private happiness of a young family and the great question addressed to Tiresias,

> Must always blood be spilt, blood spilt in rivers,
> To irrigate a harvest of gold words?...
>
> Must Chinese cities be ploughed into wet fields
> To add a pagoda-storey to their fame?
> Must Western cities be bombed to broken shells
> With troglodyte populations, that the hearts
> Of future poets beat faster? Has Guernica,
> Like Passchendaele, been razed to win a name? ('To Tiresias', p. 65)

'Yes' to all these questions reply the gold speakers.

Currey had taught at Colchester Royal Grammar School for seven years before, in 1941, being called up into the Signals. Having longed for peace until the eleventh hour, he became one of the most memorable of all World War II's soldier voices, a poet who spoke accurately about fighting with a brilliant use of the common language of engagement. When T. S. Eliot read *This Other Planet* (pp. 67–101) he told Currey that it was 'the best war poetry in the correct sense of the term that I have seen in these past six years'. Whilst observing his pupils on the rifle range he had written the first of these 'correct' war poems, with its echoes of Auden, and heralding of Keith Douglas. In 'Boy with a Rifle' (p. 78) he dwells on the exquisitely terrible relationship between man and gun. Gradually and truthfully the young schoolmaster advances from gun drill to gun war, and now no longer private rifles, but heavy guns. The sonnet sequence 'Unseen Fire' (pp. 94–5), is among the finest statements of the last war, and unforgettable. Firing-line words which for authenticity cancel all other fighting words.

> We chant our ritual words; beyond the phones
> A ghost repeats the orders to the guns:
> One Fire ... Two Fire ... ghosts answer: the guns roar
> Abruptly; and an aircraft waging war
> Inhumanly from nearly five miles height
> Meets our bouquet of death – and turns sharp right. ('Unseen Fire,' p. 94)

It is what Eliot acknowledged, this ability of Currey to say what really occurred when the soldier, at the end of a telephone, chants, 'One Fire …'. Because of his experience in radar he was made especially conscious of modern warfare being fought from a distance. This was in contrast to Keith Douglas who still saw his enemy through his gun sights.

Currey's Indian experience began when he was sent to Karachi as an artillery officer in 1943, in charge of South Indian gunners with whom he went on active service to the Burmese frontier. One of the most important periods in his life started when he was transferred to the Education Corps and sent to Belgaum. He and R. V. Gibson put together an anthology by members of the forces, *Poems from India*, based on the submissions for the Viceroy's first verse competition. The poet-Viceroy himself, Archibald Wavell, had in 1944 published the well-loved anthology, *Other Men's Flowers*. In *Poems from India*, first published in Bombay the following year, and then back home in London, the impact made by the legendary sub-continent on the imaginations of countless servicemen created its own special poetry. They had been brought up to regard India as Britain's most glorious and most controversial possession, and now they were there. Unlike most of them, Currey had been widely-travelled all his young life and when, on the eve of self-rule, he wrote *Indian Landscape* (pp. 103–39), the wonder and emphasis were different. These glittering poems belong to the pre-popular travel universe when hard-to-reach places took one's breath away, and were the subject of long letters. India enriched Currey's language. He uses the walls of a dam as a metaphor for the fragile future of this gorgeous land. He sees 'a world propped up/By boards that curve and strain' ('Dam', p. 123), the lovely dancers and the living skeletons, the Taj Mahal as 'the world's most hackneyed metaphor' and would like everything said and pictured of it destroyed so that every new visitor will be forced to 'discover/This beauty for yourself, as in a lover' ('At Agra', p. 130). *Indian Landscape* ends with a reminder of what Hiroshima and Nagasaki were like in the time of Genji 'In those yet-undevastated islands' ('A New Tale of Genji', p. 139).

As with writers everywhere, Currey had to decide early on whether to be an observer or a participant. Each has his legitimate position. By way of an apologia for the direction which he chose, Currey said:

> I was a poet and I had to go
> Into the trade I did not wish to learn;
> I wanted a corner table from which to watch
> Man's foolish courage, generous egotism.
> I did not wish to cross the dangerous chasm
> Between the eye and the heart … ('I Was a Poet', p. 145)

But he did, of course, bridging it successfully though often with pain and difficulty. And as well as eye and heart, there was learning in the ancient sense which gives access via translation to almost anywhere one would like to go. Back teaching in Colchester, Currey returned to his interest in Europe and collected his verse translations of French Renaissance poetry in *Formal Spring*. The Methodist minister's son who in the Deccan contrasted 'the rabble of competing gods' ('Ajanta II', p. 124) with the serenity of Buddha, now enters the courts of the Virgin Mary and Prince Jesus, of Romance and playfulness, knowing his way about, right down to where Rimbaud sails his 'Mad Boat'.

Beneath such headings as 'Christmas Verses' (pp. 149–66) and 'People and Places' (pp. 167–88), Currey's 'domestic' poems were more than sufficient to make him the poet of the Suffolk-Essex border, or a children's writer of genius, or a comic commentator on the local scene of the kind who had witnessed no other. More recently, 'Flashback to America' (pp. 189–202) took him to the American North-West. It is rare to find such a wandering and such a stay-at-home vision locked together, and rare for a reader to be able to range so far and wide in one poet's world.

The Heart of Exile
A South African Reading of the Poems of R. N. Currey
Mike Kirkwood

R. N. Currey (b. 14 December 1907) entered the new millennium in the house in Colchester where he has lived for more than 60 years, and within hailing distance of Colchester Grammar School, where he taught before and after the war, and is still a remembered presence decades after his retirement. Although he wrote that 'Man's roots are not in earth', he may seem embedded in a part of England where so many layers of the past have sedimented. Rooting around at the bottom of his garden in 1996, archaeologists came upon the stony face of the mercenary Longinus Sdapeze (floreat AD 50) and were able to restore this chip of identity, missing for a millennium or two, to the unbowed head of that impetuous Duplicarius Thracian cavalryman, whose richly armoured body and capering steed had been unearthed not far away in 1928.

Disjunctures, rather than continuities, reveal themselves at the core of this poet's work. Perhaps he did not seek this. There is evidence, in his technique as much as in his subjects, of a more consistent attempt at lyrics that are modest and measured, in which sound and sense elicit consummations that are as intricately implicit in their originating theme. The most 'English' of his poems work in this highly crafted, decorous way, and in these flights he reminds us that he began to write when English was an imperial literature as well as the international language that it remains. He reminds us that figures as outlandish, in their different ways, as Kipling, Conrad and Eliot were drawn to the insular heart of the Empire, and ended more English than their readers. This serener and often playful side shows up often enough to make the light verse – much of it written to celebrate family legends and occasions – assimilable as a stream that flows from the same genial source. But the poems that make R. N. Currey a significant twentieth-century poet carry a different charge. All address a theme that arises somewhere in the jumbled coordinates of our bewildering tornado of a century. Sometimes this theme stalks the personal experience of the man himself, seeming to single him out in the terrifying, random way that the madness of the storm may. At other times it finds emotional analogies in the poet's experience, so that his own unease reveals a more universal uncertainty.

This book begins with an ironic salute. The South Africa that William Plomer knew was a place visited as a young man, a time that yielded such strangely blended fruit as that lapidary poem (see p. 3); a novel (*Turbott Wolfe*) that managed to shake the complacency of a country where moral seismic charts are drawn in blood not ink; and his unlikely friendship with the turbulent Roy Campbell. Currey would meet both writers later: Campbell would claim him as a younger South African to be encouraged and (ebulliently) bullied; Plomer is remembered at the distance of a crowded room, folded within an Englishness that was different again. The Africa that Plomer and Campbell knew best (and soon retreated from) was South Africa in the very formative decade of the 1920s, when the country's political arenas, and occasionally its streets and segregated public spaces, began to be contested by the social forces that would soon make it, in Campbell's derisory couplet,

… renowned both far and wide
For politics, and little else beside

– black nationalism and proto-unionism, Afrikaner *volkskapitalisme*, ethnic rivalries that apartheid would attempt to straitjacket (and thus inflame and perpetuate), and (by the 1960s) a rampant suburban materialism that could make visiting Europeans (and even Americans) gasp. This South African melting pot was *not* the Africa R. N. Currey knew (and hence the irony of his salute, in passing at a crossroads as it were, to Plomer and Campbell). As the 1920s got under way he was sailing irrevocably away from his South African childhood. Public school (Kingswood, Bath) and Oxford (Wadham College), marriage and a war would make him English. Only then would South Africa (imagine a well-hidden long-range marksman here, if you will, and the war-remembering games of Boer and Briton that filled his childhood) claim him as its own. The first occasion was a chance supplied by an in-transit visit during the war. Then there were more deliberate excursions in 1960 (to receive the South African Poetry Prize) and in 1982; on both occasions he was accompanied by his wife, the novelist Stella Martin Currey who was also born in South Africa. But essentially the surfacing of a South African identity was an event that occurred, with seismic preludes and consequences, in his imagination.

The poems that open this book are not juvenilia. Nor are they the work of an apprentice, learning his craft and finding his voice. They are written after the poet has made a promising debut in the quintessentially English slim volume *Tiresias*, and gone on to write, in the war years, much of the mature work by which his English readers know him best. Not a setting forth, then, nor yet an arrival – and yet these poems stake out a poetic identity, opening up that 'long experience from [a] starting place' which he celebrates in a memorial poem for his mother. That poem contains another ironic salute at the crossroads, he the mother/midwife of her death in three wonderfully concentrated lines that are among his finest:

> I was her first, and with her at the last,
> The roles reversed, but my help helpless
> To halt or ease her difficult passage.
> ('Lost World', p. 6)

There is another of these crossroads in the poem that compares his own present memory of Christmas as a boy with his father's retrospect, inlaid in his own. Father and son look different ways in spatial terms, though time has curved the opposition into a unity. No winged chariot, exactly, but a pony 'lured … with lumps of sugar' and 'coaxed into his creaking cat's cradle of leather' hurries

> My father, all that tawny homeward run,
> Remembering snow as I remember sun.
> ('Remembering Snow', p. 8)

If we wonder why these displacements and polarities abound, we can answer that it's mainly a North–South, adult–child thing, the spatial and temporal accidents that define the not-unusual life of a poet born into a colonial society, and thus into a dual identity. The sonnet 'Man's Roots', however, may set our heads spinning again. It is paired in this book – not by active design in the making of the two poems, but aptly enough – with another sonnet ('South African', p. 71) that evokes the particular, place-inscribed identity whereas 'Man's Roots' subjects the entire notion of identity to metaphysical scrutiny (the poetic method, too, recalls the Metaphysicals, particularly Herbert). At one level the argument of this sonnet is plain enough:

man is a spiritual creature; his sense impressions draw him towards recognitions – religious, social, political ('Even the peasant' is drawn 'To church, or pub, or war with foreign powers') – that are 'not in earth'. Yet few readers would regard this as a sufficient reading of the poem.

It's not a simple upending, that's the trouble. A poem that repeatedly brings gravitational metaphors into play ends by spinning on its own axis, as it were: it makes a full turn, rather than the half-turn that inverts the roots. The subversion begins as early as the first quatrain, when trees and flowers are not as stolid as they should be, although they 'stand in one place'. Compare the effect of 'the intimate atmospheres/Blown through their leaves' with what happens in Wordsworth's poem when he famously tunes the Newtonian organ:

> No motion has she now, no force;
> She neither hears nor sees;
> Rolled round in earth's diurnal course
> With rocks, and stones, and trees.

If we grant that 'intimate atmospheres' circulate at a pedagogically correct distance from 'remoter spheres', it is also true that they engage us in the heretical thought that trees may not be as simply rooted as we seem to have been told they are: some communication appears to be taking place at close quarters, suggesting a rapport within space that is at odds with the mechanical model that Wordsworth has displayed (his debt to Newton emphatic in the words 'motion' and 'force', but especially in the relentless vibration of the metric scheme). Looked at in another way, what the poem does involves taking over Wordsworth's idea of nature as a moral educator, but understanding it in terms of a different model of the universe.

The next quatrain completes the subversion by undoing the certainty of the poem's opening precept from the other side of the proposition. Not only are objects rooted in earth displaying a disturbing degree of sentience; it would appear that man shows a distinct, and equally heretical, tendency to root in earth. In 'growing showers' we find him 'solid in his furrow', and the gravitational viscosity as he 'tears' himself free is palpable as well as comical.

The sestet compounds and sustains these contradictions, screwing up the tension: the spirit values have an instinctive, bodily force, are as essential to survival: these insensible couriers of sentience are indeed 'vital *tissues*'. The contradictions cannot be resolved within a dualistic schema, Lockeian or Cartesian. If the poem dramatically asserts the mixed nature of man, perhaps it also nudges us in the philosophical direction pioneered by Teillard de Chardin and others, discerning the elements of consciousness in the communication systems that begin to approach a 'critical mass' of consciousness in tiny organisms, and thus invoking a 'non-local' universe 'augured' by Blake's riposte to Newton:

> To see a World in a Grain of Sand
> And a Heaven in a Wild Flower,
> Hold Infinity in the palm of your hand
> And Eternity in an hour.

Only in some such development of thought, rooting consciousness itself in material life (God-given or otherwise) can man's roots be seen to be *of* yet not *in* earth.

As a meditation on identity deriving from place the poem has particular force in the case of this identity being transferable once imprinted, or realized as a set of moral/imaginative values. In other words it is a meditation we might expect to issue from a poet who confirms in mid-life, and at the peak of his powers, the existence of an underlying, earlier, *other* identity. It is a charac-teristic of R. N. Currey's work that this *alter ego* of childhood is not a honey-guide, luring him into a sunny world of *veld* and *vlei* and *suikerbossie* nostalgia. It is true that his 'early mythology' (p. 11), his 'legend' and 'lost world' (p. 6) sometimes shines with the freshness of a world never subjected to the day-to-day banalities of a passage through adolescence (Yeats's 'ignominies of growing up'). It is also true that his deliberate returns to the South Africa of full-blown apartheid reveal a sharper sense of Afrikaner success in revising the outcome of the Anglo-Boer war than of the wider 'Landscape of Violence' (p. 8) that had changed the meaning of 'race relations'. (He knew, of course, that 'racial attitudes, like snakes,/Coil above children as they play', just as he remembered 'the fifth-column colloquy round the well/Where the servants ate their meals': but he had left the country before the venom entered the nervous system, before the well was poisoned.)

What made his experience of psychic exile or colonial ambiguity into what he once called 'tensions of the sort that produce poetry' is, perhaps, his recognition that somewhere in his century, somewhere between childhood and maturity, a slippage had occurred that made his condition an everyday affair, that

> In the great Ocean of London, unprovided Crusoes
> On tiny, Friday-less islands wait day by day
> By aspidistra palms for friendly ships ...
> ('Outer Seas', p. 69)

Here we must anticipate that perception of the planet as 'other' which we have yet to encounter, but which was already behind the poet when he turned again to 'the Africa we knew'. We shall then be invoking this phenomenon in the context of that 'war poetry in the correct sense of the term' for which T. S. Eliot praised him so highly. Let us notice in passing, though, that a process epitomized by the mode of warfare in which he engaged was also evident to him in so quotidian a matter (heightened of course by the stress of wartime partings) as a telephone call:

> A man once lived in a village and was a part
> Of field and tree, but now his living heart
> Passes its pulses through long miles of wire
> To those who are the sum of his desire –
> For limited instants, as it were a ration
> Of love translated into speech vibration.
> ('Telephone Box', p. 85)

The 'hollowing out' or 'virtualization' of experience which is the hallmark of the twentieth century when viewed from its end has been an ongoing process. It has been recognized in different ways at different times and in different places: as existential *angst*, as alienation, as the loss of birthright by the colonized, as the commoditization of production, as the subordination of nature and women's lives by a patriarchal, technologically driven world system. R. N.

Currey's poetry registers this process from the perspective of what was in many ways a charmed individual life, protected from and outliving the worst ravages of a century that, 'destroyed so many'. Perhaps his very security sharpened this poet's empathy with his age into sensitivity to a ubiquitous flaw in the triumphant materialism of what has also been called 'America's century', and also in the apparent solidity of our own lives and identities: a tendency to slip or vanish, to be undone by danger from afar, to turn out to be no more than a tantalizing illusion.

In the South African poems that we are considering here this awareness takes many forms. Listening to his memories of Durban – where he and I, not to mention Roy Campbell and Ferdinand Pessoa, or Douglas Livingstone – waited as boys for 'Long rollers, horned like bulls' – I have been aware of the force of his closing lines in 'Durban Revisited', with their wry admission of how much may stand between us and the reassurance of our history, everything that has made us what we are:

> Once more between me and this lovely land
> There stands a barrier; it used to be
> My childhood, now it's my maturity.

In 'Rand Mine' (p. 72) the flaw is in the potentially entombing rock of the 'deep levels', in the distorted scales and pressures of relentlessly continuous technological violence, and most particularly in the perversion of communication into panic and fear, until everything reduces to the difference between the 'warning jabber' and the bursting note. It is hard to believe that Currey could have written this poem before his experience at first hand of long-range gunnery (see especially lines 12–20): 'Rand Mine' establishes, in the tissue of its imagery, a connection between the vitiation of humanity in twentieth-century warfare and a similar process within the belly of the apartheid beast. Of course it does this without addressing the political theme directly at all, and his reference to 'mine-boys' might be taken by some readers as evidence of the poet's political naïvète (Peter Abrahams's *Mine Boy*, a novel banned by the apartheid government, is a contemporary of 'Rand Mine'). But few South Africans, and even fewer Witwatersrand residents, would fail to recognize the wider social dimensions of the tension and claustrophobia the poem invokes.

It is, of course, just this connection with his roots – a buried South African identity sustained perilously at long range, yet no less vital for that – that we have been probing in the context of the South African poems. And what we have also noticed is that this 'virtualization' is often present in the poet's subject matter as well as in his dilemma as a poet. Perhaps this is the affinity that allows him to connect almost instinctively with themes that another poet might grapple with more deliberately but less successfully. To take a specific example from 'Rand Mine', we are nowhere informed that migrant workers from all over Southern Africa provided the workforce on a typical South African mine of the period; that these uprooted men were often further alienated by divide-and-rule ethnic manipulation; that severe and violent 'faction fights' were as much a feature of life on the mine as the frequent and deadly rockfalls and other accidents. Yet anyone who is even vaguely aware of these things will find that they are vividly brought to mind by the opening lines of 'Rand Mine':

> The walls jabber.

They whisper, chatter, argue,
Then jabber.
This is eight thousand feet down,
Two thousand feet below sea-level;
It's the pressure that makes them jabber –
As it does men sometimes,
Shriek, and then jabber, jabber.

There is a curious symmetry, as in the reversal of the telescope, between R. N. Currey's unerring long-range quarrying of his South African roots and the

Calculations made
For this specific exiled latitude

by which his great-grandfather Thomas Phipson

… set his glass,
His Dollond, gently polishing the lens,
Outside his house near Pietermaritzburg

in order to observe the transit of Venus in 1874 ('On That June Day', p. 4). Or, on another astronomical occasion, wondered how an eclipse (from our perspective) of the moon might be perceived (from their vantage point) by 'Lunarians – if such there be' (p. 5). These light and playful poems, and numerous others that reveal the great-grandson's own star-gazing habit, will always be read affectionately by his family (great-grandchildren now there be); the whimsy, one may reflect, also has a bearing on the deeper surveys of a poet always, as Herbert Read said, so 'exact in observation'.

The North African poems belong to a later period again and form a distinct set, unified by imperious, mesmeric cadences, 'absolute sun and shade' fortified by the colours of sunset and morning, and dramatic monologues in the manner of Browning. The poet allows us to infiltrate these rather grand and public poems that command and intimidate (Ozymandias is never too far away!) by means of a secret passage enclosed in the poem 'Fez' (p. 27). The poem leads us through

Mystery beyond mystery, a mediaeval
Craftman's nest of boxes within boxes;

all the way to

… shrill as a disciplined aviary
The spurting Koran-chorus of a school.
And then the perfumers', with tiny drops
On wrists and handkerchiefs, and birdlike cries;
And such a daze of scents in my head,

And in the middle of that maze a mosque
Closed to me as a Christian – and perhaps
Holding the brilliant throbbing plumage
Of a bird I caught as a child.

Our own surprise is as great here as that of the poet whom we have accompanied on this pilgrimage through the old city to an unexpected source. The revelation of an inner dimension, a quest within the trance-like submission to alien surfaces and sense impressions, is a very rare moment in this sequence of poems. Its gift to us is a way of understanding the creative tension that binds the sequence as a whole. Once again the hold-fast spring is the distance between the imaginer and the imagined, the buried or 'lost' identity, the sweet bird of youth that lies at the heart of all that seems most alien and closed to the traveller on his quest.

The central theme of the North African poems is empire – or empires – and the restlessness that is the *primum mobile* of each conqueror and also of the history that all the layered empires of the region comprise. These are the historical equivalents of the 'mystery on mystery', the nested boxes that make up the old quarter in Fez. And at the heart of the mystery, the mystery of mysteries, is a situation not so unlike the poet's own search for an image. If the technique sometimes suggests Browning, the imaginative unity of these poems recalls no one more than Yeats, in his most 'world historical' mood. Meditations on the meaning of Islam are inevitably at the centre of the imperial theme in this setting, and at the centre of these meditations are 'tongues of faith' that 'argued city walls from uncut stone' ('Volubilis I', p. 25), 'words of learning riding every ocean' ('Tower of Hassan, Rabat', p. 26),

... spells to harden
Our hearts to courage, bodies to desire;
                    ('Marrakech', p. 24)

– the tension between the ruling idea and the physical world it calls into being or submits to discipline.

If at times these poems seem to invoke the 'pride of power' ('Tower of Hassan, Rabat', p. 26), a desire

... to feel the stream of creation
Move right through me – to life or to death.
                    ('African Sultan', p. 28)

what they celebrate most vividly is the tension that sustains all civilizations, the suspension between the act of imagination and its object – even as it baffles and witholds consummation or a state of grace. The most commanding figures in the sequence – Marshal Lyautey in the poem of that name (p. 23) and Moulay Ismail in 'African Sultan' – may intimidate us, but the poet also allows us to see their vulnerability, along with our own, and the fragility of their 'huge stone albums' ('Volubilis I', p. 25) alongside the snapshots of our less expansive desires – 'the ball of a foot ... the flare of a hem' – all 'in time's mosaic' and the 'fortuitous glint of the sun' ('Volubilis II', p. 26).

The name of blind old *Tiresias* actually heralds the poems of R. N. Currey's youth, those in which he is most serenely English. In the best of these he is able to dip his everyday subjects into glazes that work the various chemistries of classical mythology ('Jersey Cattle', p. 44), evolutionary prehistory ('Morning Over Purley', p. 44) or Anglo-Saxon tribalism ('Reconquest', p. 45), while in 'Bicycles' (p. 45) the aspic of an exact moment when

> ... disembodied voices cry
> Into brief candle-life, snuffed instantly

delivers the

> ... whispering ghost
> Of a lost regiment

– the conjuror's pass in time perfectly synchronized with the returning sweep 'on Sunday nights' of the massed bands of cyclists first heard

> In the morning early ...
> In twos and threes....

As an opening gambit 'To His Jester' (subtitled 'A poet to his subconscious mind', p. 33) prepares us for nothing so much, perhaps, as the poet's delight in the subversion of the surface, the reworking of the elements of a familiar subject in a way that startles or surprises us. If 'Parish Church' (p. 38) is one of the most traditional of the subjects to be treated in this way, 'Pelican, St James's Park' (p. 55) is the purest example of a playful 're-make', in which the sheer liveliness of the task in hand – turning pelican to parson – absorbs and informs every stiff, hard-consonantal twist and turn of a mimetic tour-de-force. As early as the end of the first stanza, 'like' has indeed given place to 'is':

> This lank, untidy, intellectual-browed,
> Knobble-kneed, awkward bird,
> With his absent-minded glance
> Of remote benevolence,
> Is a country clergyman.

One can see – and hear – why this is the poem Dylan Thomas liked well enough to memorize and, on a memorable occasion, recite to its author on a traffic island.

Tiresias closes with poems that register the lead-up to and the onset of war. In this period of shifting alliances, international gang warfare and machinations to perfect the technology of murder, the poet begins to realize his own *rapprochement*, the alignment of imagination and technique that will bring his poetic orientation into connection with what we begin to recognize as his most characteristic and profound themes. 'Tidying a Garden' (p. 59), one of the poems that follow 'Pelican, St James's Park', briefly holds the private and public worlds at arm's length by dint of a similarly sustained and witty translation of one thing into another:

> Scrape trunk-roads, trim verges,
> Align undisciplined hedges
> On the street-frontier — I spend a
> Trifle here on propaganda!

As Spain and Guernica strike home, however, these oppositions and inversions – tools of the jester's trade – begin to demonstrate a profounder, less manageable recognition. Instead of the ironic juggling of the private and the public, the human heart and the technological killing machine are forced together, to the relentless rhythms of 'Tap-Dance' (p. 61) and 'Vaya Por Usted' (p. 62), into terrible couplings such as 'Lewis gun and black faldilla' or the mating of the passion of the bullfighter with the violent narcissism of the fascist:

> In this wide, stony amphitheatre
> Curved horns uplifted to the terrible sky
> Where the *cuadrilla* dance, sway, posture,
> Taunt and withdraw, and with parvenu swagger –
> Rattle of machine-guns the heart's terror! –
> Administer death ....

The 'Rumour of War' (p. 63) clarifies, for this poet, the gulf that is opening beween the vast scale of the coming conflict and the shrinking ambit, for ordinary people no longer armed with the crusading faith of the fanatic, of personal emotions:

> The brave illusion is sped,
> Our creed is only
> In life, and when lover is dead
> The heart is lonely.

'Modern Warfare' (p. 63) is sustained by the identification of this as a gulf between ordinary soldiers who

> Obey obscure orders in obscurity,
> Fight without knowledge

and their new, worshipped, superman totalitarian leaders.

Finally there is the entry, in 'Now That the War is Here' (p. 64) and 'Tiresias' (p. 65), of the moral territory that his war poetry will explore. Now soldiers are required by their trade to learn, beyond valour and prowess, 'high skill in homicide', to become

> ... so skilful at killing that every village,
> City, and town should win a deathless name;
> But who shall live to utter it?

They remain, despite these morally damaging demands, tied to a moral humanity. Their roots, perhaps, 'are not in earth', but in a sort of barren substitute, which is nevertheless all they have. The images that develop such metaphysical complexity in 'Man's Roots' ('he is drawn/By vital tissues, dying if they crack') are intriguingly glimpsed in these lines from 'Now That the War Is Here':

> These stunted sandbag virtues by whuch we live –
> For men must live by virtues, even when
> Bombing the helpless innocents; even hearts
> Pruned to the stump sprout virtues or else die!

Tiresias, among its lightest, most ephemeral offerings, includes a suite of star-naming lyrics. Their presence is turned to considerable effect in the 'Epilogue' (p. 64). In what is at once the jester's last fling and a shadowing of innocence, the spreading war ascends 'the darkened sky' and

> Parched Sagittarius
> With his machine-gun crew
> Prays that Aquarius
> Will get his transports through.

Stargazing was soon to shed the last vestige of genteel parody, becoming the new warfare in earnest.

'Exile' is the concept at the centre of R. N. Currey's war poetry. We have seen how the word acquires a further dimension when the poet's South African identity, planted in childhood, breaks through in the years of his maturity. We have also allowed the possibility that the question of identity had arisen for the poet at a level at once more fundamental (psychic exile) and meta- physical (relation between consciousness and the physical world) than mere national affiliation. It may not surprise us to find that the notion of 'exile' is as slippery as we have found the idea of 'roots' to be. It has lateral play, veering about as much on the horizontal axis as 'roots' on the vertical one. This play is not of a jesting, paradoxical kind, as fond as the younger poet of the *Tiresias* poems was of that sort of thing. Instead, it seems to be rooted, to use that other dangerous word, in the experience of the poet and his world. This is why we may ask whether the heart of exile does not lie in the exile of the heart.

While the opening line of This Other Planet (p. 69) glosses this central idea as 'Absolute exile to the outer seas' – a Roman phrase that will return remorselessly throughout the poems that follow, sometimes abbreviated in the place name Ultima Thule – it is not long before we have to check our compasses:

> Soldiers in trains with their unwieldy kits,
> Airmen with knapsacks and attaché cases
> In telephone-booths and post-offices, all the places
> That link up with their life as once they knew it –
> These are the obvious exiles, these returning
> From embarkation leave, half England churning

> Through crowded turnstiles to meet its fellow,
> To meet, and part with the little hollow
> Laugh that never deceives – yet what are these
> But ripples at the edge of enormous seas?
>
> ('In a Strange Land', V, p. 76)

Exile, at its heart, is not 'obvious'. The polar currents of war-time, each 'churning/ Through crowded turnstiles to meet its fellow' are a sign of massive civil displacement, yet these are not the force but its symptom. Exile, in the image detonated with such retroactive power in the last line quoted above, is not at the edge of the outer but at the centre of the inner.

Planetary 'othering' or reversal, exile from the human, a desolation at the heart of experience – this event is recorded at three main levels in these poems: it is detected as the principle of remote killing which defines the new kind of warfare; it is identified with a wider social breakdown involving the betrayal of human values; and it is felt personally, a wound shared with many others and never specified, but no less sharp for that. I shall try to explore each of these levels in turn in the discussion that follows, but it is important to recognize, taking the lines quoted above as a sample, how pervasive they all are in the poems that make up *This Other Planet*. The 'unwieldy kits' of the soldiers are associated with a wider sense of disorientation from the ordinary body world. Recruits are soon 'Dizzy with bleach',

> Yellow, and shambling, and disillusioned
> In bleach-stiff khaki and discoloured boots
>
> ('A Man Once Lived in a Village', I 'Call Up', third sequence, p. 84);

the airmen, similarly and more pointedly, are

> Men, huge beneath arctic equipment, setting out
> To remote aerial regions, whence to destroy
> Regions remote from their personal knowledge;
>
> ('In a Strange Land', VI, p. 76)

Telephone booths, as we have seen, are much in evidence in these poems, an emblem of sundering from 'life as once they knew it', because the virtualization of communication actually speaks of the loss of true contact. Worse than this is the equally ubiquitous 'little hollow/Laugh that never deceives'. The hollowing out of the social value system is given a more specific, a more knowing context here than in, say, the obvious and grander case of Eliot's 'Waste Land' mosaics. It is here that the personal level signifies. Very often the poems have the immediate quality of rueful notes to himself ('The coated taste of exile on my tongue') or to an absent partner who will read them later:

> My body is no longer mine, my mind
> So set to work on formal parrotries
> No time or energy is left to be
> The person I still like to think is me.
>
> ('A Man Once Lived in a Village', I 'Call Up', first sequence, p. 82)

The three sonnets that make up 'Unseen Fire' (pp. 94–5), all of them much anthologized, have established R. N. Currey's reputation as an important poet of the Second World War, and, in particular, a poet able to go to the heart of the experience that set this war apart from those before it: killing, often on an enormous scale but equally often of a solitary figure, from a distance too great, and by means of a technology too counter-intuitive, to permit the exercise of even that limited range of emotions said to make war vestigially 'human'. These poems are certainly a good place to start and they have been justly praised. The first sonnet in particular brings an animated, tonally expressive and down-to-earth humanity to a subject that offers for contempla-tion the antithesis of these qualities. 'This is a damned inhuman sort of war', it begins, then offers a proof of this proposition which at the same time manages to be defiantly human: 'I have been fighting in a dressing-gown/Most of the night'. That opening line, echoed in the second sonnet ('This is a damned unnatural sort of war') has a hint of parody: it speaks as much for other voices, for a judgement overheard, as in the poet's own voice, and this slight ambiguity of tone extends to the element of ambiguity in the word 'damned', for the war is indeed infernal as well the fitting object of every decent combatant's exasperated curse. Crucially, in the latter sense it can be shared by a new kind of cameraderie, and it is this 'we' that is uppermost in the sonnet sequence that makes up 'Unseen Fire'. On the other hand, the heart of the experience, the true inferno that it represents, is as deeply solitary and shocking as the last line of the third of these sonnets:

> We could not help them, six men burned to death –
> I've had their burnt flesh in my lungs all day!

If we have already noted a strong tendency towards a modest, decent Englishness in this poet's work, it is also true that in many of his most striking images, passages and poems he is a poet of the more marginal, extreme experiences of his time. Perhaps this is why the war poems sometimes seem to reach beyond bringing war up to date, extending their meanings all the way to the century's close. In a lesser-known poem he offers a sense of the 'Unseen Fire' contest that is at once ethereal and state-of-the-art technological: beyond the immediate realities of the new warfare we glimpse a world – our twenty-first century world – in which human scientific capa-bility has made the human body redundant and vulnerable, in which common-sense physical existence has yielded precedence to the theoretical materiality of particle physics:

> Searchlights with empty gestures lift their white
> Celestial sleeves, blank light without a pang
> For the thin skulls of airmen in their slight
>
> Cabins of aluminium, or the strong
> Blood-flow of men and women under glass
> And tiles and fragile brickwork; all night long
>
> We hear the planes go over, hear them pass
> Along their vaporous ceiling, separate
> As particles in an atom universe.
> ('In a Strange Land', III, p. 75)

If this vision sometimes yields (in the 1940s) such postmodernist phrases as 'replicas of life', it is also able to furnish a lasting thumbnail sketch of that triumphant twentieth-century version of *homo sapiens*, the geek:

> They don't believe in theory, but know
> How to cash in on the electron flow
> In wire conductors …
> From infancy they've felt a fascination
> For each and every form of calibration;
> They'll fix a flicker on a tube, it's reckoned,
> Down to a hundredth thousand of a second.
> ('In the Gaze of Mars', IV 'Conclusion', p. 88)

In a remarkable series of poems near the end of *This Other Planet*, this technological impera-tive is recognized as a fundamentally masculine, if not exactly patriarchal phenomenon (for his courtly and 'protective' impulses remain above the critique):

> Being a woman, you can hardly know
> The violence … which has hurled
> Man on his bloody missions through the world.
> ('Ultimate Exile', II, p. 98)

In part this recognition entails acknowledging his own masculine fascination with the technolo-gy of death in poems such as 'Boy with a Rifle' (p. 78), 'Maintenance' (p. 90) and 'Heavy Guns' (p. 91). And in an age when superpower missiles and high-level bombers mutilate the countries of errant regimes in the name of humanity, we find that R. N. Currey was forced to recognize long ago the makings of a similar dilemma, seeing that it is this

> … super-scientific race
> Of fighting men

who

> … in this barbarous
> Moment of crisis save the world for us.
> ('In the Gaze of Mars', IV 'Conclusion', p. 88)

A number of poems in *This Other Planet* – including the title poem (p. 87) – focus on the zone in which experience of the new conditions of war, when men 'have left their human values on the runway' ('In a Strange Land', VI, p. 76), infects the rest of social life. This is partly a matter of reduction, a killing back of the spirit to the stump of physical survival.

> The wind swishes through the bracken as I lie
> And listen to the long-lash bullets whip by:
> These are the alphabet, the primitive speech
> Of this new planet; grenades and bullets teach

> A man to lie still and press his face in the mud
>
> ('In the Gaze of Mars', I, 'This Other Planet', p. 87)

In these experiences his complex understanding of 'Man's Roots' was drilled and educated. Setting out to understand how the poems of a South African exile link back to the war poet who discovered Ultima Thule, a place in the heart and at the barbaric core of twentieth-century 'civilization', we may find help in another sonnet, equally taut and metaphysical, but not nearly as well known.

> I often feel, when I am on parade,
> That I have stood on one small patch of street
> So many centuries that my numbed feet
> Are rooted in the soil beneath the made
>
> Surface of asphalt; walls and houses fade,
> The long review of seasons – rain and sleet
> And snow and sun – moves past us; lost winds beat
> On boulders in a prehistoric glade.
>
> Stone walls unbuild, trees draw their branches in
> And shrink into the ground; dun uniform
> Reverts through red and green to painted skin;
> The senses shrivel inwards to a core
> Quick only to the scrutinies of war,
> The eye of lightning in the passing storm.
>
> ('In the Gaze of Mars', II 'Parade', p. 87)

All unravels here, history, evolution, geological cycles, the made and the natural. While the extended metaphor of the parade-ground review remains impeccably in place, passing the final 'scrutinies of war', we are left with a figure more akin to green man than the soldier we first enlisted.

If *in the end* the rooted green stump of consciousness is redemptive, the social consequences of the dying-back are not understated in *This Other Planet*. Remote warfare makes civilians into spectators, voyeurs: again we discover that this poet's vision has gone the distance with his century:

> How wonderful, to sit in a cinema
> And have your war brought to you …
> [landmine disposal experts]
> Moving ahead of the army and smelling out
> Like devil-dancers the mines and boobies hidden
> Under the wheel-cracked crust and crest of the sand;
> The long untidy columns of famine-ridden
> Scorched prisoners; the charred trunk and clenched hand
> Of a dead enemy….
>
> ('At This Great Distance', p. 96)

'How wonderful': the bleak sarcasm that is often uppermost (sometimes, one suspects, as a protective screen) takes a bit of getting used to after the earlier (and, indeed, the later) poems. There are lines that reflect the deracinated, *ersatz* world of the war with the impersonal, univer⁄salizing world⁄weariness of an Eliot or an Auden, acquainted with

> ... lesser disappointments –
> Dogs that ran too slowly, faithless women
> > ('In a Strange Land', I, p. 74)

and parodies of consolation –

> ... if there are troops in Samarkand
> There's probably a Naafi, and the band
> Of a regiment of Guards for dancing;
> > ('Some Little Time', p. 97)

On the whole, though, a real pain seeps through – that is to say, a deep and destabilizing personal anxiety rather than Eliot's universal 'infinitely gentle, infinitely suffering thing'. Sometimes he speaks directly of the numbness of his own exile of the heart:

> All my emotion had been drained away
> Some days before, renouncing those I loved;
> > ('Evacuation', p. 80)

This is as final, if not as stark, as:

> Nothing is new beneath the sun.
> They stood beside him with a gun,
> Gave him a minute or two to dress,
> Pushed aside his wife and son.
> Too numb with shock to show distress,
> He went with them . . . .
> > ('In a Strange Land', II, p. 75)

If his exploration of exile is to reach to the roots of a universal condition, it begins in and retains its connection with an event as deeply personal as it is ordinary, which leaves

> ... hearts uprooted
> Beside their hearths and household gods.
> > ('In a Strange Land', VI, p. 76)

He is, again, one of the modest, decent many, the 'we' who

> ... have marched endlessly from all we knew
> And thought secure and real ...
> From the home that took years to build up,
> From the loved presence of wife and children,

From the arm-chair and the peopled fireside.
('A Man Once Lived in a Village', I 'Call Up', p. 82)

And it is perhaps just because he can speak so convincingly for

The individual man and woman,
    the loved roots
Of a familiar existence
('Spring Offensive', p. 93)

– taken to be the basis of 'organized society' – that his own arrival at 'Ultimate Exile' is so extremely unsettling, providing a correlative in personal experience for that other heart of exile in the inhuman skill of remote killing. In the three sonnets that make up 'Ultimate Exile' (p. 98) there is a shocking, searing reduction of 'the individual man and woman' to any man and any woman, to the 'cruel fever' of sexual loneliness and the gendered fragility of personal identity. The three poems form a dialectical unity. The first, beginning 'A man must speak to women or go mad', holds that 'Caressing words' between men and women 'have never failed to teach/Action', at least in the 'too eager' minds of men. In which case,

What is there in a warm outburst of speech
That may not be translated into flesh?

The point of this and the other rhetorical questions that make up the sestet is the desperation signalled in the opening line of the sonnet. The second poem in the series, beginning 'Being a woman, you can hardly know', almost inevitably records an impasse, the failure of wartime communication across the gender divide:

A man has words to say you will not hear;
He has a cry you cannot understand;
He has a whisper for your single ear,
A touch for your once sympathetic hand;
But passionate words, like Gorgons, turned your dear
Grave head to stone, and stopped your ears with sand.

The dialectic opposes, not the respective viewpoints of man and woman, but the violent mood swings of the soldier lover. The desperate libertinism of the first poem is answered by the frustration and despair of the second. Male sexuality is a 'flow/Of current' closely identified here with war and death, and 'only a woman' can provide 'release'. The poet may seem close to moral blackmail here; is he not, in a sense, holding women responsible for untold violent consequences if they 'will not hear' or 'cannot understand'?

Locked into its loneliness, this male monologue cannot be rescued by a female intervention, a refusal (for example) to be blackmailed. Instead the dialectic must be completed in its own terms. The sequence of poems is dramatic, a series of pressured utterances by the same voice, from different stations in the progress of its torment. One might call it a dark version of Marvell's 'To His Coy Mistress', noticing that it has a similar, dialectical three-part structure. Whereas Marvell may end with a rousing justification of deliverance from time through pleasure, a thrilling race against the sun, Currey's third sonnet finds at the heart of exile a reduction of experience to a compulsive retreat that offers survival rather than solace:

> his time
> Is given to this one thing and this thing only:
> How to leave light of day behind, and climb
> Into the darkness of a woman's body,
> Whence to be born again, helpless and lonely.

'Is this the ultimate exile?' This is the question the last sonnet begins by asking. If it is a bleak question to be asked of all experience, it is also a question phrased by the long-distance gunner's war, and the century looming behind that.

His modest, decent, everyman's world rocked by this journey to the centre of extremity, to the core of the outermost, the poet of *This Other Planet* ends that collection with the poem simply entitled 'Song' (p. 99). If its title recalls the gentler, more amiable tenor of his earlier work, this is definitively a 'Song of One Who Has Come Through'. It is a poem in praise of balance and proportion by one who has learned that enormous risks must be taken to achieve these qualities. After the wrenching turmoil of the 'Ultimate Exile' sonnets, we come upon a love poem that walks a tightrope as love poems must, all the while pretending to be a contemplation of eternal verities:

> Nothing in life is near and nothing far—,
> Apart from love; a man can live beneath
> His roof more lonely than an outer star;
> And know a woman's beauty, a flower's breath
> Walking alone in the valley of the shadow of death.

One is not surprised to learn that this was Stella Martin Currey's favourite poem.

There are some fine poems in *Indian Landscape* and among the other poems of place which are included in this collection, and his versions of Villon, Ronsard, Du Bellay and the other luminaries of *Formal Spring* remain a standard other translators have struggled to reach. Journeying on, readers will find their travel handsomely reimbursed, but they will also understand why my exploration stops here. In India or in America, as much as in the Jamaican poems included in *Tiresias*, or indeed in King's Lynn, the poet remains at home. He takes with him his gift for 'exact observation', his well-developed interest in mythologies, customs and history's tricks of light and shade, but his heart remains unbudged, untroubled by uncertainties about where home is, far from the heart of exile.

Preparing this introduction, I spent a couple of days with R. N. Currey in Colchester. I had not met him before and we had no intermediary but a tape recorder. Our conversations 'covered the ground' fairly adequately, I suppose, yet bear little relation to what I have written here or to the thoughts, about man and work, that filled my mind when I was in his company. I was conscious then of his failing sight, and of the burden this transferred to a voice incessantly tunnelling through his labyrinth of a century to focus the attention of its listener on this latest moment, this peremptory now. The house, its three floors well stacked with books and memorabilia, might seem a large domain for a single, elderly man. Spry enough on his feet, he seemed to traverse this familiar territory easily enough by a sensory route that eluded me, just as the modulations of his voice sometimes alluded to listeners of whom I could not be aware. Our boyhoods had crossed – in South Africa, in England, even in the West Indies – but the laws of our universe decree that different times are different places. Discontinuities and exiles as intractable as that incurred by Longinus the Thracian may dispose us to praise a poet who took their measure and, in Roy Campbell's phrase, 'taught their Gorgon destinies to sing'.

Chronology R.N.Currey

1907   14 December Ralph Nixon Currey born in Mafeking, South Africa, eldest son of John Currey, Methodist minister sent from England as Chaplain with British troops at end of Anglo-Boer War, married to Edith, née Vinnicombe, whose grandparents on both sides had arrived in Natal in 1849, the year of settlement.

1907–10   Mafeking

1911–14   Johannesburg

1914–17   Boksburg

1917–21   Ermelo ('Vaaldorp' in BBC drama)

1921–7   Kingswood School, Bath

1922   Parents in Jamaica for eleven years (RNC visited them twice)

1927–30   Read Modern History, Wadham College, Oxford B.A. 1930, M.A. 1935

1930–1   Diploma of Education, Oxford, with teaching experience at St Paul's, London

1931–4   Teaching on short term contracts, at St Paul's, Mill Hill, Whitgift, Merchant Taylors London, Cheltenham Grammar School; tutor to Oscar Deutsch family

1932   Married Stella Martin, journalist, novelist and play-wright, daughter of J. P. Martin, author of children's classic *Uncle*

1934   Appointed to Colchester Royal Grammar School to teach History and English

1936   Birth of James
Appointed Head of English

1940   Birth of Andrew
Ambulance work in Colchester
Tiresias (Oxford University Press, London)

1941   Called up to join Royal Corps of Signals
Trained in Ossett and Huddersfield on field wireless and telephones. Lance-Corporal. Passed Electrician Signals exam
OCTU at Llandrindod Wells

1942   Commissioned in Royal Artillery. Served as Second Lieutenant in heavy artillery and radar in Cheshire, Somerset, Devon, Cornwall and Kent. In command Radar Unit, Margate

1943   Sea to Cape Town, train to Durban and ship to India
First Lieutenant
Transit camp at Ranchi, near Calcutta. Karachi to train

south Indian recruits in Royal Indian Artillery

Visited temples in Madura and Ramaswaram, south India

Active service on Burma frontier with Madrassi gunners

1944 Transferred to Education Corps at Senior Officers Cadet School, Belgaum

Passed exam in Urdu. Captain, then Major.

Winner, Viceroy's All India Poetry Prize

1945 Work on Army Publications at *Times of India*, Bombay, including giving news of atom bombs at Hiroshima and Nagasaki

Visited Udaipur as State guest

Brief period in Viceroy's HQ in Delhi to clear publication of *Poems from India* (edited with R. V. Gibson), Oxford University Press, Bombay (republished by Oxford University Press, London, 1946)

This Other Planet (Routledge, London)

1946 Return to England by air for demobilisation from army. Summer – broadcasting for BBC and other freelance work. Autumn – return to Colchester Royal Grammar School as Head of English

1947 *Indian Landscape* (Routledge, London)

1948 *Between Two Worlds* verse drama (BBC Third Programme; new production 1951)

1950 *Formal Spring* Translations of French Renaissance Poems (Oxford University Press, London)

Family visit to Morocco

1951 *Poets of the 1939–1945 War* (Longmans, Green, London for the British Council and National Book League; revised 1967)

1959 South African Poetry Prize (jointly with Anthony Delius and Sidney Clouts)

1960 Lecture tour round South African universities

1961 *Return to Vaaldorp*. Verse drama (BBC Home Service)

1967–79 President, Suffolk Poetry Society

1968 *Letters of a Natal Sheriff: Thomas Phipson* (Oxford University Press, Cape Town)

1969 Visit to USA. *Flashback to America* Verse Sequence

1970 Elected Fellow, Royal Society of Literature

1973 *The Africa We Knew* (David Philip, Cape Town)

Retired from Colchester Royal Grammar School

Chairman, Public Library Colchester Literary Society

1974 Visit to Tuscany

1974–5 Winter in Macnabs' house, France

1982 Golden Wedding Anniversary; Visit to South Africa

1989 *Vinnicombe's Trek* (James Currey, London)

2001 *Collected Poems* (James Currey, Oxford)

I

To Andrew & Elspeth

The Africa We Knew

The Africa We Knew
(David Philip 1973)

That was the Africa we knew,
Where, wandering alone,
We saw, heraldic in the heat,
A scorpion on a stone
William Plomer

These poems were written at different times during my writing life. They have been placed at the beginning, reflecting my mother's South African family and my formative first thirteen years. The chance passage through the country on my way to India during World War II re-established my poetic connections with my roots. After the war South African poets helped me develop these associations.

I would like especially to acknowledge the help of my mother Edith, my father John, my wife Stella, my son James, Michael Arkwright, A. A. Balkema, Ray and Yvonne Burl, Biffy and Hilary Burl, Guy Butler, Roy Campbell, Fab and Guido Casale, Jack Cope, Robert Gittings, Norah Henshilwood, R. G. Howarth, Iris Linder, Roy and Rachel Macnab, Mavis Orpen, David and Marie Philip, Frank Quirke, Ronald and Douglas Vinnicombe, and Cecil and Freda Wood.

In a life spent mostly in England, I have done a great deal of research into the lives of my ancestors, including biographical studies of Thomas Phipson and Tom Vinnicombe. These could not have been accomplished without my return visits to South Africa, and the generous help of family and literary friends. Many of those listed in those two books have also given me great help and encouragement with my South African verses.

South Africa

In Memoriam: Roy Campbell

He grew where waves ride nine feet high
Like Zulu impis up the beach,
Crested with sound, and every boy
Must watch for the whites-of-eyes of each.

Long rollers, horned like bulls, would gore
Into the whinnying groins of sand,
And every boy, a matador,
Must hold his courage out, and stand.

He learned to watch the rush and lunge,
And feel his feet, and wait until
The instant came for him to plunge
Into the envy poised to kill;

To plunge and come through to a world
Of triumph on the other side,
Where he is lifted up and whirled
Down the long combers of his pride.

The Africa We Knew
Listener
Natal Witness
Sydney Bulletin
Roy Macnab: *Poets in South Africa*
(Maskew Miller 1958)
Guy Butler: *A Book of South African Verse*
(Oxford University Press 1959)
Jack Cope & Uys Krige:
Penguin Book of South African Verse (1968)
K. M. Durham: *Two Roads* (Juta/Arnold 1969)
BBC, SABC broadcasts

Durban Revisited 1943

After these weeks at sea, my native land:
I stand and stare at the remembered Bluff;
Enough that long green skyline for a boy,
The joy of those high breakers, their huge roar
The lift-in of the tide, upon the shore.

My forefather in eighteen-forty-nine
Put down his family here; since then his blood
Has flowed up almost every fertile valley;
But many of his sons, through circumstance,
Lost his intense and civilized tolerance.

By chance we ride at anchor in the Bay
A day or two, and may not go ashore;
Once more between me and this lovely land
There stands a barrier; it used to be
My childhood, now it's my maturity.

The Africa We Knew
Poetry Commonwealth 1948
Roy Macnab: *Poets in South Africa*
(Maskew Miller 1958)
Guy Butler: *A Book of South African Verse*
(Oxford University Press 1959)
Howard Sergeant: *Commonwealth Poets of Today*
(Murray 1967)
M. C. Andersen, S. G. Kossick &
E. Pereira (eds): *A New University Anthology of
English Poetry* (Oxford University Press,
Cape Town 1993)
BBC, SABC broadcasts

On That June Day

'*The last transits of the planet Venus were on June 5th 1761 and July 3rd 1769, the next to be on the 9th proximo (as we all know) and the next on the 6th December 1882. After that there will be none until the 7th June in the year 2004; and where shall we be on that June day?*'

Thomas Phipson, writing at New England, Pietermaritzburg, on 16 November 1874

The Africa We Knew
Contrast 15, 4 (3), 1967
British Council for
Harvard Poetry Room 1972
BBC, SABC broadcasts

Where shall we be on that June day?

On the 9th proximo, for this event,
He rose at half-past four and set his glass,
His Dollond, gently polishing the lens,
Outside his house near Pietermaritzburg,

The place New England. Calculations made
For this specific exiled latitude.
He held a broken shard of window-pane
In the feathery tip of a tall candle-flame,
Soft-surfacing it with smoke.
At first, the clouds being low in the south-east,
He quite despaired,
But just at seven o'clock the sun broke through.

Assisted by his Dollond's higher powers,
He watched the planet slide towards the sun;
It seemed to him a trifle pear-shaped when
It breached the sun's bright rim. Its egresses
Internal and external both took place
Exactly at the calculated time—
Proclaiming yet again his God's secure
And punctual ordering of the universe.

He was not there in eighteen-eighty-two
To watch the next prompt transit of the sun;
Neither, I think, were we.
Where shall we be in the year two-thousand-and-four
On that June day?

If Such There Be

'… by means of which Lunarians (if such there be) would behold
our globe as a dark spot surrounded by a circle of dull, hazy,
reddish-brown light…'

Thomas Phipson, writing in the The Natal Mercury
of the 1870 eclipse of the moon.

Beneath the fiat of our great Creator—
Which cannot but impress a thinking mind—
Controlling as he does the planets' motion,
Last night's eclipse of the moon took place
With praiseworthy punctuality. We would call it
A large eclipse. The moon passed through
The obscure centre of earth's shadow;
Yet after midnight, at the darkest moment,
The disc of the satellite could still be seen
Wearing a lurid, dull and smoky hue
Like London streets in a November fog,
Or veld here in Natal beneath grass fires—
Let readers take their choice of similes—
So the Lunarians—if such there be—
Would see our distant globe as a dark spot
Surrounded by a haze of reddish brown,
Giving sufficient light—if they've good eyes—
For seeing lunar objects close at hand
During the total eclipsing of *their* sun.

A century has passed, and new explorers
Circle the moon in silver argosies,
Put out long legs to walk a stranger desert
Than any Doughty* knew—perhaps, in an eclipse,
When earth slides in between them and their sun
Stare back through a nostalgia of distance
At our globe in its haze of reddish brown,
Which gives sufficient light—as they've good eyes—
For seeing lunar objects close at hand—
But also, in that leprechaun atmosphere,
Recalling to those steady, sceptical minds
Vague glow-worm rumours of Lunarians,
Making them peer round furtively to see
If such there be.

Contrast 1967
British Council for
Harvard Poetry Room 1972
BBC, SABC broadcasts

*Charles Montagu Doughty (1843–1926), whose
work vividly records his travels in
Arabia Deserta

The Africa We Knew

The Africa We Knew
New Coin Poetry 2 (2), 1966
Michael Chapman: *A Century of South African Poetry* (Ad Donker 1981)
SABC broadcast
South African Poetry Prize 1959

Lost World

In memory of Edith Currey, died March 1959
Born Pietermaritzburg 1881

She died in England, in the early morning,
A long experience from her starting-place.
The brilliant silver mirror of her death
Seemed the right symbol for her life, but gave
Too landlocked and unruffled an impression.

The simple commendation of one age
Is technicolor cliché in the next:

She was small and gay, with a hand for horses;
She rode side-saddle without a snaffle:
She turned the muzzle of her small revolver
To pierce, beside a panic of African women,
The flicker of a mamba along a verandah
Towards a child. In a lonely place
She grouped a caveat of holes on a target
For those who looked for a sign. These legends
That spark from the hooves of her earlier years
Wear the habit of a lost convention.

I was her first, and with her at the last,
The rôles reversed, but my help helpless
To halt or ease her difficult passage,
Her life-long habits of thought for others
Still there in flashes of maternity;
Her smooth white cap of hair recalling
The cape of comfort that brushed to the waist;
The worn hands, folded in death, out-reaching
My span of years to touch the legend.

She opened her eyes on the sleepy hollow
Of Rip-van-Winkle Pietermaritzburg,
Where waters ran under weeping willows
Through channelled streets. Her grandfather
Had written comparing it with Babylon
In layout, not in sin—the jail stood open,
The graves were few, he found the natives
Fine fellows 'shrewd as merchants upon "Change".'
He built a handsome house with an observatory
But lost it among the stars. Her father
Ran waggons up-country, built solidly-founded
Churches of character, gave sidelong glances
At diamonds and gold. At seven she saw
Water sold in the streets of Johannesburg.

She came home in plaits from her boarding school
To a veld at war. Her father and her brother
Took sudden separate ways to the frontier.
She, with her mother and the younger children,
Lived on a knife-edge of local friendship
And outside frenzy on a dwindling farm,
Where war requisitioned horses and oxen.
When a commando, boys they had known,
Rode in for food and songs round the piano,
She played a new song, *Soldiers of the Queen*—
Her hands were merry but her eyes were tactful:
This is a story that fits like a glove
On the hands I knew. One moonless night
With trolley-wheels drawn up from the well
And thin mules lent by a friendly enemy
They crossed the nerve-taut lines. A chronicle
Where war draws in the lines of character
Must give a far too definite impression!

At seventeen she put up her hair
And trippled down in her riding-habit
To pass the barbed-wire picket of the new
Camp for burger families—innocent still
Of every overtone but improvisation.
In a marquee, equipped with shelter,
She led wild children and bearded youths
Through jogging songs and jingling tables—
Her riding-crop the symbol of order
But never of Empire. Among the waggons
She visited the families she had known,
Brought news to mothers of commando sons.

A photograph of not long after
Shows her as small and well-proportioned,
The face beneath the fantasy of flowers
Unformed as yet by suffering or fulfilment.
After the war her over-ridden heart
Sent her to Britain for recuperation
And lessons in painting. She married on her return
Out of the world that is now my legend
To the world I have come to share.

She was small and gentle, with a will of kindness.
She rode her love of animals and children
With easy rein, without a snaffle.
Her sensitive touch gave life to broken toys,
To oils on canvas, notes of a piano,
And all the kinder nuances of words.

The Africa We Knew

(Landscape of Violence)
The Africa We Knew
Contrast 1 (3), 1961
Jack Cope & Uys Krige:
Penguin Book of South African Verse (1968)
British Council for
Harvard Poetry Room 1972
Michael Chapman: The Paperbook of South
African English Poetry (Ad Donker 1986)
BBC, SABC broadcasts
Danish Radio 1973
South African Poetry Prize 1959
Stephen Finn & Rosemary Gray (eds): Broken
Strings: The Politics of Poetry in South Africa
(Maskew Miller Longman 1992)

(Remembering Snow)
The Africa We Knew
Contrast 1 (1), 1960
Thwaite, Plomer & Corke: New Poems (PEN)
(Hutchinson 1961)
Jack Cope & Uys Krige:
Penguin Book of South African Verse (1968)
Jack Cope: Seismograph (Reijger 1970)
A. Rowe & P. Emmens: English through
Experience (Granada 1974)
Guy Butler & Chris Mann:
A New Book of South African Verse in English
(Oxford University Press 1979)
British Council for Harvard Poetry Room 1972
Ernest Pereira: Tellers of Tales: Singers of Songs
(Pat Lubbe 1981)
Annette Stones: Give Me More Words
(Book Studio Johannesburg 1986)
Syd Gosher & Tony Pannell: Inside Poetry
(Kagiso 1995)
Stephanie Nettell: Collins Christmas Treasury
(Collins 1996)
BBC, SABC broadcasts
South African Poetry Prize 1959

The fountain of her gaiety spilled over
From family and friends to men and women
In thirty places in three continents.
Her heart, which failed her at the last, had travelled
Through seas of every pigmentation, lands
Of every human contour.

A story that broke surface at her death
Tells of a solemn invasion of husbands
Into a laughing concourse of wives:
'The merry wives', she murmured, and the comment
Gives an exact impression.

Landscape of Violence

Where racial attitudes, like snakes,
Coil above children as they play,
And every brown and white child wakes
Beside a sloughed-off love one day;

Where politics like hailstorms ride
And tear the future from the trees,
And every rider caught outside
Must pray between his horse's knees.

Remembering Snow

To-day I think of a boy in the Transvaal
Spending his Christmas Day at the krantzes
Where the khaki drought of veld, cleft open,
Held festivals of water in a fern-green canyon.

We dived fork-naked into crystal pools,
Explored behind the maidenhair waterfalls,
Eating our Christmas pudding beneath the grace
Of feminine willows on the vivid grass.

My mother lured the pony with lumps of sugar;
We coaxed him into his creaking cat's-cradle of leather,
My father, all that tawny homeward run,
Remembering snow as I remember the sun.

8

Southern Stars

Wherever man voyages
Be sure that he will find
Symbols and images
Of what he left behind.

Past Capricorn we steer,
And soon the Telescope
Shows a new hemisphere
Beyond our northern hope.

Under the Southern Cross
The Flying Fish whirr and dip;
The moonlit waters toss
Argus the Southern Ship.

The Swallow takes the Fly,
The Crane stalks up and down;
Peacock and Toucan vie
To wear the Southern Crown;

The shy Chameleon hides;
The Centaur thunders by;
The southern Phoenix glides
Up through the re⁄born sky.

South Africa

The Africa We Knew
Observer c. 1940
Contrast 15 4 (3), 1967
M. van Wyk Smith:
Shades of Adamastor: Africa & the Portuguese
Connection (ISEA, NELM 1988)
South African Poetry Prize 1959

The Old Manse, Transvaal

The Old Manse, with its shovel⁄hat verandas
Flat fore⁄and⁄aft, was guarded on the south
By a double file of even⁄shouldered fir⁄trees
That faced the assegai winds with disciplined growth.

On loud black nights we'd hear them changing pickets,
But they'd be back next morning—when we'd swarm
Around those kindly giants' resinous pockets,
Or, sticky Tarzans, swing from arm to arm.

The tallest stood near to the house, to rear of parade,
Above the fifth⁄column colloquy round the well
Where the servants ate their meals; from his glossy cockade
The manse looked fragile, not defensible.

The Africa We Knew
New Coin Poetry 2 (2), 1966
BBC, SABC broadcasts
South African Poetry Prize 1959

The Africa We Knew

The Africa We Knew
New Coin Poetry 2 (2), 1966
BBC, SABC broadcasts
South African Poetry Prize 1959

Spanish Influenza 1918

I waited for my father in the trap
Outside the wire-fence cemetery where he laid
Away from all but memory Mrs Petrie
Mother of six with whom we often played.

He had no choice but to take me; our two servants
Were grey with fear and fever, and my mother
Stretched on the threat of going. All that week
His funeral services followed one another.

That odd parade of European bones
Beside the shabby location, above the vlei,
Was something to take for granted, side by side,
In ranks, convenient for Judgment Day.

I *Saturn*

Mr van Niekerk, small and saturnine,
His glinting eyes like mine ball-bearings,
His little waist, for vanity or support—
How could we know?—held in by corsets,
Stood like a ruler by my desk, resentful
Of the weak heresies of former teachers,
Forced my soft formlessness with sullen fury
Through the strict rituals of arithmetic;
Fitted, as I have realized long years later,
A working frame of vanity and support.

The Africa We Knew
Standpunte 23 (2), 1969
BBC, SABC broadcasts
South African Poetry Prize 1959

II *Local Deity*

Our headmaster, nicknamed Gin—
'Gin' for 'Ginger'—was tall and thin
But never aloof; you'd see him go
Down on one knee by a boy to show
Just how a marble should be propelled—
By finger and not by thumb; he held
Didactic views on this rule of thumb;
The finger of Afrikanerdom,
The thumb of the imperialist!

Standpunte 23 (1), 1969
BBC, SABC broadcasts
South African Poetry Prize 1959

He wore a snakeskin round his wrist,
And on his head a wide-brimmed hat;
He pushed it back when he came to chat
With Miss du Plooy in front of the class,
His faded gold by her new brass;
And stood there basking in her sun
His right knee dusty, his fly undone.

III *Juno*

Miss du Plooy was, I suppose,
A Juno of a woman. Her opulent gold,
Piled on her head in coils of serpents,
Spelt toils of love to young men-teachers,
To us spelt temper. When her shrill peacock
Screeched frustration, these hissed us into stone.

New Coin 1966
Standpunte 23 (2), 1969
SABC broadcast
South African Poetry Prize 1959

But there were days when thunder waited
For Miss du Plooy. With jovial swagger

The Africa We Knew

Flashing his whip across the window
Hammering the roof—while we stared embarrassed
To see her cringe, her hard gold melted,
Her cruel eyes covered before the god.

IV *Virgin Huntress*

New Coin Poetry 2 (2), 1966
SABC broadcast
South African Poetry Prize 1959

In English that was not her native tongue
Miss Meiring read aloud from Gordon Stables;
All I remember is the vague suggestion
Of splendid seas that beat on distant beaches;
I read it later, and they left no jetsam;

But for a year I lusted to possess it,
And know again the delicate enchantment
Of words and images that she conveyed
In English that was sweet upon her tongue;
I did not know that *she* was the enchantment.

She was a virgin priestess to Diana,
Hunting in bookish leaves on moonlit nights,
But she was gentle, half-approachable,
And made her oracles sweet upon her tongue:
Her name conveyed to me an English spring.

V *Chosen People*

London Magazine 1961
Guy Butler & Chris Mann:
A New Book of South African Verse in English
(Oxford University Press 1979)
BBC broadcast
South African Poetry Prize 1959

Mrs van Rensburg, in her short square person,
Re-lived for us the myths of her dour nation.

Her close-set eyes surveyed, as from a trance,
The history which, she told us, was romance.
It was the Will of God: a small boy's hand
Thrust in a dyke preserved the parent land.
It was the Will of God: the Portuguese
Discerned a rock of hope in stormy seas;
Diaz, da Gama, sailing round the Cape,
Gave the long continent its perfect shape;
Tacked down a carpet to the East, in stages;
Created a round globe in seven pages.

So far the dim, romantic origin—
And then her trumpets blew the Dutchman in!
When Jan van Riebeeck landed to be warden
Of a few cattle and a kitchen-garden,

She stood beside him, privileged to see
In that small bargaining group the land to be;
The Tavern of the Seas, the half-way station,
Hung out as sign a fine new constellation,
The Southern Cross, her focus from now on—
The Great Bear dropped into oblivion.

We saw her bosom rise, her nostrils swell—
And now she welcomed Simon van der Stel;
His exiled Huguenots, their first sour wine,
Were further details in the Grand Design;
The Flying Dutchmen of this coaching stage
Seemed to be blowing in a golden age.
Alas! their white-walled Groot Constantia dream
Was splintered on a clumsy English scheme
To free the slaves, to draw the frontiers in.

She held her shoulders back, thrust out her chin;
Gallows and trust collapsed at Slachter's Nek—
She cursed, and spat, and went with the great Trek.

The great Land-hunger March—the sixteen-spanned
Waggons that pointed to the inner land.
In calico bonnet and complexion-veil
She trudged by hooded wheels that ground a trail
Over the Dragon-passes to the high
Wine-heady emptinesses endlessly
Rolling towards a northern Promised Land—
Met the invading hosts and made her stand.

Like those far dykes with which her ancestors
Had faced the sea, the waggon-rings and squares
Fronted the tide of tribes that crossed the plain—
And she was in the thick of it again,
Packing in thorn-bushes with bleeding hands
Between chain-fastened wheels. And now she stands
Passing the loaded muskets to her men:
Pour in the powder, ram it down, and then
The wad, and last of all the leaden shot—
And now, wet rags because the barrel's hot!

But we had been there with her since the crust
Of the horizon's rim broke into dust:
The running impis with their silver line
Of assegais, their short-shaft discipline,
Striding towards us under plumes of dust;
The great bull's forehead low, his long horns thrust

13

The Africa We Knew

Curving to right and left to close us in,
The full-chest bellow swelling to a din
That swayed around, above us—nerves like wire
Waiting to see the markings clear—and fire.

She told us how her father once had lain
Hidden, and watched an impi cross the plain:
The mat-boys first, in running rank on rank
With rolled-up mats and cooking-pots, their lank
Long limbs and bodies moving easily—
The squires these, the warriors-to-be;
And then the knights themselves, with shield and spear
And loping ankle-tufted stride, were there.
They passed for hours, ran forty miles that day—
And won a battle at the end—he'd say.

Mrs van Rensburg had us with her there;
She lifted loaded muskets till her hair
Fell from its pins about her glowing face—
She stopped the war to put it back in place.

 Old Colley had his try
 Of course he had to die;
 No Englishman shall ever cross the Vaal!

She did *not* have me with her when she fought
A British column ambushed in some poort
Or helped to stalk them on Majuba Hill—
Crouching behind their beards they reached the rim
To find the naked square drawn up for them—
The graves of Colley's men are white there still!

Or when she side-slipped continents and read
Of 'British regulars' who 'fired and fled'
At Lexington, from Longfellow's *Paul Revere*;
But when her history had come this far
God's will, romance and documents were one;
There was no pardon underneath the sun
For any side but God's. I jibbed once more
When she was *veldkornet* in Kruger's war:

 Joubert and his sons
 Kruger and his guns
 No Englishmen shall ever cross the Vaal!

Still in my mind her monologue of wrongs
Is mingled with the words of burger songs
In Dutch and English—making clear
That words, like blood, can mingle and cohere.

Hoera! Hoera! Die burgers het gestaan
Die Engels wil die franchise *hê*
En Equal Rights *daarby*
No Englishman shall ever cross the Vaal!

VI *Halo*

Pastor M'Gadi's startling blackness
In my father's study, taking tea,
His smile for me as white as the saucer
Balanced like a privilege on his knee.

Pastor M'Gadi in the drab location
Reading his letter by his gap of door;
Waiting by my horse, I watched his pigeons
White as the paper from my father's drawer.

Pastor M'Gadi's brilliant blackness
Laughing in the sun by his pigeon-cote,
Wearing his fluttering halo of fantails
White as the celluloid about his throat.

Contrast 1 (3), 1961
Jack Cope & Uys Krige:
Penguin Book of South African Verse (1968)
Guy Butler & Chris Mann:
A New Book of South African Verse in English
(Oxford University Press 1979)
Michael Chapman: *The Paperbook of South*
African English Poetry (Ad Donker 1986)
British Council for
Harvard Poetry Room 1972
BBC broadcast

VII *Lesson in Murder*

I drew the smooth round pebble back;
    I felt the strong release;
I did not know that thud would crack
    The thin bones of my peace.

Contrast 15 4 (3), 1967
Robert Gittings: *Poets and Poetry*
(BBC 1961)
Rhodri Jones: *Themes: Conflict*
(Heinemann Educational Books 1969)

The jewelled bird fell from the tree,
    Half-fluttered to my feet;
The others snatched it up to see
    If any warm pulse beat.

They filled the leafy air with cries,
    Re-lived the redstart thrill,
Ruffled a rainbow in my eyes;
    While I stood sick and still—

The Africa We Knew

And, head averted, bent and took
  Another five smooth stones,
With catapult fingers cocked a snook
  At aching greenstick bones.

Those Were the Games!

Robert Gittings: *Poets and Poetry*
(BBC 1961)
J. Skull: *Themes: Sport & Leisure*
(Heinemann Educational Books 1970)
Rhodri Jones: *Preludes: Work and Play*
(Heinemann Educational Books 1971)
Standpunte 23 (1), 1969
All under the title 'Marbles'

Now that our fertile acres yield
Instead of crops a football field,
Or, groomed and levelled, primly don
A score-board and pavilion;
Now dark-green jersey and white flannel
Are ferried over sea and channel
On headline dates to some habitual
Accepted and unvarying ritual
Of over, kick-off, whistle, scrum,
I watch, but wonder what's become
Of all those joys of a former day—
The simple games we used to play.

The mesmerism of spinning tops—
Made by ourselves, not bought in shops;
The flick that lifted them in air
On to one's palm, still spinning there,
Swaying on hard earth or soft hands;
The home-filed point, the rifling bands,
The ridgy winding of the string;
The knack that made them whirr and sing;
The skill that with one drilling fling
Cleft rivals—earned the name of king.

Marbles, despised where goal-posts rise,
Shone brightly in our homelier eyes:
Glass marbles from the dented throttles
Of strangled soda-water bottles;
Clay marbles minted long ago
And passed as current to and fro;
Ballbearings from the stamping mines
Diverted to our mild designs;
And *goens* of lead poured molten in
The matrix of a blacking tin.

Carefully with a foot we drew
A straight smooth path, and, kneeling, threw
Our cluster of clays, to see them rest
Like brown eggs in a shallow nest;
With what a crack our *goen* of lead
Fell on the stragglers from this bed.
Or on some space of veld we'd trace
Our conjurer's circle, gravely place
Our green glass stakes, and from the ring
Propel our steel-ballbearing king;
With what a Zulu click he'd call
The raided cattle from the kraal.

Or *kennetjie*, the willow-click
Of round hard stick on round hard stick;
The sleight of hand and knee and foot
That poised the shorter piece and put
It high in air to take the crack
Which sent the whole field racing back;
The tingling palm, triumphant shout
Proclaiming that the striker's out.

Leapfrog, astride a pile of caps;
Leapfrog, along a line of chaps,
Heads down, with shoulders pressed well home
Forefather of the rugby scrum;
The long horse leans against a wall;
The clutching riders sway and fall
Or sway and ride; and from the press
Show fingers, ask the horse to guess.
'Five?' 'Four.' So we're the horse again;
Our ten legs bend beneath the strain.

In all these games the rule of law,
The well-tried ritual held the floor;
Everyone playing knew by heart
The sortilege that ruled the start,
The subtleties of turn and score,
The throw that earned the one throw more,
The sequence of strokes that *had* to be,
The custom-hallowed mystery
By which both tops and conkers yield
Their total of scalps when they are killed.

The Africa We Knew

So, in those golden-tawny days
When every season brought its craze,
When by some instinct we would know
What pastime would be all the go;
Like savages, who jog and grunt,
Then, chanting, all rise up to hunt,
We'd wait until an impulse came
To lift us up into the game:
The plain joys of a former day
The simple games we used to play.

Going Home
A Memory of c. 1919

New Contrast 94 24 (2), 1996

Back from our June
Of sun and breakers
At the dark end
Of our up-country journey,
Met by my father
On the open platform
At the whistling centre
Of a freak snowstorm

My mother and the three of us
Laughed to see
His clerical hat
Tied on with a puttee;
The oil lamp showed
A snowy blanket
Slung across the front
Of the family trap.

Our horse held his head
To the side and counted
As we pressed our weight
One by one on the step,
And then with a crunch
And a snort leaned forward.
One of us shouted,
'It must be Christmas!'

Hottentots' Holland

South Africa

Why is this country behind Cape Town
Called Hottentots' Holland?

For Mavis Orpen
New Contrast 72 18 (4), 1990

The Dutchmen at the Tavern of the Seas
Called their home mountain by the name of Table
Suitable to a tavern, and a welcome
Seamark for skippers sailing from the Indies.
They walked the ridge along their harbour,
Enjoying the masts of ships at anchor
And the sails of argosies at sea.
What interest had they in the savage mountains
That gave them their Hottentot servants—
Yet, needing a name for the area, reasoned thus:
The harbour and the snug streets of Cape Town
Are our Holland, those *lelike* mountains
The Holland of the Hottentots.

Noonday Game, South Africa

Once it was buffalos,
Rhinos and hippos
By whom this noonday
Game was played;
Now it's the cars of human beings
That nose each other
Out of the shade.

New Contrast 1994

Gecko, near Durban

When you step inside from the hot veranda
And the morning glory of the jacaranda,
And open the designated door,
It streaks across the ceiling or the floor,
A flash of apricot that's called a gecko,
A smooth loo lizard with a long pale neck⌐o;
It glides behind the pedestal or curtain;
Its morals, like its movements are uncertain,
A smooth Levanter with a name like Greco
You wouldn't trust his word or take his cheque⌐o
I'd hardly class him as a friend of mine.
And yet, he adds a lustre to the shrine

New Contrast 94 24 (2), 1996

19

That we must visit daily. On my way,
If I must find excuses, I don't say
I'm going to see a man about a dog;
But only murmur, too low to raise an echo,
'I'm going to take a decco at the gecko!'

Flamingoes at Welkom

1982

This red flamingo feather calls me back …
But first reminds me of a Highveld Boer,
Whose name, of course, was Rip Van Winkel,
Who found a horseshoe on the empty veld,
And spat on it, and threw it over his shoulder,
Then went to sleep, they say, for seven years,
And woke beside his horse's skeleton,
In sight and sound of golden horseshoe Welkom.

This tiny feather, not more beautiful
Than a white hen's dipped in red ink,
Wings me back to a shallow depression
Our Rip Van Winkel might have called a pan.
A width of water, unembroidered by rock or tree,
Outside the lucky horseshoe town of Welkom,
Where mineshafts reach below sea-level
For gold and more gold, pumping, pumping out
This brackish water that feeds a favourite
Species of algae; so that flights of flamingoes
From painted pools in Natal or Namibia
Have settled in this place as colonists;
Knobble-kneed, they walk in the water,
Wet-feathered, stand in it; and, when a car
Brings visitors from Welkom out to see them,
Newcomers like themselves to this bare place,
They lift into the air, flying creakily
Showing a flash of red nostalgia
For their gorgeous, crammed home-waters.

South African Folk Rhymes

From Afrikaans rhymes remembered by Thomas Vinnicombe (1854-1932)
from childhood in the Transvaal and recorded
in R.N. Currey: Vinnicombe's Trek (1989)

Tricky Dick

My saddle and my bridle, and my fine new horse
With the blaze, and the tail cropped short, of course!
I bought them yesterday from Tricky Dick;
They're good for nothing — I must sell them quick!

My Splendid Gelding

My splendid gelding, my joy and pride;
A star on his forehead, and a joy to ride!
Just look at the beautiful hair on his head—
It's frizzy, like fine worsted thread!

High-Heeled Shoe

Johnny, Maggie high-heeled shoe,
Tonight's the night of nights for you!
Just sit up, and say your say;
Then go and ask your parents rightaway!

The Bogeyman Will Come

The bogeyman will come
If you don't lie still;
The bogeyman will come
Over the window-sill;
Your dappled cow has a coat like silk
And gives such sweet and lovely milk;
So go to sleep, lie still;
And here's the carpenter, Uncle John,
To nail your doggy's tail back on.

My Heart Is So Sore

I sit on my horse
I feel worse and worse;
My mind's in a whirl
When I think of my girl;

I sit on my hands
And think of my lands;
I sit on the pole
And think of my soul;

I sit on a stool
And feel a great fool;
I sit in a lather
And think of her father;

I sit in the waggon
Her ma's such a dragon;
My cows are so skinny
My debts are so heavy.

I sit on the spokes
And think of my folks;
It's all gone too far
It's time to tell Pa.

Go To Sleep My Monkey

Sleep, my little monkey,
Husha Hushaby
Outside now a lambkin
On four white feet trips by;
Tickle, Tickle toesies,
Piggies in the beans,
Ducklings on the meadow,
Goslings in the greens,
Calves are in the clover,
Foals are in the hay—
I wish that you were older;
You'll be a help some day!

North Africa

Search for Morocco

Seven invasions, seven dynasties,
Seven cruel and splendid histories,
Seven dictators, seven capitals
With chanting minarets and silent walls.

The Romans, like the French, came to make roads;
The Carthaginians came for trade and war;
What brought the Berbers is a mystery
As strange as their occasional blond hair.

Islam, that brought the Arabs, baffles us,
Being infidels with no beliefs at all;
Their motives, like their mosques, are closed to us;
And each new dynasty that built a wall

Shared with this faith a common restlessness
That raised up gross Meknes and dappled Fez,
Grey Moulay Idriss, ochre Marrakech,
And Rabat ruling from white offices.

And now the restlessness that brought them here
Diverts the Gulf Stream Drift of History,
And throws back on the shores of Africa
A New World's voyages of discovery.

The Africa We Knew
Guy Butler: *A Book of South African Verse*
(Oxford University Press 1959)

Marshal Lyautey*

My roads stretch out
Into a tamed interior;
My body lies
Beneath a Muslim dome in Christian soil.

My roads are rivers of trade,
My ports are open;
The soldiers rule by flags instead of blood—
Holding the ring for warlike tribesmen.

* *Colonial administrator, sometimes called the
Rhodes of North Africa.*
The Africa We Knew
Guy Butler: *A Book of South African Verse*
(Oxford University Press 1959)

The Africa We Knew

My snow-fed rivers
No longer race to the sea,
But stroll abroad beneath white birds
Among new farms and forests.

In a green corner of a Civil Service garden
Where Arabs scythe the grass,
I feel the miner's pick, the controlled explosion,
The engineer's step on the new dam.

My feudal, feudal world should be quite perfect;
My sergeants and my Berbers know their places;
My *caïds* administer justice, but new nomads
Disfigure the land with shanty-town disgraces.

I tried to make a marriage of convenience
Between the Cross and the Crescent;
But the voice of Marx, professional seducer,
Corrupts the veiled platonic bride.

My still hand still protects
The murmuring mosque, the shrill *medersa*,*
The sweated craftsman and the spluttering fountain,
The flawless stupid face behind the veil.

* Muslim university.

Marrakech

The Africa We Knew
Contrast 1 (3), 1961
Jack Cope & Uys Krige: *Penguin Book of
South African Verse* (1968)
Poet July–August 1968
South African Poetry Prize 1959

Joseph Ben Tachfin came from the Sahara
With Potiphar's wife and army, crossed the plain
With a desert Arab's sensitive nose for water,
And an eye that saw the whole long way to Spain.

He brought his restlessness to Marrakech
Across the desert, over the High Atlas,
Then cut these wells and conduits for the fresh
Water to float this lily, this oasis,

This scatter of dark-leaved tents, these walls of ochre,
This quivering frieze of white-pavilioned mountains,
These date-palms of a desert tribe's nostalgia,
The princely palaces, the private fountains,

And the great public square, that unkempt garden
That glows at dusk with men who breathe out fire,
Weave necklaces of snakes, or spells to harden
Our hearts to courage, bodies to desire;

Floating on water, held in air like glass,
Bright in the glitter of the untouched snow—
The restlessness that thrust across the pass
Made this a stage, with further yet to go;

For lily out of lily, against the sunset,
Grows the Koutoubia, imperial tower;
It looks to the Giralda in Seville, and Rabat,
Backwards and forwards to the Muslim hour.

Zone of Insecurity

For hours we drive across a restless region
Where ochre casbahs crown each formless hill,
And glare with windowless non-recognition
At blank-faced casbahs that are enemies still.

Beneath dark clouds among these Berber valleys
The mediaeval world is full of horses,
Untrimmed and shaggy as their tall, spare riders
Bearded and easy in their long burnouses.

This hill is alive with horses, haltered, tethered,
Or grazing freely round a crowded square
Where men with horses are buying and selling horses
For riding and for breeding—and for war.

The Africa We Knew
Standpunte 23 (2), 1969
South African Poetry Prize 1959

Volubilis I

South of the fabled pillars of Hercules
Where, among hills, the morning glory throngs,
Phoenician traders built Volubilis
Not with their hands but with their chaffering tongues.

The Carthaginian morning slid away
On stone-crushed oil from the olive trees.
The stolid Romans spent their half a day
In pasting up prosaic memories

In huge stone albums: bath, and victory arch,
Virgins, and dogs, and fish from the Great Sea
That once their fathers passed. How quiet the march
Of century on stealthy century—

The Africa We Knew
Jack Cope & Uys Krige:
Penguin Book of South African Verse (1968)
South African Poetry Prize 1959

Till Islam came, and tongues began again,
The tongues of faith that talked the tribesmen down,
That talked the townsmen out across the plain,
And argued city walls from uncut stone.

Volubilis II

The Africa We Knew
BBC broadcast
South African Poetry Prize 1959

Here, among African olives and morning glories,
Where fish swim out from coelacanth centuries
To glint again in mosaic, I think that I see—
Among these knee-high walls of colonial Rome—
A casual pattern of feet, the ball of a foot
Pressed down on this pattern of scales, the flare of a hem;
And outside in the etched groove of the street
The curve of a tilting wheel, a hoof, a fetlock . . .
While all above, free arms and living faces,
Are lost with roof and arch in the crumbled sky.
    A pair of feet in a fountain, carved stone feet,
    Divinities side by side, devoutly sandalled,
    Lakshmi up to the ankle, there cut off;
    And women with outstretched arms and upturned palms
    Dropped petals of prayer on the trance of waters,
    With dancing gesture conjuring the goddess
    Whose feet alone I saw.
Imprisoned, like these fish, in time's mosaic,
We swim in the brief, fortuitous glint of the sun.

Tower of Hassan, Rabat

The Africa We Knew
Standpunte 23 (2), 1969
South African Poetry Prize 1959

I am a teacher teaching a boy.
In the name of Allah the Omniscient
I kiss the hem of learning and begin:
Yacoub the Victorious built this tower
And rode each day up the curving ramp
To look out over his land and ocean . . .
Sometimes, in the spell of repeated words,
A teacher becomes the thing he teaches!
Sometimes I have no way of knowing
If I am sitting with a boy on a bare
Hard stump of stone lifted above
An ugly stubble of broken pillars—
Or if I am an emperor,
Looking down from sixteen extra

Quivering hands of height, a mane
Beneath my bridle, down and down
Over the newly-carven parapet
Over the prostrate praying roofs
And chanting courtyards of my fine *medersa*—
My words of learning riding every ocean,
My pride of power on the corsair sea.

Fez

Mystery beyond mystery, a mediaeval
Craftsman's nest of boxes within boxes:
In streets like tunnels roofed with reeds,
Mottled with absolute sun and shade,
I jostled animals, foot-passengers,
And opened up the jewellers' box, whole streets
Pillared with golden bracelets. Then I found
The dyers' box, with pageantry of skeins
Lining the route, and scarlet thighs.
And then the leather-workers', arabesques
Dancing on grave Morocco, bargainings
Blessed with orange-blossom. Inside that,
A carpenter's box, of noise and cedar-wood—
Within, shrill as a disciplined aviary,
The spurting Koran-chorus of a school.
And then the perfumers', with tiny drops
On wrists and handkerchiefs, and birdlike cries;
And such a daze of scents in my head,
And in the middle of that maze a mosque
Closed to me as a Christian—and perhaps
Holding the brilliant throbbing plumage
Of a bird I caught as a child.

The Africa We Knew
Michael Chapman: *The Paperbook of South
African English Poetry* (Ad Donker 1986)
Contrast c. 1961
South African Poetry Prize 1959

Fez At Sunset

Light colours the walls.
Those troglodytes in the cliff below me
Are urchins at a lit shop-window;
And I myself, the twentieth century,
Confronted, through this trick of time,
With the original of the Duc de Berri's
Lunar, illuminated Book of Hours.

The Africa We Knew
Contrast c. 1961
South African Poetry Prize 1959

The Africa We Knew

That single shepherd with his little pipe—
The thin noise comes to us as it has done
To others on this hill, in the hour of sunset,
For a thousand years. This far-off shouting,
This crying, this beating of tin and copper,
Have risen like hymns in a minor mode
To gods forgotten in the mind
Remembered in the blood.

African Sultan

Standpunte 23 (2), 1969
South African Poetry Prize 1959

I'm Moulay Ismail, Sultan of Meknes.
Killed seven Europeans, did you say?
I've killed my hundreds, my thousands, I never counted:
But I am always impartial: I have killed
Black men from the Sahara, white men from the sea;
Girls of every gradation of colour,
Chocolate, and orange, and rose-petal pink
I like to see the pallor take possession
Where I can only caress.

I have a harem — don't interrupt me!—
Of fifteen hundred women. And a stud
Of fifteen thousand for my splendid negroes;
But the pick are my harem! I have invited
Louis of France to send me one of his daughters.
He sends me watches, jewelled weapons,
A thousand royal regards—but he declines!

Why does he decline? I am austere.
I drink no wine. Eat very little.
Spend much time in pious observances.
Why does he decline? Don't interrupt me!
I am impatient. I cannot wait
To see a building grow, to feel
Desire come climbing back into my veins.
It makes me mad to wait.
Raze the building!
Kill the concubine!
I like to feel the stream of creation
Move right through me—to life or to death.
Whenever I rest from lust my solace
Is killing, always killing.
I kill a man a day, a man an hour;
I chain-kill men until I have no pleasure

From individual killings.
I killed the builder of my Bab Mansour
So that my gate of gates should have no fellow.
I kill men as they help me to my stirrup;
They leap to catch my spittle—and their lives
Follow it as it flecks upon the floor.
And all the while my negroes stock my territories,
And all the while I build and build
Barracks and brothels, palaces and stables,
Mosques and forts and dams and granaries,
High gates with pillars from Volubilis,
My one incomparable Bab Mansour,
And this poised weight of arrogant wall on wall
Meknes, my city,
Built to stand for ever.
I am the Sultan, Moulay Ismail. All
The walls I build shall stand for ever. All.

II

Tiresias

To Stella

Tiresias & Other Poems
(Oxford University Press 1940)

The poems in this section were written in the years between my coming to England in 1921 and the beginning of World War II. While at Kingswood School, Bath, and Wadham College, Oxford, I paid two visits to my parents in Jamaica and went on a school course to the Sorbonne at Caen where I began my interest in translating French verse. I also made an Easter trip to Italy which enabled me to spend a summer vacation as a tourist guide around the Italian lakes, where we later spent our honeymoon.

I had helpful advice and encouragement from friends, editors and writers, who continued to support me through the war. Among those who gave me special help were John Arlott, Ralph Kilner Brown, Lord David Cecil. L.J. and Gwen Cheney, Gerald Cluer, Tom and Sally Currey, H. A. C. Evans, Malcolm Ford, A. F. Hall, Francis House, G. L. Jones, E. C. and Lynton Lamb, Philip Mairet, Norman Martin, Edward Thompson and A. C. Ward.

Acknowledgements show poems as having also appeared before 1940 in
Dublin Magazine
John O'London's Weekly
The Listener
New English Weekly
Penguin Parade
The Sunday Times
Time and Tide
The Argosy

To His Jester

A poet to his sub-conscious mind

Tiresias
New English Weekly c. 1940

Good fool, my fool,
Licensed to fill
My court of sleep
With shape on shape

Of unguessed fear,
Twisted desire,
Mocking distortion
Of ambition;

Licensed to root
Escaping feet,
The arms of love
Hold up in leaf;

Raise maize-seed teeth
To bladed death;
Hurl straight wings down
With Phaethon;

Cruelly burlesque
Day in a mask
With lips of horn
And eyes of stone:

A fool, I know,
Saw Xanadu,
A fool Ezekiel's
Living wheel;

And, should you pass
The caves of ice,
Sway in the whirl
Of wing and wheel,

Why then, good fool,
Say what you will
By night or day
To prophesy—

But, if you must
Still jest and jest,
One sock and one
Worn buskin on,

Tiresias

Or, like some fools,
For cap and bells
Solemnly don
Cap and gown,

Mime on, good fool,
Burlesque your fill—
Licence to mock
Lasts till I wake.

Angelico Gold

Oxford Magazine c. 1928
Stella Martin Currey: *One Woman's Year*
(Nelson 1953)

After the rain laburnums
Are loaded with yellow snow,
And buttercup fields are painted
With gold of Angelico

Who never was in England
Yet magically could shew
The green and gold of English fields
On the walls of San Marco;

And when he painted heaven
Would have his angels blow
Trumpets of gold on English lawns
Rain-washed an hour ago.

Laburnum I

Oxford Magazine 1928

When Jason drove for Colchis
Through the sounding seas,
He did not know the secret
Of the Golden Fleece;

And when Medea whispered
Of the yellow flame
That dies when it is stolen,
He told it not, for shame.

Long furrow home to Iolchos
The sturdy Argus cleaves;
But the rowers have no knowledge
Of the shrivelled leaves.

The poets knew a curse came
Home with the argosy;
They never knew the secret
Of the Golden Tree.

Tiresias

Buttercups

They lead the invasion every Spring,
A golden army, with tall spears
And plumes of light‑green grass, and bring
Their dandelion stalks to stand
Like flag‑poles, marking conquered land
Until high summer's force appears.

Observer 1935

Old Sailor

I lives in a cottage by the shore
With my old parrakeet;
On either side of my front door
Are shells set in concrete;
I grows two rows of sunflowers
With seeds for the birds to eat.

1921

My parrakeet is a tropical bird;
He grew up far away
With poinsettias and paradise birds,
But be that as it may,
Of all the lovely things he's seen
He hasn't got much to say.

My sunflowers are suns to me;
To him they're only food;
He may have a very wonderful brain,
But his speech is rough and crude;
He says his say again and again;
And what he says is rude.

He screams 'Hell's bells!' as he cracks seed‑shells,
And 'Buckaroo, old sport!'
But there is nothing he says that tells
Of foreign land or port;
And every day my sunflowers
Hear words they didn't ought!

35

Tiresias   Old Jake's Tales

I *The Tea Race*

This story and the two that follow were told to R. N. Currey by a very old sailor, who died in the next bed, in Charing Cross Hospital in 1928.

From the way folks talk of the *Cutty Sark* and the *Thermopylae*
You'd think them clippers the only ships that ever raced with tea;
But while there's no denying them a queenly sort of grace
They don't come up to a steamship if you really wants to race.

Hurrying up to Foochow with the engines stamping hard
And the hold all empty and clean for the tea, you'd be a queer card
To think of the sailing clippers then; when Dick me fo'c'sle mate
Caught in a rope and went overboard of course we couldn't wait.

Them Chinks can pack a basket of tea where someone like you or I
Couldn't put in a box of cigars. Like ants, but orderly,
They packed in tea to the hatches—everything else was junk—
And didn't go off in their sampans till they'd filled up me dead mate's bunk.

We knew there were prizes for all aboard the first ship to get home;
And we took her out of port ahead of even the *Flying Foam*;
We watched the *Flying Foam* fall behind all day and into the night
When her lights grew dim and wobbly and disappeared from sight.

We were working up steam at Singapore when she came in for coal;
Off Aden we sighted a craft like her, but she signalled *Orient Goal*;
We started dividing the prizes and each laying bets on his whack,
Till we found at Suez that the *Flying Foam* had passed through six hours back.

She got home first, in record time, a day ahead of us,
And when we'd heard the way of it we'd sit in the bars and curse
The *Flying Foam* for signalling false and not showing no fair play—
But all of us knew that our luck went out when we didn't stop that day.

II *Bringing the Parrot Home*

1928

I've been some queer trips in me time, with a tug to Monterey,
With herds o' drunk and kickin' steers from Massachusetts Bay,
With pearlers findin' a livelihood between the police-boats comb,
But the funniest trip was the one I had bringin' the parrot 'ome.

I hates the dirty screechin' things, but my Maria she said:
'A bird'll be company for me when yore as good as dead,
Somethin' to speak to while yore away!' I thought: 'My stars it will,
And somethin' to swank to the neighbours with!' But I bought her one in Brazil.

36

Speak! I worked like a nigger cook to learn that bird to speak!
She'd sit quite still till I came up close, then have at me with her beak.
'Oh Blimey, what a life!' I'd say, and shut the cabin-door,
(Maria being particular!) and wait until after I'd swore.

Then I got me monkey. Now he was a lad with charms!
He came on board on a nigger's leg, clingin' with legs and arms;
He bit the hand which fed him, the bos'n's who sold him me;
And I fixed him up on the boat-deck where the skipper'd let him be.

I used to go up twice a day with sorft bananas and bits;
For only to see him at his tricks would send you off into fits;
But when the gulls came wheelin' round he'd cling to my legs in fright,
So once when a flock o' them joined the ship I took him below for the night.

I tied him up near that parrot—and that was the end of it!
I came orf watch to find him loose, pluckin' her bit by bit:
She conked out naked and shameless like, with a 'Blimey, what a life!'
But I couldn't have taken her home like that—she's particular, is my wife!

III *The Good Old Days*

The *Mary Ann* she leaked like a sieve, but we got her to Tenerife
And took aboard an English pair what used to know the Chief.
The husband had got the blamed DTs and took his Spanish knife
And chased around in his shirt and boots after his poor little wife.

He tried to stab me as he passed and stuck his knife in the wall;
I coshed him then, and knew he was dead directly I saw him fall.
We sewed him up in a canvas sheet with some lead, the bosun and me,
And when the skipper had read his bits we dropped him into the sea.

We stood there quiet and respectful-like while the wife she piped her eye;
Then suddenly, as we turned away, she lets out a horrible cry,
And, to the skipper, who held her up, 'What'll I do?' says she,
'A hundred sovereigns was in his belt when you slipped him into the sea!'

The bosun and I we kicked ourselves, and every man of the crew
(Who thought they'd have their share of it) came round and kicked us too;
But the Old Man roared out, 'Man the pumps!' The old ship's creaking stays
Was letting the water in again—for them was the good old days!

Tiresias

Tiresias
New English Weekly c. 1931
John Adlard: *Poet's England: Essex*
(Brentham Press 1984)

Parish Church

A haloed, shadowless, pre-Raphaelite church;
A picture remembered from childhood, yet most strangely
Naked of gravestones, and not introvert
Behind blank walls, but glowing steadily outwards.

The enormous choir, tier upon tier of surplices,
Sang ceaselessly; while numberless men and women
Crammed the pew-less nave, brimmed over on to the meadow,
Jostled and laughed as on a railway station,
Stood there with infants in their arms, rocked cradles,
Their children chasing each other around the pillars.

In the transparent transept, through a carved screen,
Some forty clergy robing, in statuesque attitudes;
Some handsome, one with symmetrical black ringlets
Set at inch-distance on his head; some ugly,
Mean, snivelling and sly; and all remote, all dusty:
About their feet the children chasing each other.

Against an arch a beggar, a Cabinet Minister
I saw once on a College Barge in Eights Week,
Shaking hands loftily; the same monocle,
But chipped; the same frock-coat, but dusty;
The same long, hanging chaps, but quite unshaven.

The verger interposed: 'So you're a stranger !
We haven't had a visitor since the day
We tidied the gravestones away behind the copse ...
You're right, we're crowded out with all these children;
There were fifteen of them in one tomb alone ! ...
Yes, sir, those are our vicars for thirteen centuries ...'

Carp Pond, Fontainebleau

The normal life of carp is 200 years

Remote with yellow age, like Chinese seers,
or golden-young as patriarchs, Ishmael
and Abraham, who at their seven score years
gat sons and daughters—this, I think, knew well
which silken dairymaid was Antoinette,
l'Autrichienne, unapprehensive yet,
and missed the fine white bread-crumbs when she fell;
this, almost, the young Francis, who would run
from pedant Venuses to fling a stone
at bellies lucent-parchment in the sun;
'le vieux gros blanc,' Methuselah, has known,
as through green window-glass, distortedly,
round Charlemagne on Big-foot Bertha's knee.

Tiresias

Tiresias
New English Weekly 1932

Cock-Crow

This sudden cockerel who stood
Across the smoke-gold dawn and crowed
Became the bird who hid the sun
Crowing in morning Babylon;
The Talmud cock whose brazen plumes
Curved fanwise up the beaten roof
Of heaven in shadowed bas-relief,
Out-stretching fire-scalloped tips
To east and west in the eclipse;
His spurred feet on the earth; his comb
Touching the zenith; his huge voice
Making the heart of God rejoice.

Tiresias
New English Weekly 1938
Jack Cope & Uys Krige:
Penguin Book of South African Verse 1968

Independent c. 1932
Modern Travel c. 1932

Garage

Engines
intricate almost as the human body
steel⁄hearted, wire⁄nerved and iron⁄sinewed
able to go rough⁄used and crudely mended
but when they're cared for, trained and tuned
sheer joy.

Boys
lying beneath them in the oil⁄mud of the floor
rolling in the grease that's life and breath to steel
(sooted and no clean patch of wrist to rub the eyes)
standing in pits
working unfulfilled
at engines filthy with ill⁄use
jammed pistons, broken bushes.

Men
with fingers hard⁄black as their spanners, able
to peel off piston⁄rings like rind from apples,
to cut neat holes in steel as women cut button⁄holes
yet nimble enough to take the tiniest bearings
and set them round a dimpled swivel⁄joint
like the small silver balls on Christmas cakes
able to fit the debris from a box
into a whole that coughs and starts again
and runs with an athlete's beauty in trained eyes.

Speed

Independent c. 1932

Swiftly spinning world,
Adam could never know
Nor Tree of Knowledge show
How dizzily you whirled;
He saw the clouds lie curled
Along the quiet blue,
He saw the morning pearled
With still ear⁄rings of dew.

He had no way to see
How dizzily you swung
Until the years had hung
A new Forbidden Tree
With bright new fruit that he
Could taste and give to Eve—
And see as planets see,
Perceive as stars perceive.

Dizzily spinning world
The cities come and go,
The trees and buses flow
Hiding, revolving, swirled
Away—impetuous world,
Where is our quiet garden?
Adam and Eve are hurled
Out of a second Eden.

Dionysus

After they'd torn him down and buried him,
setting the Childless God in his niche,
those who had prayers they could no longer pray
cried craftily:

Tiresias
New English Weekly 1936

He is too great! Hang Him high, hang Him high;
give us the Virgin Mother to hear our cry!
(She has a child, she knows the wild
desire of the prayers we can no longer pray!)

But some still cried: The mild
seed planted secretly, grown quietly,
has nothing to do with the wild
lavish scattering, profligate rioting
of Dionysus, Dionysus.

So they have dug him up, and, dancing, sing:
God older than the Greeks, of more than wine,
we worship thee with the fierce disquieting
profligate rioting of ancient Thrace;
phallos and thyrsus, music harsh, entrancing
graceless dancing, udders of shambling kine
and loaded vine, women's and corn's wombs thine;
we fuddle our wits with wine and sleep, and chase
Christ and the Virgin apace in our wild dancing.

Dionysus says: They cry,
Fertility, fertility,
and worship barrenly;
they should have let me lie.

Independent 1935

Requiem

The light behind these trees
Makes their bare branches black,
And throws across the stars
The net which holds me back.

The wind in this dead bush
Sets the leaves whispering
The harsh, dry words that mock
My heart's imagining.

The gleam on this wire fence
That climbs the long hill's brow
Goes tight-rope dancing where
I never may go now.

Joshua, Paedagogus

Tiresias
New English Weekly 1936

'Joshua, Joshua shall lead them on,
shall lead our children to the Promised Land,
where milk and honey flow, and gold grapes grow
in such gargantuan clusters in the sun
that two men faint, they say, in carrying one ...'

They used to bake bricks for bronze Rameses,
content with flesh-pots, wanting but for straw,
for forty years, between far oases,
manna-provided, pillar of cloud before,
with slow, circuitous Moses trod the sand;

protected, guided through the cloven seas—
chariots struck wheel-less, corpses on the shore—
murmuring, murmuring for the olive trees
of Thebes and Memphis, shuffling before
the golden calf in unkempt saraband.

'Joshua, Joshua shall lead them on,
shall lead them on to mud-walled Jericho,
and, giving them trumpets, show them how to blow!'

Firstborn

This two months' infant plays such parts
As Caliban and knave of hearts;
When cleaned and fed and in the mood
A ladies' man, and then a rude
Bedouin belching thanks for food;
A frog when bathing, straddle-legged,
A cat when sneezing, a bald-egged
Roll-chinned, neck-tufted politician,
Demagogue-lunged; but his commission
Is mostly that of monarchy.

At once on his accession he
Titles conferred by birthday grant
On mother, grandfather and aunt;
Showed royal thirst, since he began
A six or seven bottle man;
An oriental potentate
Carried from place to place in state;
A Bourbon holding grand levee
And changing twenty times a day;
An uncontrollable Angevin,
To shout and slobber is no sin,
To sleep in public, shamelessly,
To kick his boots off, royally,
And chew his bedding; in the night
Summoning aid by divine right,
A Stuart, assuming all day long
That the king can do no wrong.

A grocer first, in flattery,
Accorded him this royalty.
'How is His Majesty?' he said
And I was short with him, instead
Of hearing through his sugared tones
The roar of one-and-twenty guns.

Tiresias

John O'London's Weekly 1937

Tiresias

Tiresias
Listener 1937
Philip Larkin: *The Oxford Book of
Twentieth Century English Verse* (1973)
*Guildhall School of Music and Drama
Anthology* 1974

Jersey Cattle

In rosy-fingered dawn they go
Beneath my window through the street
The kine that Homer used to know
With shambling gait and trailing feet.

Dappled with gold their ridged backs rise
And fall like waves; each white horn curls
Like a ship's prow; the heifers' eyes
Are brown and soft, like a young girl's.

An island in the wine-dark sea
Gave them first grazing; Jupiter
Assumed their shape; their sire was he
Who fathered golden Minotaur.

Their shambling gait and trailing feet
Raise sea-girt Ithaca again,
As they pad through the village street
With a sound like heavy rain.

Morning Over Purley

New English Weekly 1936

Air green as water fills this valley now,
Brims up the terraced hills and drowns the tops.
In moving light green-crystal without flaw
Buildings of coral climb the long sea-slopes,
Crustacean houses cling to the sea-steeps,
Through glaucous weeds washed walls like pebbles glow.

Fishes, once birds, from swaying bushes fly;
Blunt eels, electric trains, nose aqueous trees;
Sea-creatures now, horse, car, and lorry trace
Their silver belly-tracks on the sea-floor;
Above, through glass-green water, finned and sure,
The monsters of the deep sail gravely by.

Moated Farm

New English Weekly 1938

Something could be made of this: the pond
Banked up with concrete; wisteria;
Gravel on the muck churned up by the cattle;
The house rebuilt with turrets to be in keeping;
Swans instead of ducks; a peacock ...

The house is of ancient brick with a mansard roof;
Against the tawny-green trees the tiles are old rose,
Horses are russet silk, cows black-and-white velvet.
The ducks are absurd villagers on holiday:
Youths speed-boating across the pool;
Girls, white as swans, vividly lipsticked,
Treading over the slush in orange galoshes;
Wives, heads sunk in brown bodices,
Fluffing to show the surprising lining of purple;
This mallard, in dove-grey morning coat, light spats,
His sleek head shot emerald velvet,
A bloom on it like grapes, out-dandies the peacock.
   ... The new by-pass is opening things up nicely;
   Light should be cheaper ...
   Why not a drawbridge !

Tiresias

Reconquest

Once a year the East country
Remembers its ancient master:
The fluid corn,
The grey-green swirling oats and luminous barley
Brim up between banked hedges—
The strong tides join and sweep irresistibly over
Houses and telegraph-poles
Till only the towered poplars and islanded cathedrals,
Lincoln, Ely,
Look to the Pennines and High Germany.

Tiresias
Sunday Times
G. Rostrevor Hamilton & John Arlott:
Landmarks
(Cambridge University Press 1943)
Shell Guide 1943
Stella Martin Currey: *One Woman's Year*
(Nelson 1953)

Bicycles

In the morning early I hear the dry
Crisp sigh of phantoms as they pass
In twos and threes, wind through stiff grass;
And disembodied voices cry
Into brief candle-life, snuffed instantly.

On Sunday nights the whispering ghost
Of a lost regiment passes by
In bands of fifty, rhythmically
Giant-striding brittle air, a burst
Of song, lit woodbine-ends, behind them tossed.

Tiresias
Sunday Times c. 1936
John O'London's Weekly 1937
Spectator c. 1939

Tiresias

Tiresias
Sunday Times 1937

Radio Play

Shakespeare, who did his scenes in words,
Morning on tip‚toe, barren heath,
Pinnacled mansionry of birds—
Immune so from pale artifice,
The theatre's rigid miracle,
The cinema's two‚dimensional death—

Would think that a Pygmalion's skill
Gave Prospero life, whose new device,
Still hiding instruments in air,
Can paint in music countries where
Actors are free as Ariel, round
The scenes with curtains of bright sound.

The Individualists

New English Weekly 1937

Complacent, self‚assured, with green
Narcissus eyes they gaze into the fire,
With slow indifference arch for a caress,
Stoic and satisfied, curl up for sleep,
Sadistic, stretch a claw.

What secret impulse turns them out to cry
In such wild agony, in such despair,
Desolate, disillusioned, with no sense
Of polished reticence?

Realist, have they probed the skies,
And found them lethal fire and ice, and air
Hollow beyond conceit? Have they looked through
Life at the sovereign lust which now they serve
In masochistic torment, with no sense
Of civilised pretence?

House-Proud

Tiresias

John O'London's Weekly 1936

She keeps her house, both out and in,
As bright and clean as a new pin;
Her linen is as crisp and white
As the Himalayas by moonlight;
Her furniture and brasses shine
With secret moon and unguessed sun—
What moment, then, has she to spare
For an unburnished head of hair?

He keeps his garden neat and trim
As a Scots Calvinistic hymn;
With rolling, mowing, puts to school
The lawn to make an emerald pool;
And, since his life is a crusade
Against each pagan leaf and blade,
What moment has he left to clip
The strange growth on his upper lip?

The Brothers

Observer 1937

Old Matthew, shaping his box-tree,
Balances on his steps and clips
Staid animals and urns and ships,
Poplars like those of Lombardy,
Cypresses of the Appenines,
Noah's ark firs, Black Forest pines...

Meanwhile Mark's wayward scissors shape
The visitors to his small shop;
Butcher to have his beard trimmed,
His ship's prow beard; the postman there
With his great upturned urn of hair,
Looped ears for handles; our lion-limbed
Tawny-maned landlord; Cobbler Joe
Whose parting is a double row
Of Lombard poplars; Grocer Vines
With straight hair like Black Forest pines;
Policeman Peters, from whose ears
Sprout toy shrubs and Noah's ark firs;
Old Giles, whose grey moustaches hang
Like willow-pattern, period Wang.

Hey, Nanny Nanny!

The children on this exclusive beach
Have, as I calculate, a nanny each.
Nanny! they shout.
Nanny! they cry.
We don't want to come out!
Really, I'm as dry as dry!
Nannies argue plaintively
While parents standing by
Cry, Nanny, Nanny, Nanny!

Nanny, mother undefiled
Of child after child after child.
Others marry,
Others carry and deliver, it's true;
But that's about all they do do.
Oh Nanny, run!
What *were* you doing, Nanny,
To let him sit about so long in the sun?
Mother's work is over in one;
Nanny's work is never done.

The old-fashioned nanny
Stayed on
In the same place,
Helped out the mother who couldn't stand the pace
Of annual fruition;
Had, besides bed and board,
Something of the reward.

Nanny, Nanny,
Compared with a billygoat's wife, a real nanny,
You know sweet Fanny
Adams about life;
Madam's the wife,
You're just the nanny;
And, with those gaunt, goat-like hips,
That long-suffering face and those hesitant lips,
You stand little chance of ever being a granny,
Nanny!

But this is for the wife to read,
Not you, poor Nanny, Nanny,
Na-a-a-anny!

Seaside

When sea and sky take colour from the sun
And earth goes clothed again in green,
By opposites we all are seen
To rid ourselves of clothing and to run
In our own shape and naked, save that we
Wear strips of blue and green like sky and sea.

Star Sequence

Star Circus

In January the sky
Becomes a circus-tent;
Twin-brother John and I
Stare to our heart's content.

Unicorn, Lynx, and Bear
Are in the star-dust ring;
The Mammoth Million-Star
Circus is in full swing.

The ramping Lion defies
Orion, who cracks his whip;
Great Bear stands up and tries
To give his Ward the slip.

The wide-legged Charioteer
Goes round upon one wheel;
He skids, and Cassiopeia—
The idiot!— gives a squeal.

'But the real fun begins,'
Announces Cepheus,
'When those two Heavenly Twins
Ride round on Pegasus!'

Everyman 1934

Observer 1939

Tiresias

Observer 1937

Dangerous Sky

Now February is here
Twin-brother John and I
Dare not go out at night
For fear of the sky.

The tough hunter Orion
Is hunting the Great Bear;
The Small Bear and the Lion
And the wild Bull are there;

The Big Dog and the Small Dog
To chase us for our sins;
And here comes Cassiopeia
With Castor-oil for Twins.

March Skies

Observer c. 1938

In windswept spaces stars
Play tig for all they're worth;
The floundering Hydra tries
To run the Crab to earth;

The Crab makes for the Lion,
Then sideways swiftly spins,
Grabs at the Unicorn
And fastens on the Twins;

The Twins snatch at the Lynx,
Miss him and touch Great Bear;
Then stop to watch the Dog
Chasing the mad March Hare.

April Fool

* *'Boöthes is sometimes called the Bear-ward.*
Auriga is the Charioteer.

'Boöthes', the Twins cry,
'Your poor old Bear's been drowned!'
And to Auriga, 'Hi!
Your back wheel's on the ground!'

They shout at Hercules,
'Your sandal's come undone!'
His glance falls to his knees
As they turn round and run.

50

May Evening

About the Maypole now
Cepheus and Cassiopeia,
The Swan and Dragon go,
With Great and Little Bear.

Hercules tunes his Lyre;
The choir-boy Twins begin
To lead the starry choir;
Bootes' bass joins in.

The clustering stars are white
As hedges thick with may;
They'd like a may-queen, but
Shy Virgo runs away.

June Stars

On June nights the desire
Of young stars is to throw
A party at the *Lyre*
And then go to the zoo.

It is, without mistake,
A special kind of zoo,
With Lion and Bear and Snake—
But a Snake-Charmer too!

It has the usual Dolphin—
In a glittering pool, of course—
But what do you say to a Dragon?
And to a Flying Horse?

✧

Tiresias

Tiresias
Observer
Thomas Moult: *Best Poems of 1938*
(Cape 1939)

c. 1938

Lament for Frost in May

O, weep for my potatoes, they are dead!
Lovelier were they to me than air-hostesses,
They stood up in rows like footballers introduced to
    Prince Philip,
They held out their arms gracefully, like ballet-dancers,
But the frost seized them, and they are dead—
Like sea-birds in an oil-slick,
Like Pavlova in the 'Dying Swan'.
O, my potatoes, I'm very disappointed in you;
When they warned me you were sub-tropical, I said,
Surely the potato, the homely potato
Is dependable, is tough,
Is able to stand the rough-
And-tumble of the weather, but I see
The delicate lettuce and the fragile pea
Still stand where you have fallen,
O, fair-fallen, O, cut off
In the green promise of your vegetable youth.
Those whom the gods love die young—
It's clear that the gods
Love spuds!

Early News-reel

The camera that never lies
Calls up this horde of fly-blown ghosts
To agitate dead limbs in base
St Vitus parody of the past.

Accelerated goose-steppers
Are like a madman's marionettes;
Curtseys are shaken into capers
A general's stride into a trot.

O world-emblazoned royalty,
What shabby reach-me-downs you wore!
And how did words of fealty
Rise through such barriers of hair?

Time is a snob, and never kind
To any but extreme age; thus
Victoria is re-enthroned
And these inherit her abuse.

All ages suffer from the tongues
That gossip after they are dead,
But no past age had so obscene
A witness at its masquerade.

Tiresias

Song in the Hebrides

The soil so poor that we must set
Sea-weed in crevices of rock
To bed our few potatoes; scrape
Thin stony furrows for our oats;
Raise scanty crops and stunted sheep
Under salt spray; dig out and stack
Wet peats for cottage fires; scale
The cliffs for sea-gulls' eggs; drive keels,
Like ploughshares through green tides, to bring
Reluctant silver from the sea;
Water and land being barren, sow
The fallow tracts of air with song.

Tiresias
Denys Kilham Roberts: *Penguin Parade*
no. 4, 1938

Gulls, Yorkshire Coast

These strange-tongued fisherfolk, the first invaders,
Screamed down from populous towers
Sheer as Manhattan. This was no Vinland,
Green and unpeopled, that guarded the grainland.
From the crammed Empire State they clamoured,
From the dizzy Flat Iron as the armoured
Prows grounded, and linden shields swung inland.

Tiresias
Time and Tide 1938

Still foreigners, still crying their outland words
At sea-lords become sea-side landlords;
Fishermen longshoremen; land-rapers
Tillers and reapers; plundering grainland,
Wailing over the bungalows on the foreland,
Launching against round coble-loads of trippers
Grey sails and foam-white prows from pale skyscrapers.

Tiresias

Tiresias
New English Weekly c. 1938

Dawn Chorus

No Matins choir
Of yawning monks:
Hedge-rested friars
Offer thanks,

Come from Provence
And lands beyond,
To Providence
In a new land.

In pearl-grey light
I cannot see
A hood or habit
To know them by

Grey friars or white—
I cannot tell,
Or what their Latin
Voices call.

St Francis' thrush,
St Dominic's swallow?
In vain I wish
To name and follow

Each brother's note,
Liquid and sure,
In the clear-fluting
Barefooted choir.

Pelican, St James's Park

This lank, untidy, intellectual‑browed,
Knobble‑kneed, awkward bird,
With his absent‑minded glance
Of remote benevolence,
Is a country clergyman.

His piety fills the same
Loose angularity of frame;
His grave quiet presence
And ascetic, bony features
Show quality of breeding;
His sedentary scholar's flitches
His solitary wading
Through the philosophies, and brooding,
Eyes astride the long beak
Stretched over his book,
Showing, as his glance passes
Over the reedy, the papyrus pages,
Over the well‑kept sedges,
Effect if not actuality of glasses.

He keeps a fountain pen
Beneath a wing,
And, let me tell you one other thing,
The trousers, from which pond‑water drips,
Bear the indentations of his cycle‑clips.

Tiresias

Tiresias
Denys Kilham Roberts: *Penguin Parade*
no. 8, 1941

Final Grief

Eyes look through glass on final grief.
Fingers stretch out, but cannot touch.
Hands of the living cannot reach
The living past this crystal gulf.

Beyond invisible walls of glass
The marbled dead lie so remote
That no adventuring hand puts out
To test the tiny foot of space;

No fluttering hand puts out to try
That glacial sea; but from the cold
Immaculate bergs beyond, a hard
And glittering wind blows solidly.

Tiresias
New English Weekly 1940

Tiresias

The living try, through walls of glass,
To touch a man upon the arm;
Enclosed in ice, he watches them
Lean toward him, posture and grimace.

Faust to Helen

Tiresias
Dublin Magazine 1939
Thomas Moult: *Best Poems of 1939*
(Cape 1939)

Apart even from the mouths of fire
That grin at me from each path's end,
Have I not bought you far too dear
For palpable air and solid ground?

Was this the face? And was the face
That launched the ships a legend too,
A poet's song; so that I choose
The shadow of a shadow now?

I hold you in my arms so close
That mingle, mingle, O, we must;
But what's behind your empty eyes,
Where does your virgin heart keep tryst?

Solidity, the old man's friend,
Will take his blessing from my chair,
My hand, my glass; and I shall find
Contact with nothing except fire.

One Night Before the Dawn

Tiresias
New English Weekly 1937

One night before the dawn I found the Plough
Obsolete, ineffectual, on its side;
Charles' Wain a derelict box-on-wheels;
Great Bear crude scratchings on a smoky wall
That failed to hold their quarry:
The trinity
An amateur's futile cabbalistic sign
That let the devil out.

Come to the fair! Come to the fair!
Come and see life⁄in⁄the⁄raw at the fair!
Men and coconuts covered with hair;
Women big⁄bosomed, and tough, and raucous;
None of your second⁄hand hocus⁄pocus
Of celluloid figures and vulcanite voices,
But flesh, and biceps, and sweaty faces,
Uncovered collar⁄studs and bully braces;
Come to the blare and glare of the fair;
Come to the fair! Come to the fair!

When I passed by the fair today
The women were folding the beds away;
The coconut⁄shy girl, spick and span,
Was dusting her bijou caravan,
Setting out plates and a new⁄ironed batch
Of rose⁄pink serviettes to match;
The Mexican gun⁄woman, if you please,
Had a china dog on her mantelpiece;
While Madam Fortuna was reading meekly
The recipe pages of 'Housewife's Weekly'.

Tonight, two youths in the shabby swings;
A country couple throwing rings
For household ornaments; a squawk
Of factory girls on the cake⁄walk;
A sober few, who spurn the ground
From animal pews on the merry⁄go⁄round;
A boy at the turntable grill; a few
Young men in khaki going to view
The headless calf, the giantess,
The ladies in Montmartre dress;
Two shrieking girls on the giant slide …
While hundreds on hundreds queue to ride,
Suburban, under painted stars,
At two miles⁄an⁄hour in bumping cars!

Come to the fair! Come to the fair!
Come and see life⁄in⁄the⁄raw at the fair!

O Fons Bandusiae!

After Horace

Bandusian spring, more glittering than glass,
Worthy our offerings of wine and flowers,
    A kid I'll bring to you
    Whose young horn-swelling brow

Foretells both love and battles—but in vain;
This offspring of a wanton flock must stain
    With his rich crimson blood
    The cool depths of your flood.

The burning season of the fierce dog-star
Cannot affect you—you have coolness for
    The bulls tired from the plough,
    The flocks that wander too.

You shall be honoured among famous springs
Especially when I sing of the oak that clings
    Beside the hollowed stone
    Your murmuring stream leaps down.

Prayer for Professional Skill

After the prayer of Saladin's court physician, written in 1180

Time and Tide 1939

Preserve my body's strength, O Lord, and send
Me strength of soul to labour tirelessly
In helping rich and poor impartially,
Both good and bad men, enemy and friend.

Let me not think I know enough, but find
Leisure and zeal to work unceasingly
In mastery of our great mystery—
Since art moves ever onward with man's mind.

I thank Thee, Lord, that Thou hast chosen me
To tend Thy creatures in their life and death.
I go now to my work. O, let Thy breath
Inspire me, Lord, in what I do today
Lest it should come to naught, for nothing may
Prosper, however small, apart from Thee.

Machine-guns, songs of revolution,
Sounded elsewhere; revaluation
Of unfamiliar currencies stilled voices
In the basement, interrupted kisses;
Turned attics that held children
To junk-rooms; in the garden
Let proletariat grasses
Take possession.

My five-month plan
Will make this pot-verge run
Straight as old rolling-stock
Allows to Vladivostock
Beyond the pear-tree; clip
This overgrown Ural slope;
Scrape trunk-road paths, trim verges,
Align undisciplined hedges
On the street-frontier—I spend a
Trifle here on propaganda!
Tear down new-green corruption
Of vines strangling laburnum;
Struggle with army-growth
Of ivy, whose new strength
Threatens the fence, while yet
Its strands hold it upright;
Postponing root-and-branch
Destruction till the pinch
Lessens with acceleration
Of production.

Rake over the Ukraine
Of this untamed lawn;
From new frame-factories
Plant out marigolds, sweet peas,
But first, utilitarian lettuces;
Stretching entanglements
Of black threads round the plants,
Instead of mumbo-jumbo
Of swaying scares—a row
Of sparrows underneath.

And with
A handful of baize strips and rusty nails,
Recrucify plum-trees on sunny walls.

Tiresias

Tiresias
Dublin Magazine 1938

Laburnum II

There are no words for this mad yearly
Glory, this short spendthrift splendour,
This reminder of the country investing
With bursting rose and rhododendron
Our Maginot line of road and pavement;
Earth rent with bayonet⁄bladed grass; the sun
Bursting from this sky⁄branching mine.

During the static moment of exploding
The Wooden Horse in Troy, whose belly holds
Green water⁄meadows buttercup⁄starred;
Mustard across a valley; broom; the year's pageant
Of hanging golden lanterns, vertical banners;

The ram whose sunset⁄fleece raised Jason's sail;
Unsoiled gold of saint⁄painting Angelico;
El Greco's honey⁄gold; Byzantine haloes;
Jupiter, hidden in gold rain, demanding
Danaen entrance; golden⁄haired Rapunzel's
Dear ladder up the ivy; the gold hair
Of mermaids in green water; yellow coins
Lolloping looping down while the gold diver
Drives like a shaft of light; gold of lost ships;

Gold hoarded by Pluto, by Proserpine
Wildly spent. First beauty squandered
On hundreds in a night. Pods of lost youth.

Spanish Weather⁄cock

Tiresias
New English Weekly 1937

Peter's penance, weather⁄cock,
Still unstable as the Rock
When God built upon it; symbol
Of the mind that's always nimble
In denying, thrice denying:

Vested cities for bread crying;
Iron⁄bowelled harpies dropping
Hell of trees and pavements leaping,
Houses twisting, gas⁄mains bursting,
Towers leaning, torn streets grinning,
Chimneys falling, grey dust crawling
After stiff⁄winged shadows, spreading
Over broken dead for bedding;

A boy running, a girl dancing,
A wife planning, a man planting,
Obscure millions only wanting
A sure footing in quiet renting.

In a pub—was it?—denying
When men spoke of it, then going
Out among the laughing, thronging
Crowds in town for the Passover—
Herod's pageant or Passover?
Barabbas and his gang in clover
Drinking, shouting ... A cock crowing.
Cruel penance, weather-cock,
Veering Peter became Rock;
When will we, who have denied you
Pray to hang head-down beside you?

Tiresias

Tap-Dance

Tip-a tap-a, tip-a tap-a;
Jaunty in the spotlight's glare,
Shake a nimble foot, entrap a
Wisp of rhythm, light as air:

    Castanets and jade mantilla;
    Ivory tongues that chatter chatter,
    Lovers' matters, in guerilla
    Warfare chatter, chatter, chatter.

Wood and leather cry together,
Quicker, slicker, dancing there;
Stepping rapid, features vapid,
Mouth ajar and eyes astare:

    Lewis gun and black faldilla;
    Iron tongues that clatter clatter
    Leaden matters, in guerilla
    Warfare clatter, clatter, clatter.

Tiresias
John O'London's Weekly 1937
Frank Whitaker & W. T. Williams: *Saturday
to Monday* (Newnes, 1938)

Tiresias
Dublin Magazine 1939

Vaya Por Usted
Dance of the Dedication of the Bull

Curved arms, curved horns uplifted.
Angle of lovely head and neck, of the charging shoulder.
Beauty, swiftness, grace of limbs' movement
Underlined by death.

Controlled display of the red cloth—
The rustle of castanets the heart's beating!
Withdrawal. With a single
Art-concealing movement
Of hands, thighs, snakes'-tongue feet darting,
Evading death ...
The crash of castanets the heart's laughter!

In this wide, stony amphitheatre
Curved horns uplifted to the terrible sky
Where the *cuadrilla* dance, sway, posture,
Taunt and withdraw, and with parvenu swagger—
Rattle of machine-guns the heart's terror! —
Administer death,

Dedicating to aliens
This long-suffering, bewildered people; towns brimming,
No room underground; roads crammed;
Men, women and children trudging numbly
Towards shelterless shelter, uncertain safety.
Curved horns uplifted uncomprehendingly,
Fallen forward in death-agony.

Rearmament

New Leader 1937

There should have been no more flying in formation,
Marking the broad arrow on the sky,
No more marching in column
With hands upraised against a new crucifixion.

Rumour of War

They sang on the outermost road,
    And laughed when taken,
Their women were prouder than God
    To be forsaken;

But to us, if we should be driven
    To equal hell,
Can no saviour vision be given,
    No miracle;

The brave illusion is sped,
    Our creed is only
In life, and when lover is dead
    The heart is lonely.

Modern Warfare

The men
Obey obscure orders in obscurity,
Fight without knowledge of result, lose comrades,
Grumble at the sun, cold, lice, lack of women,
At everything except the leaders,
Whom, rather than admit the worst of a bargain,
They worship.

The leaders
Argue by telegraph, microphone, newspaper;
Deduce advantage from defeat, victory from silence,
Out-yell each other's Te Deums;
Sacrifice men, money, strategic position
For a debating point.

Tiresias

Tiresias
Poetry Chicago 1940

Now That the War Is Here

Now that the war is here, thank God
For merciful close perspective, blocking out
Façades of peace which otherwise would dwarf
These stunted sandbag virtues by which we live—
For men must live by virtues, even when
Bombing the helpless innocents; even hearts
Pruned to the stump sprout virtues or else die!

In this diminished world we must acquire—
Although our small hearts ache, weak sinews crack—
Unplumbable courage, numb endurance,
Blind sacrifice, high skill in homicide.
God help us, peering close in Lilliput
At giants of seven inches, still to see
Only their pigmy splendour, their mouse magnificence.

Epilogue – Planet Mars

Observer 1939

Somewhere the planet Mars
Burns with an angry glow;
And the great host of stars
Take warlike stations now.

The constellations pass
Across the darkened sky:
Auriga's armoured cars;
Hercules' infantry;

Silver-winged Pegasus
With his strong squadrons seen;
Cetus and Delphinus—
Warship and submarine.

Parched Sagittarius
With his machine-gun crew
Prays that Aquarius
Will get his transports through.

To Tiresias

Tiresias
New English Weekly 1939

Tell me, Tiresias, tongue among the dead:

Must always blood be spilt, blood spilt in rivers,
To irrigate a harvest of gold words?
Must Troy be burnt, Troy-town be sacked and gutted,
Eight cities sacked, the ninth mean mud-wall stand
Seven years of siege to make amoral Helen
Immortal, and shed splendour on the spears
Of crafty herdsmen from a remote island?

Must newer armies die, thousands at Suvla
(Within a hail of Troy), at Gaba Tepe,
To give a new continent dignity, and lay
The gritty dust on the name of Gallipoli?
Must blood be uttered in hymns of sacrifice,
Bodies be battered into bone-manure
And dug into the ground, to nourish laurels
For an unbalanced upstart or an obscure town?

Must Chinese cities be ploughed into wet fields
To add a pagoda-storey to their fame?
Must Western cities be bombed to broken shells
With troglodyte populations, that the hearts
Of future poets beat faster? Has Guernica,
Like Passchendaele, been razed to win a name? ..
For whose wreath is race racked in the name of race,
Long lineage cracked and torn up by the roots?

In man's imagination, that great cemetery,
Walks no ghost without blood?
Must every shade—of man, or woman, or town—
Be heavy with blood or slighter than the air?
We are so skilful at killing that every village,
City, and town should win a deathless name;
But who shall live to utter it? ... Must we still pour
The blood of millions out in shallow trenches?

Must you have blood, Tiresias, to speak?

III

This Other Planet

To My Father

This Other Planet
(Routledge 1945)

These poems cover the first years of World War II: my voluntary service, followed by my call up to the Royal Corps of Signals and service with the heavy anti-aircraft guns and radar of the Royal Artillery.

    I had valuable help and encouragement from John Arlott, T. S. Eliot, Malcolm and Jane Ford, Brian and Jenny de la Harp Meyer, Herbert Reed, H. A. Saunders, W. J. Turner, and Ronald and Douglas Vinnicombe.

Acknowledgements show poems as having appeared before 1945 in

English

The Listener

New English Weekly

Poetry Chicago

The Spectator

Exile

Outer Seas

Absolute exile to the outer seas:

This Other Planet
New English Weekly 1941
Roy Macnab with Charles Gulston:
South African Poetry (Collins 1948)

There, at the day's end of miserable toil
For bodily half-comfort, which of us
Would drive self-pitying comparisons farther:
You, with no barricading grand piano,
No musketry of 'cello and violin,
Artillery of gramophone records—
Firing round notes from a home-made flute?
Or I, with no pen-and-paper council,
No household regiment of books,
Drilling raw verses on the sea-wet sand?

Who has not wished to make Tristan da Cunha
In a small boat, alone, and let the world
Go fooling on with cabinets and dictators—
Receiving the odd newspaper, of course,
And coming back to write about the rough
And touching innocence of the fisherfolk?

Compared with Tristan da Cunha the Antipodes
Seems a mere week-end jaunt; Antipodeans
Walk upside-down, it's true, but right themselves
And bring their cockney tongues, like coals to Newcastle,
When Bradman and his boys come to London;
Return then to the Europeanization
Of their inverted country: colonnades,
Bastards of the Acropolis; sheep
Out of the ewes that stuffed the Woolsack; cricket,
White blades of willow among pendent gum-trees.
Only the fauna are original:
The kangaroo with palaeolithic tail
And carpenter's front pocket; winged jackasses;
Swans Villon thought impossible, black as soot;
Koala bears like bunchy-nosed old ladies
Reeking of eucalyptus; platypuses
Who hate their duck-bill compromise, and hide
From European eyes—and blackfellows,

Who threw their spears and kept them, thrifty men;
They'd like to have more of these little men,
But slew them thoughtlessly before demand grew;
Still, copies of their boomerangs can be bought,
Carved with Australian animals and flowers!

Compared with this the surf of Tristan da Cunha
Seems pleasantly remote—or terribly so?
Ultima Thule or Tir-nan-Og?
Devil's Island or the still-vext Bermoothes?
Why is there this shaking at the knees
At the mere mention of the Caribbees—
Unless, of course, you've been there? Is it just
The attraction of a spiritual nudity,
Free of all rates and taxes, times of trains,
Where you can stretch as when your clothes are off?

Air-routes now
Constrict the ball of earth, bringing Hawaii
Almost to picnicking distance; yet we still
Lean out, as leaves to sun, towards those places
That keep the flavour of distance. Is exile possible,
Absolute exile to some triangle between air routes,
Unshrivelled yet by speed?

Not exile within an Empire, to some half-homeland
Of machines, like giant imprisoned rabbits, stamping
In galvanized-iron hutches, kicking up white hills,
Crushing out gold, that, locked again underground
As tight as in the quartz, yet runs in the veins
The boom-and-slump varicose veins of the world ...
Nor a land of reapers handling prairie-gold
Along an endless chain to train and ship ...
Nor of elephants, twin tusks like swivelled guns,
Steaming upstream against a fleet of teak ...

Not exile to a neighbouring country where
Meanings are black-and-white, the nuances lost,
Where postmen wear berets, tables are set in the street;
Where clothes, houses, and newspapers
Grow on new branches from familiar roots ...

Not mere uncomfortable travel, copy
For future reminiscences, but exile
Utter and desolate to outer seas?

In the great Ocean of London, unprovided Crusoes   *Exile*
On tiny, Friday-less islands wait day by day
By aspidistra palms for friendly ships;
Or on square slabs of weather-beaten rock
Desert, deserted, watch blind ships go by;
Their neighbours are not men but elements
That throw shell-fish up sometimes, but more often
Destroy shelter, drench through to the skin,
Cut off all human communication, create
Moon-crater isolation on this planet.

Man's Roots

I

Man's roots are not in earth; while trees and flowers   *This Other Planet*
Stand in one place, the intimate atmospheres   *English*
Blown through their leaves, and the remoter spheres   Roy Macnab: *Poets in South Africa*
Of space whirled round them every twenty-four hours,   (Maskew Miller 1958)
                                                           Guy Butler: *A Book of South African Verse*
Even the peasant, who, in growing showers,   (Oxford University Press 1959)
Stands solid in his furrow, at times tears   Michael Chapman: *The Paperbook of South*
His boots from clinging mud, and slowly fares   *African English Poetry* (Ad Donker 1986)
To church, or pub, or war with foreign powers;   BBC, SABC broadcasts

But, as a ship, or migrant bird, or deer
Moves in a limited orbit, driving back
On pre-determined courses, so with man;
His many-branching lungs are roots in air;
His eyes, mind, lips have roots; and he is drawn
By vital tissues, dying if they crack.

II *South African*   *This Other Planet*
                                                                  The Africa We Knew
His eyes are rooted in these accidents   *English*
Of soil, and crops, and buildings: mealie-fields—   Roy Macnab with Charles Gulston:
Massed shafts and blades of assegai: cowhide shields—   *South African Poetry* (Collins 1948);
Split cobs with grain-row markings; vast extents   Roy Macnab: *Poets in South Africa*
                                                                   (Maskew Miller 1958)
Of plumes wind-tossed with Zulu discontents;   Guy Butler: *A Book of South African Verse*
This endless undulating khaki veld,   (Oxford University Press 1959)
Where upon sun-dried earth the ants have built   J. G. Brown: *Verse for You* (Longman 1966)
Their kraals of domed and hut-like tenements.   BBC, SABC broadcasts

Now Europeans, the last invaders, bring
Their even undulations in square roofs
Of corrugated iron, and hear the ring
Of hailstones on them—the stampeding hoofs
Of cattle, curved horns crowding; dour as ants,
Pile up square dumps beside their tribal haunts.

III *Rand Mine*

To Ronald Vinnicombe
Killed in mine accident c. 1940

This Other Planet
The Africa We Knew
English
New English Weekly 1943
Roy Macnab with Charles Gulston:
South African Poetry (Collins 1948)
Roy Macnab: *Poets in South Africa*
(Maskew Miller 1958)
Guy Butler: *A Book of South African Verse*
(Oxford University Press 1959)
BBC, SABC broadcasts

The walls jabber.
They whisper, chatter, argue,
Then jabber.
This is eight thousand feet down,
Two thousand below sea-level;
It's the pressure that makes them jabber—
As it does men sometimes,
Shriek, and then jabber, jabber.

The wall is low here,
The passage full of the noise of machinery,
Hundreds of mine-boys, iron-wheeled trolleys,
The sudden impact of blasting;
And then this casual readjustment
Of millions of tons of rock,
With a tearing as of steel plates, a gun-report
Followed by this lunatic,
Straining, complaining jabber.

'You can tell by the note when they're going to burst,
Rocketing inwards;
This is still the warning jabber!'

A prick in the earth's crust,
Two of the four thousand miles to earth's centre;
But the piled plateau of the Highveld,
The Drakensberg mountains,
The South Atlantic and Indian oceans
Press on me as the walls
Jabber, jabber.

IV *Jamaica*

Exile

This Other Planet
New English Weekly 1943
Poetry Chicago 1943
English

The sun sets over this most lovely bay
Crimson beyond the palm‑trees; at my feet,
In this small chattering patch of dusty street,
Between the frontless Chinese shops, the gay

Excited stalls where khaki hands display
Their rows of gaudy bottles, women squat
Among their rags and market‑wares, men shout
And argue in the rum‑shop over the way.

The clattering street‑car passes with the light.
In momentary twilight a hush falls
Over the cavernous shops, the shadowy stalls.
Between the car‑lines a young negro stands,
And stamps bare, dusty feet, and jerks his hands,
Twanging a jew's‑harp in the sudden night.

Sounds hold a man in tether: all night long
Bat, croaking lizard, in off‑harmony
With whistling frog and cricket, rhythmically
Throw whisper, shriek, croak, hum—vast choric song

Of negro freedman?—pipe, and curléd tongue,
Leg‑fiddle, husky throat incessantly
Across the velvet quiet as vividly
As firefly shuttles across darkness flung.

Behind the humming foothills promise of light
Shows bamboo plumes in outline; with a slight
Movement of baton brings fresh voices in;
Cocks, hens, and horses, crows, and cows unite
With a million shadowy dogs in this vast din
To greet the steady sun mile‑running in.

V *Fireflies: Home Thoughts from Jamaica*

Tonight the stars have left the sky to call
Field 1937
A season of masked dance and carnival
Down here on earth—on every side you see
Innumerable fireflies tirelessly
Doffing and donning visibility
In golden arabesque, bewilderingly...

This Other Planet

The darkening stands at Twickenham when the play
Draws to an end on a midwinter day,
And every instant, stabbing tiers of grey,
Thousands of matches flare and fade away.

VI *European*

This Other Planet
English

Wherever the industrial counterpane,
Patterned by blind machines, has not yet spread,
The buildings rise like plants out of the bed
Of local soil, these northern columns strain

Upwards like pine trees crowding close as rain;
Those in the south stand wide apart to shade
All those who must walk in their urbane arcade
A southern dome flowers over a wide plain.

Houses wear local wood and local stone;
Men shapes of bough, women of leaves and flowers;
Out of grey stony fells grey walls are grown;
These sheep their grey and these brown fleeces beat;
Gravely the Norman soldiers used to wear
Upon their heads their castles' conical towers.

In a Strange Land

I

This Other Planet
New English Weekly 1943
Maurice Wollman: *Poems of the War Years*
(Macmillan 1950)

How lovely are the waters of Babylon,
Removed three thousand years, three thousand miles!
The weeping willows green in the dusty plain,
And, in the dusk, to the crickets' insistent buzz,
The sounds of harps and weeping, without pain
For us, at this great distance, after this time ...
But in the sun-baked houses, the terraced gardens—
The wonder of the world—under the lash,
And under the metalled club of the sun,
Under the bas-relief eagles in the terrible square,
They remembered Jerusalem,
Cool in the dusk, crowned with olives,
Friendly stone shaped familiarly,
Enriched with the usury of distance;
How could they sing the songs of Zion
In a strange land?

Only their children, who had not seen her,
Sang the songs of Zion by the waters of Babylon;
Songs that were symbols now of lesser disappointments—
Dogs that ran too slowly, faithless women,
The repeated slights that fell to aliens.
By the waters of Babylon, in the cool dusk,
They sang the songs of Zion in a syncopated measure,
Danced, kissed, and forgot Jerusalem.

II

Nothing is new beneath the sun.
They stood beside him with a gun,
Gave him a minute or two to dress,
Pushed aside his wife and son.
Too numb with shock to show distress,
He went with them, and saw the sun
Go backward, gathering scattered fire...

This Other Planet
New English Weekly c. 1939

III

Searchlights with empty gestures lift their white
Celestial sleeves, blank light without a pang
For the thin skulls of airmen in their slight

This Other Planet
New English Weekly c. 1940

Cabins of aluminium, or the strong
Blood-flow of men and women under glass
And tiles and fragile brickwork; all night long

We hear the planes go over, hear them pass
Along their vaporous ceiling, separate
As particles in an atom universe.

As separate as stars are, held apart
And drawn by invisible tensions, each a dry
Crystal of sound infusing through the quiet,

Each a permanganate grain successively
Staining the bowl of quiet, which, growing still
And clear, is stained again immediately;

Unmelodramatic as a dentist's drill
Whose fine attrition grinds, and flakes, and breaks,
Just misses the raw nerve with infinite skill
Yet jars the skull. A sudden flash awakes
Moon-powdered roofs; windows in gleaming tension
Chatter like teeth; doors rattle; the earth shakes;

Dead on the nerve with little intermission
A single gun barks at the long procession.

This Other Planet

This Other Planet
New English Weekly c. 1940

IV

The air, the glare,
Air full of the glare
Of planes, of rhododendrons;
No patch of shade in which to hide
Except beneath those rhododendrons.

The brilliant sky a rhododendron bush
Turned inside out, a peacock's tail of eyes,
Each arrogant as a peacock, each a sun
Detached from molten skies
Falling as down the barrel of a gun.

Along the road the bomb-bursts, livid bushes
Planted and flowering in an instant;
Flowering among the velvet, glossy-splendid,
Sun-spotted, sheltering rhododendrons.

V

This Other Planet
New English Weekly
Poetry Chicago 1943

Soldiers in trains with their unwieldy kits,
Airmen with knapsacks and attaché cases
In telephone-booths and post-offices, all the places
That link up with their life as once they knew it—
These are the obvious exiles, these returning
From embarkation leave, half England churning
Through crowded turnstiles to meet its fellow,
To meet, and part with the little hollow
Laugh that never deceives—yet what are these
But ripples at the edge of enormous seas?

The millions of Germans in Russia that have no leave,
The millions of Russians, our armies in the East,
The prisoners of war with their depressed
And shabby replicas of life, the grave
Family men who didn't want the war,
And the young who loved at first sight, but love no more.

VI

This Other Planet

Men, huge beneath arctic equipment, setting out
To remote aerial regions, whence to destroy
Regions remote from their personal knowledge;
Drawn by the running feet of petrol explosions
In light metal cabins through austere air,
By fleecy ice-cliffs and through vaporous space ...
Whether these find Ultima Thule or tread a beat
As usual and prosaic as a bus-route,
They have left their human values on the runway.

These, too, are exiles, these who sent their son
Out of their crushed and broken land to aliens—
Aliens in speech, in thought their fellow-countrymen—
And plan to follow him. He will be fed,
And clothed, and bred, with leaves that reach to them
But roots apart from them;
Within their frontiers their hearts are exiles;
And these, the thousands who have sent their children
Unwillingly to greater safety, knowing
That every mile of the train's unpublished journey
Carried off not their children but themselves;
All these are exiles;
And those whose sons and husbands fight in ships,
And planes, and removed places, carrying off
Uprooted hearts, and leaving hearts uprooted
Beside their hearths and household gods.

Stretchers

*A stretcher-bearing squad based on
the Colchester Royal Grammar School
Sixth Form was responsible for removing
casualties from ambulances during air raids.*

Among Strangers

New English Weekly c. 1940
Poetry Chicago 1941

For a short time after his death
A man retains his semblance; friends come in
On tiptoe, peer at the pale, parchment face
And think: O death, what dignity has death
Conferred on him! Carry away a picture
That blurs as surely as the buried features.

I knew this man
For minutes only of the intimate day
When he, apart from friends, life lost
Began to put identity away;
Death is, like birth, convulsive, but decay
Gradual as pregnancy.

We lifted him down from the top rack of the ambulance
At eleven o'clock at night in pouring rain;
Rain on our hands, torch shining under the hood,
We eased the stretcher out so as not to catch the blankets,
And carried him in to the white electric light:

His pale domed head fallen back, the glazing eyes
Half-shut, huge hands oblong as oars

This Other Planet

Flattened against the blue serge sides,
The jersey fitting like a skin. Nurses removed
The blood-caked blankets, the pathetic sea-boots
That, holding still his shape, seemed amputated:
In light reflected from glazed walls decay
Began to form a foetus.

Cold rain had fallen all day. At seven that morning
An enemy had swooped out of the squally sky.
Bullets had spattered like rain off the wet deck,
Had caught him in the knee, the neck, the shoulder.
He lay in a fo'c'sle berth while the waves lifted
The bows of the tiny drifter and crashed them down,
Crushed lead on bone.
He came ashore in a dinghy, hardly aware
Of the rain on his numbing face, on the hands at the oars.

He died in the ambulance. All we could do for him
Was to carry him in for the nurses to wash his limbs,
Midwives at his premature death.

Boy With a Rifle

This Other Planet
Listener c. 1939
Keidrych Rhys: *More Poems from the Forces*
(Routledge 1943)
Andrew Sinclair: *The War Decade*
(Hamish Hamilton 1989)
Andrew Sinclair: *War Like a Wasp*
(Hamish Hamilton 1989)

*The Cricket School at Colchester Royal
Grammar School was converted into a small-bore
rifle range, where boys were instructed by masters.
Stella Currey was also instructed.*

Pacifist must find an answer,
League of Nations, Super-State,
Every pattern of New Order;

Rifle-virgin, dedicate
To this yard of metal, slender,
Strange and lovely as a mate.

Trigger gravely curved and tender
As a lover's lips, a rod
And a thimbleful of thunder

Carrying life-and-death, and shod
With the speed of instancy,
Exquisitely just as God.

Neat as trigonometry;
Mortal flesh to an immortal
Element swears constancy,

Cheek pressed closely to the fatal
Beauty, and the quivering shy
Finger on the tender petal

Of release, the ecstasy
And agony of consummation,
Cardboard iris, human eye

Checked in slightly-swaying motion
Their brief unity to put
On record. How but by this weapon

Or the million-spawn irate
Machine-gun or the Rabelaisian
Cannon can we sublimate

Youthful energy and passion?
Find an answer, victor-nation.

Searchlight Battery

Michel Angelo would understand
And appreciate your job.

This Other Planet
New English Weekly 1941
A. C. Ward: *Grim and Gay*
(Oxford University Press 1942)

He had to lie for several years
Upon his back, his long brush feeling
Life stir behind a shadowed ceiling:
Prophets and sibyls in the spandrels;
Serpent; and Flood; and Cain's and Abel's
Sacrifices; and muscular angels;
God in a swirl of heaven creating
Adam, extending His generating
Arm and hand, like an artist's brush ...
When through the Sistine doors with a rush,
Beard aflame like the Burning Bush,
Came the blaspheming, shouting, railing,
Sexagenarian Julius, scaling
The dizzy ladder, to dance gyrating
On that high platform, and try to grab
And throw to earth the procrastinating,
Death underrating
Artist through whom he planned to be
Set up in immortality
As pope and patron—and kept in arrears.

This Other Planet

And you, lying back, your long brush feeling
The ceiling behind the clouds, are filling
In line and colour of the outline traced
On your patch of sky by these lightning-paced
Death-dealing shapes—these, Signorelli's
Metal-winged devils with lurid bellies;
These, he nor Michel Angelo
Nor even Leonardo ever planned,
Earth-ranging, avenging,
All but Sistine-Roof-spanned
Armoured archangels.

Boys from Colchester Royal Grammar School
went to Kettering, Northamptonshire,
in September 1940

Evacuation

I had no right with them, no sort of right.
My troubles were so slight compared with theirs.
All my emotion had been drained away
Some days before, renouncing those I loved;
And now this chance was sending me quite near them!
It seemed a light thing then to leave my house—
My books and manuscripts—and take a train
To a town I did not know—responsible
For other people's children. I could feel
No sympathy—I was too numb for that—
But was amused to see how chance had picked
Boys that I knew quite well, an excellent bunch,
With only one whose troublesomeness stuck out
Like a pyjama-tassel from his suitcase.
I didn't give a damn, and laughed to find
Good friends with me as colleagues; in fact it seemed
Exactly like a novel in which you meet
Each of the characters again in heaven—
Or else in prison. I couldn't understand
How the events that took me by the collar
Under a week before could so pamper me!

For days we had been conscious of ships massing
In dusty Ostend, and Boulogne, and Calais—
Places of happier memory—of planes
Attacking in armadas, losing heavily,
But coming still with undiminished fury;
For weeks I had been working to a time-table
Strange and exacting where curved siren-calls
Instead of bells marked periods; my feet were flat
With carrying stretchers down steep stairways,

80

Helping to empty the hospital. Straining quays
And capes and beaches circled us
From Brest to Norway, reaching out to seize
And crush us over ever-narrowing seas—
Green balks now, moats no longer; and I smiled
To find myself in a novel of escape.
I hardly felt the boys' preoccupation
When they sat quiet a moment. I was too tired
To be unselfish. Imagination
And heart dozed side by side in that railway carriage.
The boys laughed and ate, and played like puppies—
There was no holding them—but soon they started
The never-ending question: 'How many stations?'

How many stations? We went half way round
England to half-traverse it; the boys groaned
At each digression, cheered to pass a truck-load
Of shot-down German planes, and ate, and wrestled,
Read bloods, and slept against each other's shoulders,
Asking repeatedly: 'How many stations?'
How many miles?
How many miles to Babylon, porter, porter?
How many stations more to Xanadu?
We passed an airfield with its safety-belt
Of broken columns suggesting monuments
To men cut off in their prime, and, in the dusk,
We passed an airship station, with hangars
Like giant Noah's arks in the Tigris plain.
We travelled under the moon for hours drawn out
By ignorance of the time when we should arrive.
At last, in the dark, a porter said, 'Next station!'
At last—but this was no arrival home,
Swift welcome, bath and bed. In the black station
Which we had thought of as our destination
We stood with coats and cases in a serpent
That spread along one platform, through a subway,
And down another—and sometimes moved a little.
Then buses to a school; and here we moved
With coats and cases down long passages
Past tables where we showed identity cards.
We went
Upstairs at one o'clock to the bread and cheese
Boys were too tired to eat; my selfishness
Wore thin before those green, exhausted faces.

We dragged our things to a classroom three floors up,
Laid down our single blanket on the floor,

An overcoat on top, and tried to sleep,
And did sleep too, though for some little time
A snarling bomber circled overhead.

Next day, after the serpent had been searched
For lice and infectious diseases, we waited
For billets to be found; by supper-time
The last boy of our batch was fitted in
A dozen being taken in a bus
From road to road, and hawked from door to door.

This was a slight adventure beside those
That many have met these days, and, as I say,
I had no right there ... drained of sympathy.

Signals

A Man Once Lived in a Village

I *Call Up*

This Other Planet
Poetry Chicago 1943

To drill raw verses on the sea-wet sand?
This was a pleasant fancy in the days
Before my exile; now I have no right
To drill my toes or the fingers of my hand.
I am enclosed, cribbed, cabined, and confined;
My body is no longer mine, my mind
So set to work on formal parrotries
No time or energy is left to be
The person I still like to think is me.
At the day's end of miserable toil
The bodily half-comfort in my power
Is to lie by the shore for half an hour
And watch the hostile waves on the wet sand;
Or sleep, or dream, and, dreaming, wake to find
The coated taste of exile on my tongue.

Railway journeys mark off phases of existence.
We travelled all day in trains, slowly converging,
Each with his obvious suitcase, on to the office
Where a soldier took down our names with infinite slowness.
Grey moors and climbing houses, factory chimneys.

The man in the corner said: 'I've never seen
So bleak a countryside!' He came from the South.
The old man travelling with us: 'Yes, I know it.
They send you for five weeks to break your heart!'
Arriving, we were marched to our billets,
To the endless formalities of attestation,
At last to our meal; in these last weeks
We have marched endlessly from all we knew
And thought secure and real; marched to the barracks
For food, equipment, clothing, and medical examination;
To fatigues, pickets and battle-drills; up and down,
About turn, quick time, slow time, double,
Right incline, left incline, the sentry's futile beat
Up the pavement and down again, right about, left about,
Lifting the heels like a guardsman, check pace, halt;
Marched on the spot, but always farther and farther
From the home that took years to build up,
From the loved presence of wife and children,
From the arm-chair and the peopled fireside.
All these recede. Now backless benches
And wire netting bunks give comfort;
Good comradeship, trivial joys and sorrows in common,
Shared photographs and beer and fish-and-chips.
No intolerable hardship, but a life
Of ceaseless driving—drill, P.T., fatigues,
Blanco, and blacking, and silvo, and rifle-oil;
No privacy, no moment to read, to think,
Even to wonder how the war is going:
A penny buys a paper—or a cup of tea.

A trivial thing, this marking of phases by dress:
The first putting on of long trousers,
The first putting on of uniform —yet I'm sure
The symbolism as well as the heat affected us.
We marched through the streets in threes, self-conscious
And glad this would be the last time in civilian clothes.
It was hot, our food overdue, and we were excited.
In the stifling heat, smelling of bleach,
We stood in rows by our kit-bags, took off our clothes
By numbers, picking up the socks,
The leather bootlaces and collarless shirts
Of our new existence; some sixty men
To be fitted with two battle-dress suits, one cap,
Two pairs boots, one greatcoat, to be handed denims,
Gym things, and shaving things, and underclothing.

This Other Planet

In the swimming heat of that green cage
We crushed them into our kits with civilian clothes,
And stumbled out into the afternoon air
To stare at each other,
Yellow, and shambling, and disillusioned
In bleach-stiff khaki and discoloured boots
And stiff ungainly convict caps—
The barracks a factory and reminiscent
Of an American prison.
Still in greatcoats, we formed up on the square,
Boots stumbling and slithering, on one shoulder
Our kit-bag, a miscellaneous package
Beneath the other.
Dizzy with bleach, we moved off in ungainly
Column of threes, enduring
From step to step, wondering
If everything in the army would be like this;
We were relieved, almost happy, when one man fainted.

II *Training Depot*

You're all enthusiasm at the start,
But in the first month we'll break your heart!

You hold up your head and think you can take it—
You don't know just how tough we can make it.

You come and go; we're on the spot,
We know what reserves of strength you've got.

We know all the ways to make you squirm—
Cut out the man and leave the worm.

You're willing to work until you drop;
You'll learn how to dodge before we stop.

You're used to having your conscience clear;
You mustn't expect that luxury here.

Until you're seasoned a sense of sin
Will follow you out and follow you in.

You're ready for anything—in reason
But to ask for reason here's high treason.

You're wanting to help to win the war—
We'll teach you to wonder what you're fighting for!

There was a recruit who said: You figure
To tame lions here; well, I'm a tiger!

This is a democratic country, see;
You might tame lions, but you won't tame me!

He called the orderly sergeant a twister;
He told the C.S.M. to call him mister.

He was here two months, or maybe three,
And all that time he was on C.B.

He wouldn't let the army change his ways,
So they sent him to the glasshouse for a hundred days.

When he came out he wouldn't salute,
And he dropped his rifle on the colonel's foot.

We'd have had to have a special picquet
For him alone, so he got his ticket!

We hear he's shut up in a padded cell—
Rather a pity, as we liked him well.

Our theory is simple, though hard to batter in:
There's no other way to teach you discipline!

III *Telephone-Box*

Here are navel strings that hold men tight:
Wire labyrinths between red telephone-boxes
And private sets; tall honeycomb gear that foxes
The layman even more than nature's sleight—

Of-hand within the womb; for night by night
Behind small Georgian panes the severed sexes
Stand close, and smile; a shabby strand of flex is
A flock of homing pigeons in full flight.

A man once lived in a village and was a part
Of field and tree, but now his living heart
Passes its pulses through long miles of wire
To those who are the sum of his desire—
For limited instants, as it were a ration
Of love translated into speech vibration.

85

IV

A young man has a way of life
  That changes each day;
Circumstance
  Decides his way.

An old man has a way of life
  Lined in with brick;
Push him out of his rut,
  You'll kill him quick.

A man of thirty to forty years
  Can change his way of life,
But he's as full of regrets
  As a man with a second wife.

Get into the army, young man,
  And put your mind to sleep;
Sharpen up your wits—
  Your mind will keep.

Or so they tell me, but I saw
  A mind unpacked one day;
The moths had got at the edges,
  The centre had rotted away.

I *This Other Planet*

This other planet, nearer than the moon,
Has nothing romantic about it; jagged mountains,
Deep rainy valleys, mossy fountains—
But these are for fighting over; you soon forget

Their rugged beauty and grandeur when you are wet
Through to the skin, and dragging a Lewis gun
Sideways across a cliff, or trying to run
Up a long slope with it; this afternoon

The wind swishes through the bracken as I lie
And listen to the long-lash bullets whip by:
These are the alphabet, the primitive speech
Of this new planet; grenades and bullets teach
A man to lie still and press his face in the mud,
Or run till his eyes are full of the colour of blood.

This Other Planet
Poetry Chicago 1943
K. M. Durham: *Two Roads*
(Juta/Arnold 1969)

II *Parade*

I often feel, when I am on parade,
That I have stood on one small patch of street
So many centuries that my numbed feet
Are rooted in the soil beneath the made

Surface of asphalt; walls and houses fade,
The long review of seasons—rain and sleet
And snow and sun—moves past us; lost winds beat
On boulders in a prehistoric glade.

Stone walls unbuild, trees draw their branches in
And shrink into the ground; dun uniform
Reverts through red and green to painted skin;
The senses shrivel inwards to a core
Quick only to the scrutinies of war,
The eye of lightning in the passing storm.

This Other Planet
Maurice Wollman: *Poems of the War Years*
(Macmillan 1950)

Yet, even in exile there are living moments.
Robinson Crusoe looked from his stockade
Past all the poor things that he had made,
His sure prosaic pride, in sudden boredom

With everything except the sense of freedom
Of ocean breakers, lacing every shade
Of turquoise, aquamarine, and glittering jade
With white, obliterating the dull currents

Of his small faithful stream; so, on parade,
In this dim cobbled channel between mills
I look beyond the immobile stockade
Of khaki caps and shoulders at the hills,
A short clear strip above the street-end roof
And free white clouds out of a former life.

III *Firing Range*

High on these moors the hand of man is shown
In this square reservoir, an inland sea
Wild with white waves but held securely
By concrete sides; our marching files are blown

Sideways by wind, and each man is alone
Shut off by gritty air; against this scree
We set up symbols of our enemy
And hump up ammunition to shoot them down.

Up in the butts they stand out of the wind,
Change targets underneath the whip-lash crack
Of bullets, move their discs from side to side,
Patch the huge tattered bull—this tiny black
Pinhead that dances on a foresight's end
Above a concrete line on the hillside.

IV *Conclusion*

This other planet, in the gaze of Mars,
Has curious flora and fauna, ripe for wars;
The grass is hessian, the trees are brass
And leathern men interminably pass
With hands at the salute ... these are the men
Who estimate a plane's position, then
Look to the future, as with second sight,
And snap out future bearing, time of flight;
They know by instinct how to put a shell
Seven miles up, and calculate as well
The instant of explosion, arc of curve,
Allowances for droop, for drift or swerve,
And heat and pressure at the point where
The shell will burst—you'd think they'd been up there!

Their hearts are dynamos, their quick brains glean
Figures as smoothly as a bank machine;
They don't believe in theory, but know
How to cash in on the electron flow
In wire conductors; know how to repair
Ten marks of telephone, and with a pair
Of avometer pointers quickly vet
A dozen different types of wireless set.
Batteries wet and dry are their delight;
They'll come at any hour of day or night
To adjust a magslip pointer, mend a wire …
And engines, engines are their hearts' desire!
They've never nursed an animal, but know
If a generator coughs just what to do;
From infancy they've felt a fascination
For each and every form of calibration;
They'll fix a flicker on a tube, it's reckoned,
Down to a hundred thousandth of a second.
Sometimes, I swear
They are not men but bloodless parasites
Planted by Martians on electric nights
To undermine humanity and replace
It by a super-scientific race
Of fighting men!
These are the men who do but cannot think;
They eat, and there's no doubt that they can drink
And even laugh at limited types of joke
And argue points of fact; for, from the smoke
Of technical argument I've yet to hear
Of the birth of one idea….
They'll learn the joy of words and images;
And even, given time,
The joys of rhyme;
At present they are in the early stages;
Their speech is coprophile; in metaphors
Turned on the muddy tongues of many wars,
And dead alike to meaning and disgust,
The bastards of pure science are discussed …
These men are janissaries; brain and hand
Service this world they only understand
In terms of cogs—yet in this barbarous
Moment of crisis save the world for us.

Artillery & Radar

Gun Park

I *Maintenance*

This Other Planet
New English Weekly 1942

In this fantastic world each death's machine
Is beautiful, the bore of every barrel
A hollowed spiral, like an exquisite jewel—
A lit match adds a bloom like crêpe‑de‑chine;

*N.C.O.

In the predictor telescope a clean‑
Cut image of a jewelled Number One*
Stands out upon the platform of his gun:
As fine a miniature as you have seen.

These jewelled men, from a devoted heart,
Offer up worship to each slick machine,
And yet their ritual phrases are obscene;
The barrel's full of excrement, they say;
And, as for copulation, every part
Shows potency recalling Rabelais.

II *Check Dials and Line Up*

This Other Planet
New English Weekly 1942

We hold strange matins and strange vespers here.
In the first morning and last evening light
Lay our four guns upon an aiming point—
Some landmark our East window!—start our queer

* Gun Position Officer

Utilitarian parody of prayer.
The G.P.O.* priest and his acolyte
Intone the motif for a counterpoint,
Returned by Numbers One with impeccable ear.

From each gun‑pit in turn responses flow
With ritual smoothness as the Numbers One
Speak for the circling layers on their gun.
Number Four, set bearing ... says the G.P.O.;
Then: Go to bearing ... Amen to our prayer
Of readiness for the daemons of the air.

III *Heavy Guns*

This Other Planet
New English Weekly 1942

We speak an alien language to the guns,
Using the shouted words they understand,
Bearing, Q.E., and Fuse, for on demand
They'll follow a delicate pointer as it runs

About its dial, and move their oiled tons
With silken ease to gestures of a hand;
Traverse right! Depress! Make answer through the grand
And sonorous voices of their Number Ones.

On the word 'Fire' they speak, these lordly ones,
Their splendid devils' language, with long tongues
Of blinding flame and thundering iron lungs—
But they are devil-slaves, Aladdin djinns;
They keep the deadly letter of their command,
Exult to kill their masters out of hand.

IV *Firing with Heavy Guns*

This Other Planet
Poems of Today (Macmillan 1951)
Victor Selwyn: *Poems of the Second World War*
(Dent 1985)

They laugh like fallen archangels, these four guns,
Utter their searing blasphemies of flame
And thunder that seeks to take in vain the name
And power of God; they flash hot vivid suns

From every side, and all four firing at once
In one clean salvo separately clout
Your head from side to side; they laugh and shout
And make the sandbags leap with their loud tones.

They are the fallen archangels, this the hour
In which they taste some memory of the power
With which they stormed the frontiers of heaven.
The four rounds burst together, seven miles high
Quite close—good shooting, but they have not even
Begun to climb the immense heights of the sky.

Military Funeral

The people who pass in the street
Make no lasting pattern.
Even those who pass daily
Each along his own peculiar beat
Draw lines that gaily
Criss-cross in the mind
For a moment only.

And now the lonely
Body on the flagged truck passes by
With officers leading,
And a long column of men slow-marching by,
Slow-marching,
Emphasizing,
With each held step the transience of mankind.

Under his uniform
He was a civilian.
He had his individual beat
Along this street,
Obliterated now by marching feet.

Training

The rhythm of seasons is irrelevant,
The beauty of the buttercups has no part
In this routine which we must get by heart,
This fragment of a planned development

Of vast and overwhelming armament.
Sunlight and rain impinge no more than thought,
Unnoticed are laburnums and their short
Flourish of absolute accomplishment.

Beyond the tall guns are the changing fields
Obedient to the rhythms of life and birth;
The green and golden sequences of earth
Have no place in our drills; the mountain yields
A useful aiming-point; the season's rent
Effective man-power, growing armament.

Mixed Battery

Artillery & Radar

This Other Planet

This curious replica of a prairie town;
Verandah'd huts, and shabby offices,
Canteen and cookhouse, wooden storehouses.
And smoky sleeping quarters here set down
Slap on the edge of nowhere, mushroom-grown
For fifty men and eighty A.T.S.,
Has yet achieved a certain synthesis,
Become a community upon its own ...

Set here to serve four guns; the instruments
Are manned by girls, big-bottomed in their slacks,
Who pass with gunnery data some pretence
Of normal life to men who bend their backs
Over the rounds they tend like infant sons—
The arrogant servant-masters of the guns.

Spring Offensive

This Other Planet
Poetry Chicago
Keidrych Rhys: *More Poems from the Forces*
(Routledge 1943)

We buy the beauty of the spring
        with the mind's anguish;
Those who stand before the rush
        pay with their blood.

Pink almond blossom breaks the ice,
        frees armoured wheels;
Buttercups and laburnum
        fill quisling purses.

Skins that should be sensitive
        are raw;
Nostrils are scorched by the scent of flowers,
        eyes blink.

The noise of aeroplanes
        stains the blue;
Far promise of peace upon earth
        contaminates the ear.

We have seen the fragility of houses,
        the guts of palaces,
The fluidity of the lines and squares
        of organized society.

This Other Planet

The individual man and woman,
      the loved roots
Of a familiar existence
      quiver and blur;

Our children are held in common, and the tribe
      alone exists;
Ants hurry from the crushing foot
      and some survive.

Those whom spring sunshine most intoxicates
      have foreseen
This disintegration of springtime
      for fifteen springs;

Foreseen spring sunshine setting free
      the upper ice;
The almond blossom loosening
      the avalanche.

(Unseen Fire)
This Other Planet
Roy Macnab with Charles Gulston:
South African Poetry (Collins 1948)
Poems of Today (Macmillan 1951)
Ian Hamilton: *The Poetry of War*
(Alan Ross 1965)
Brian Gardner: *The Terrible Rain, War Poets
1939–45* (Methuen 1966)
D. R. Beeton & W.D. Maxwell-Mahon:
South African Poetry: A Critical Anthology
(UNISA 1966)
John Rowe Townsend: *Modern Poetry* (Oxford
University Press 1971)
British Council for
Harvard Poetry Room 1972
Philip Larkin: *Oxford Book of Twentieth
Century English Verse* (1973)
Michael Chapman: *A Century of
South African Poetry* (Ad Donker 1981)
Jon Stallworthy:
The Oxford Book of War Poetry (1984)
Victor Selwyn: *Poems of the Second World War*
(Dent 1985)
Andrew Sinclair: *The War Decade*
(Hamish Hamilton 1989)
Michael Foss: *Poetry of the World Wars*
(Michael O'Mara 1990)
Desmond Graham: *Poetry of the Second
World War – An International Anthology*
(Chatto & Windus 1995)
Victor Selwyn: *The Voice of War* (Michael
Joseph 1995)
A. D. Harvey: *A Muse of Fire*
(Hambledon Press 1998)
Frequent readings, most recently BBC 1998

Disintegration of Spring Time

Unseen Fire

I
This is a damned inhuman sort of war.
I have been fighting in a dressing-gown
Most of the night; I cannot see the guns,
The sweating gun-detachments or the planes;

I sweat down here before a symbol thrown
Upon a screen, sift facts, initiate
Swift calculations and swift orders; wait
For the precise split-second to order fire.

We chant our ritual words; beyond the phones
A ghost repeats the orders to the guns:
One Fire ... Two Fire ... ghosts answer: the guns roar
Abruptly; and an aircraft waging war
Inhumanly from nearly five miles height
Meets our bouquet of death—and turns sharp right.

II

This is a damned unnatural sort of war;
The pilot sits among the clouds, quite sure
About the values he is fighting for;
He cannot hear beyond his veil of sound,

He cannot see the people on the ground;
He only knows that on the sloping map
Of sea‑fringed town and country people creep
Like ants—and who cares if ants laugh or weep?

To us he is no more than a machine
Shown on an instrument; what can he mean
In human terms?—a man, somebody's son,
Proud of his skill; compact of flesh and bone
Fragile as Icarus—and our desire
To see that damned machine come down on fire.

Artillery & Radar

This Other Planet
John Lehmann: *Penguin New Writing*
no. 21, 1944
John Lehmann: *Poems from New Writing 1936-
1946* (John Lehmann 1946)
Roy Macnab with Charles Gulston:
South African Poetry (Collins 1948)
Burton: *Exercises in Criticism*
(Longman 1956)
Ian Hamilton: *Poetry of War 1939–45*
(Alan Ross 1965)
D.R. Beeton & W.D. Maxwell‑Mahon:
A South African Critical Anthology
(UNISA 1968)
John Rowe Townsend: *Modern Poetry*
(Oxford University Press 1971)
Michael Chapman: *A Century of South
African Poetry* (Ad Donker 1981)
Victor Selwyn: *Poems of the Second World War*
(Dent 1985)
Andrew Sinclair: *The War Decade*
(Hamish Hamilton 1989)
Michael Foss: *Poetry of the World Wars*
(Michael O'Mara 1990)
Victor Selwyn: *The Voice of War*
(Michael Joseph 1995)

III

We've most of us seen aircraft crash in flame,
Seen how the cruel guardians of height,
Fire and the force of gravity, unite
To humanize the flying god and proclaim

His common clay; by hedge and field we came
Running through the darkness, tried to fight
The solid wall of heat. Only the white
Lilac of foam could get us near that frame—

That frame like a picked fish‑bone; sprawled beneath—
Charred bodies, more like trunks of trees than men;
The ammunition began to go up then,
Another and more glittering type of spray;
We could not help them, six men burned to death—
I've had their burnt flesh in my lungs all day!

This Other Planet
Roy Macnab with Charles Gulston:
South African Poetry (Collins 1948)
D. R. Beeton & W. D. Maxwell‑Mahon: *A
South African Critical Anthropology* (UNISA
1968)
Michael Chapman: *A Century of
South African Poetry* (Ad Donker 1981)
Victor Selwyn: *Poems of the Second World War*
(Dent 1985)
Victor Selwyn: *The Voice of War*
(Michael Joseph 1995)

This Other Planet

This Other Planet
New English Weekly 1942
Guy Butler: *A Book of South African Verse*
(Oxford University Press 1959)
Jack Cope & Uys Krige: *Penguin Book*
of South African Verse (1970)

At This Great Distance

How lovely are the waters of Babylon
Removed three thousand years, three thousand miles;
The weeping willows green in the dusty plain,
And, in the dusk, to the crickets' insistent buzz,
The sound of harps and weeping, without pain
For us, at this great distance, after this time …

How wonderful, to sit in a cinema
And have your war brought to you; El Alamein,
A barrage like a black Niagara of sand,
A creeping giant holding by the hand
Pygmies who fall—and rise to run again:
The lurch and slither of a reptile band
Of belly-dragging tanks; strange sarabande
Of Engineers with long divining-wand
Moving ahead of the army and smelling out
Like devil-dancers the mines and boobies hidden
Under the wheel-cracked crust and crest of the sand;
The long untidy columns of famine-ridden
Scorched prisoners; the charred trunk and clenched hand
Of a dead enemy; the urgent shout
Of a sergeant to a devil-choir of guns;
All the excitement, all the thrill
Of modern warfare, the chase and the kill—
And the triumph! To watch with pleasantly-scalded eye
The spit-and-polish sporrans swinging by
Skirling *Cock o' the North* for victory—
And all for two shillings; sit in your seat
And never feel the brazen heat of the sun,
And the daze, and the beat, and the stun
Of the guns as they fire; the oven-heat
(Under the riveting hammer of the sun)
Of tanks rank with the stink of oil;
The smell of roasted flesh, that sweet sick smell;
The sick plague of flies spawned by the sun;
Sand like hot embers in the eye, in the groin.
The blind whirlpool of sand obscuring the sun;
The long hot monotonies, preoccupied
With sand in the limber, sand in the chamber,
Sand in the brakes, in the gears, in your hair;
The men that bear the burden and heat of the day
Have these thrown in and nothing extra to pay:
But the delicate edge between triumph and defeat
And the personal danger of death don't go with the seat—

Nor yet the occasional coolness after heat
And the occasional clear, bare
Unbelievable austerity of desert air,
Jewelling edges of sand, while mountains as far
As fifty miles away stand suddenly near
And pink as rose-petals in water,
O water—O the sheer
Cool of a pool leaf-hidden from the sun:
How lovely are the waters, the waters of Babylon.

Some Little Time

Exile of the body or of the mind?
The war has loaded the dice, so that we find
There are no Tir-nan-Ogs to visit now
Except strategic ones, to which we go
Willy-nilly, regardless of our whims;
Iceland, where poets sang nostalgic hymns
To glacial austerity says No!
No beer, no flicks, no women; in fact, No!
Try living in small hutments in that bare
Land of the six-months-twilight atmosphere
Without these universal pastimes, or
The subtler pleasures you are fighting for—
For instance, books that take you round the world
And meanwhile leave you comfortably curled
Before a fire; go, and see what sense
You can make of nude Nature, what defence
Offer against crude man; for if it's true
That you like realism it's there for you;
An enemy has cut through each distinction
Except between survival and extinction;
Your body and brain are learning how to fight;
You can't be on the gadabout each night
With imaginative authors—so the pundits say,
And certainly *they* contrive to pass the day
With technical pottering, technical argument,
And poker for relaxation—I have spent
Some little time with them! … And now I go
To Tunis or to Norway, as drafts blow!
Algeria used to be a place to go
On holiday cruises; you can keep it now!
Deserts, and palms, and paupers off the leash;
A swirl of mendicants, Baksheesh, baksheesh!

This Other Planet

Malta, Gibraltar, Alex, Cairo
Have learned to cater for troops; their soiled goods go
With crude economy from hand to hand,
And there are commodities too in Samarkand
On sale or hire, for some caravan
Has spent the night there since the world began;
But now if there are troops in Samarkand
There's probably a Naafi, and the band
Of a regiment of Guards for dancing; there will be
Places where soldiers with impunity
Are robbed and stabbed ... and these are the high lights;
The normal diet consists of days and nights
With guns and equipment and men who have no root
In places where loneliness is absolute.

Ultimate Exile

I

This Other Planet
Jack Cope & Uys Krige: *Penguin Book of South African Verse* (1968)

A man must speak to women or go mad,
And hands and lips must take their cue from speech;
Caressing words have never failed to teach
Action and cruel fever to the blood;

The gentle tones of friendly tongues have made
To our too eager minds such great and rich
Implicit promises that we must reach
Towards a heaven that we might have had.

Where is the nice distinction in all this?
Why is this word a word, and that a kiss?
What is there in a warm outburst of speech
That may not be translated into flesh?
Why should not tongues and hands and limbs be one
And petals all lie open to the sun?

II

This Other Planet

Being a woman, you can hardly know
The violence of the blind lust which has hurled
Man on his bloody missions through the world,
The frustrate strength behind each cruel blow;

Only a woman can release the flow
Of current, which, dammed up, has often whirled
Hell from the darkness of men's minds, and skirled
Its wicked pipes, and let its devils go.

A man has words to say you will not hear;
He has a cry you cannot understand;
He has a whisper for your single ear,
A touch for your once sympathetic hand;
But passionate words, like Gorgons, turned your dear
Grave head to stone, and stopped your ears with sand.

III
Is this the ultimate exile no man born
Can find return from, save for moments only,
By which each living man must wander lonely
From the convulsive moment when he's torn

Helpless into the light; and every dawn
Turn blinking from the glare towards some kindly
Dream of enfolding darkness, of the only
And multifoliate rose without a thorn?

The more a man's alive the more this steady
Search for the heart of darkness, and his time
Is given to this one thing and this thing only:
How to leave light of day behind, and climb
Into the darkness of a woman's body,
Whence to be born again, helpless and lonely.

This Other Planet

G. M. Miller & Howard Sergeant: *Critical
Survey of South African Poetry* (Balkema 1957)

Jack Cope & Uys Krige: *Penguin Book of
South African Verse* (1968)

Gareth Cornwell:
South African English Poets
(National English Literary Museum 1985)

Artillery & Radar

Song

There is no joy in water apart from the sun,
There is no beauty not emphasized by death,
No meaning in home if exile were unknown;
A man who lives in a thermostat lives beneath
A bell of glass alone with the smell of death.

There is no beauty like that seen from a cliff;
The beauty of women comes and goes with a breath;
A man must offer the beauty of his wife
In sacrifice to give his children breath—
The children will walk on their folded hands of death.

Nothing in life is near and nothing far—,
Apart from love; a man can live beneath
His roof more lonely than an outer star;
And know a woman's beauty, a flower's breath
Walking alone in the valley of the shadow of death.

This Other Planet

Roy Macnab with Charles Gulston:
South African Poetry (Collins 1948)

Maurice Wollman: *Poems of the War Years*
(Macmillan 1950)

Francis Meynell: *Weekend Book*
(Nonesuch 1955)

Francis Meynell: *By Heart* (Nonesuch/Cygnet
1965)

Jack Cope & Uys Krige: *Penguin Book of
South African Verse* (1968)

Roy Macnab: *Poets in South Africa*
(Maskew Miller 1958)

Guy Butler: *A Book of South African Verse*
(Oxford University Press 1959)

99

This Other Planet

This Other Planet
Brian Gardner: *The Terrible Rain, War Poets*
1939–45 (Methuen 1966)

Local Leave

In three or four or five weeks' time when I
Am out in Tripoli or Libya,
Or somewhere on the way to India,
I shall be listening quite convincedly

To lists of what we'd do if only we
Were back in England—where we'd go to eat,
And what we'd go to see, and how complete
A perfect day beneath a kinder sky.

Ironic, for tonight was my free night.
I'd waited for it all the week. I spent
An hour waiting for the bus. I went
Around closed shops in heavy, sleety rain,
Queued uselessly for flicks, came back again
To spend my Saturday evening on the site.

Well-Deck 1943

Over the bow-wave Over the bow-wave
Smoothly sliding Smoothly sliding
Two plump porpoises Two plump porpoises
Ambled away Idle away;
Sleek shire horses Sleek shire horses
Mother and daughter Mare and filly
Groomed tails plaited Silk tails plaited
With ribands gay With rainbow spray.

Away from the well-deck Away from the close-packed
Packed with the pitiless Human predicament
Human predicament Gravely heraldic
Shabby and grey That bare-back day
Over the bow-wave On dauphin histories
Smoothly sliding Dolphin fantasies
On that bright morning With slithering knees
I rode away. I ride away.

100

Or were those cruppers
Gentle dolphins
Gravely heraldic
Gliding away
Dolphin and dauphin
Darling dolphin
To rule an ocean
Of a former day?

Over the bow-wave
Away from the trooper
With slithering knees
On that bare-back day
On gliding histories
Plunging fantasies
For one long moment
I rode away.

IV

Indian Landscape

To Denys and Vivien

Indian Landscape
(Routledge 1947)

I was posted to India in 1943. I trained South Indian troops in artillery at Karachi and served with them on the Burma front. After my transfer to the Education Corps at the Senior Officers Cadet School at Belgaum, I was sent to take over army publications at *The Times of India* in Bombay.

I co-operated with R. V. Gibson in producing *Poems from India*, a forces anthology, and this brought me into contact with the Viceroy Field-Marshal Viscount Wavell and his son, Archibald John Wavell. I owe a great deal to these three people, and also to Lawrence Brander, Philip Chester, Rudolf von Leyden, Denys and Vivien Milburn, Stuart Piggott and Jimmy Ramamurthy. I owe a debt of thanks to Herbert Reed, who made sure that *Indian Landscape* was published in 1947, a time when publishers were ceasing to publish poems of the war period.

Acknowledgements show poems as having also appeared before 1947 in

Dublin Magazine
New English Weekly
Penguin New Writing
The Spectator
Poetry Chicago
Army Digest
Indian Army Review
Madras Calling
Illustrated Weekly of India

Several of the poems were also broadcast on Voice of India and the BBC.

For five days from the racks of a troop-train
We stared at what was new—or had we known,
As old as sin and older than mankind!
The countryside was featureless, too wide
And flat for us to grasp; all that we saw
Was men and women and beasts in the brown fields
Working or soaking in the muddy pools....
At station after station our close view
Was mendicants, small children with bare bellies
And practised voices, women with a whine
Mechanical as eyes' movement to and fro,
And men with shrunken limbs or twisted feet;
One tall old man had small vestigial arms
And ran beside us flapping like a crow;
'Baksheesh,' he cried, the children cried 'Baksheesh',
And scrambled in the filth between the rails
For coins thrown down to them. A woman raised
Her claw-like hands for food; a kite curved down
And snatched it from her... We, like savages
Blind in a civilised room to all but fire,
Saw nothing else but this: the dogs with scabs,
The children foul with sores, the platform black
With flies that rose in clouds to meet the sun—
A belt of plague across a continent.
Some human touch would make you fling a coin
And then regret it—for they'd snatch and thrust
It in a dhoti-twist without a sign
Of gratitude, but only a swift move
Sideways to catch another sahib's eye.
Some, it is true, showed pleasure, and touched hands
In prayer to us, extended suppliant arms
And touched their heads; but these embarrassed us:
Promoted suddenly from men to gods
We looked down on the world and hated it.

Monkeys we saw one day, obscene with mange;
Vultures in hundreds fouled one tiny hill;
Boys brought a dingy mongoose out to fight
A dull and listless cobra; once we saw
Two elephants with howdars, cock-eyed towers
Swaying as in an ancient tapestry!
Sometimes a woman in bright robes would come
With gently swaying steps through the station gates
And squat among the luggage on the ground;
Nearby a peacock scrabbled in the dust.

Indian Landscape

After four days the country rose in steps
Patterned with green-edged tanks and paddy fields;
Men carried coracle hats against the rain
And pushed their wooden ploughshares through wet mud;
Women up to their knees, with sarees tucked
Into their waist-bands, planted out green shoots...
One painted sunrise all the terraced world
Was delicate as a willow-pattern scene.
This too was new to us; for few had seen
So wide a segment of the world before;
We could not take it in.
The waits at shabby stations in thick air,
Poisoned by the undersides of trains,
Gave us our first impression: Bengali boys
Who quarrelled for our bags at the journey's end
Were typical, typical; and how they stank!

Bengal

1 *World Under Water*

Indian Landscape

The lawn-like paddy-fields, asbestos mountains,
And patchwork quilt of tanks suggest a world
As rich as Little Claus' peasant fancies—
The world that little liar said he'd seen
Beneath the river, where the atmosphere
Was lush and heavy, and the cattle grazing
Among the water-meadows huge and fat ...
And oh, the girls that sang among the grasses!

Down here the air is heavy as a cloak,
The hornéd cattle small and gaunt as goats,
The goats like dogs, and all these vivid fields
So starved for centuries that their thin crops
Provide no flesh for men like skeletons ...
While songs are hard, and shrill, and tell of grief.

106

I look across the gap of centuries
At this strange individual, short and square,
One of the archer-caste, with matted hair
About his shoulders, but without a bow—
He'd hardly have the strength to draw one now!
I come to buy three geese, lovely as swans
Against this squalor, bargain with small stones:
The morning passes in these processes.

Women peer out from the low alley-way
Between two hovels; there are sudden men
In empty paddy-fields; the naked boy,
Who helped to run this fleet of white sails down,
Sits on a struggling head; as we talk on,
His tentative finger prods a shell-pink eye.

3 *The Sweeper*

This is where East is East, and where the West
Speaks empty words that none will understand:
Upon the frontier these stand:
The sweeper with his brush of straw,
The jackal and the vulture and the crow,
These guard the land—

> *The sweeper with his brush of straw*
> *Worships a clique of gods so low*
> *They shun the temples and ride out*
> *On wooden horses with the rout*
> *Of grotesque demons that one sees*
> *On fringes of lost villages—*

These guard the land from change; the cookhouse *naik*
Salutes, and wags his head from side to side,
Says he'll make clean, but these decide:
The sweeper whom no threat can touch,
The vulture, the hyena and the pi,
These override—

> *He whom all other men despise*
> *Is lord of life, being lord of flies;*
> *The rajah pales before his breath;*
> *The brahmin bears his curse of death;*
> *He turns in less than seven years*

Indian Landscape

Indian Landscape
R. N. Currey & R. V. Gibson:
Poems from India
(Oxford University Press 1945)
British Council for
Harvard Poetry Room 1972
Andrew Sinclair: *The War Decade*
(Hamish Hamilton 1989)
Andrew Sinclair: *War Like a Wasp*
(Hamish Hamilton 1991)

Young subalterns to crashing bores;
His subtle hold on all of us
Turns pretty women querulous—

These sabotage our plans; we go our rounds
And gasp to see the blitzkrieg speed of flies,
Explode and try to organise;
The sweeper does not worry much,
The jackal and the kite-hawk and the crow,
If someone dies.

—From hideous pits his larvae rise;
His shabby kite-hawks fill the skies;
His vultures swoop on burial towers;
His jackals nose the half-burned pyres....

4 Unconsidered Bodies

Unconsidered bodies
Ride the tides
Of holy rivers
Down the Ganges
Past Benares steps,
Godavery, Cauvery,
The River Kistna.

Under a dam
Dedicate to Allah
Blessed by Vishnu
Serving provinces
With light and water
I found a body
Stretched across a rock.

Coolies working near
Saw but ignored it;
Nobody wanted it
Even for record.

1 *Desert Colour*

This is an utterly dead and desolate land
Drained by the sun of colour; in the glare
The baked earth bare of grass, the spreading sand
And dusty shrubs are drab; in this fierce air
No light-and-shade or colour can exist.

A camel lies beneath a shadeless tree
As dead-white as the ground; a buffalo
Merges his drab invisibility
Into a neutral bank beside a flow
Of wide and lifeless waters; faded dust

Hangs in the air above this mud-walled town
Of windowless houses with blind doorways where
Even the shabby children who have grown
To womanhood inside do not appear.
There is no hint of life in all this vast

Wilderness of no-colour—till the sun
Declines; and roofs are red, and bushes green,
And girls' eyes suddenly sparkle, and the dun
Of camels and cows and robes is briefly clean
And glowing as a child's face after rest.

Indian Landscape
Phyllis M. Jones: *Modern Verse 1900–1950*
(Oxford University Press
World's Classics 1955)

2 *Chinese Airman's Defence*
A Chinese airman was court-martialled
for machine-gunning a camel

It's hard to sound convincing, but I swear
I was deluded by some ancestor
Sitting up there beside me on that rare
And exquisite morning of the middle air
(Where demons live), above the austere spaces
Of desert that was once an ocean floor,
A spreading sea of sand with leaf-vein traces
Of runnels that poured off when first the land
Rose from the water; dried and flattened hills
Groined with cactus, and a shining road
Leading to the straight and sudden walls
And jewelled pattern of a green oasis,
A little fertile world around four wells,

Indian Landscape

109

Indian Landscape

Some five square miles of perfect miniature
Set in a flawless crystal atmosphere;
Then, as I dropped, a beast heraldic there
Against hard grass, a creature you'd not see
In all the normal world, stump-leggéd, long
Of neck, a circular body, and a strange
Small head of such unguessed-at potency,
It was a dragon as far as I could see;
I fired one burst and killed the beast as clean
As your St. George would with the same machine;
Not holy-water spray but silver fire
Crumpled that living monster, foam not flame
Fell from his lips ... but thirty centuries came
And sat beside me with that ancestor.

3 *Burial Flags*

Indian Landscape
R.N. Currey & R. V. Gibson: *Poems from India* (Oxford University Press 1945)
Ian Hamilton: *Poetry of War* (Alan Ross 1965)
Robin Skelton: *Poetry of the Forties* (Penguin 1968)
Alan Ross: *Colours of War* (Cape 1983)
Michael Foss: *Poetry of the World Wars* (Michael O'Mara 1990)
British Council for Harvard Poetry Room 1972
Prizewinner, Viceroy's Verse Competition 1944

Here with the desert so austere that only
Flags live, plant out your flags upon the wind,
Red tattered bannerets that mark a lonely
        Grave in the sand;

A crude oblong of stone to hold some mortal
Remains against a jackal's rooting paws,
Painted with colour-wash to look like marble
        Through the heat-haze;

Roofed casually with corrugated iron
Held up by jutting and uneven poles;
The crooked flagpoles tied to a curved headstone
        Carved with symbols—

Stars and new moon that are the only flowers
To grow out of this naked earth and sky,
Except these flags that through the windy hours
        Bloom steadily,

Dull red, the faded red of women's garments
Carried on sudden camels past the sky—
Red strips of cloth that ride the dusty heavens
        Untiringly.

4 *Desert Goats*

Sind Desert

These desert goats inherit the grave poise

Indian Landscape

And carriage of their masters; flowing robes
Protect impartially from sun and wind
And the hard morning cold in which men squat
Huddled round fires under low stone walls;
Their trousers are as wide as those designed
To hide the New Messiah; matted beards
Cover their eyes in shifting tides of sand.

They hold their heads up like the prows of ships
Through cactus reefs and whirlpool coils of sand;
Their antique figureheads are crudely turned,
Their long and lanky ears hang down like ropes;
To-night their clustered horns above the thorn
Are sloping masts beneath the Muslim moon.

5 *Chowkidar* *

* *Caretaker*

We took him over with a derelict site

Indian Landscape

With goat-horn cactuses, and spiky thorn,
Four hold-fast gun pits staked to take the guns,
And half a dozen huts; he lived alone
In what had been a guard-room with his fire,
His dechies and his bread-iron; stately goats
Passed by with plumes of dust twice every day;
He prayed to God, he said, and liked it there.

His carriage showed he'd been a soldier once;
He spoke from six-foot-four with deference,
Asking politely for arrears of pay
And for an issue blanket; his dyed beard
Marked up a trip to Mecca, his carved head
Some sixty years of desert sand and wind.

6 *Troops' Cinema*

Catcalls communicate

R.N. Currey & R. V. Gibson: *Poems from
India* (Oxford University Press 1945)

Unsatisfied desire,
But the hot cutie

Andrew Sinclair: *The War Decade*
(Hamish Hamilton 1989)

Eludes the grasp;

Indian Landscape

Only those youths
Who feed on shadows
Shall hold her beauty
In their arms;

I feel frustrated—
And bored almost to tears—
Returning to duty
Beneath familiar stars.

Letter Home

... It's hot to-day, damned hot to-day, and the wind comes
    over Sind,
A fiery, sandy, cactus wind, a strangely ghostly wind;
It wails round naked pillars and four-square concrete posts
While the framed vista of sand and scrub fades into the hot
    mists.

No ghosts are here, but ghosts are there, in turbans and rags
    they ride
On the wavering ghosts of camels that died by the roadside,
Mountains of flesh that vultures found and jackals and pi-dogs
    tore,
That stank a moment, and putrified, and crumbled in flowing
    air.

Where are you from? Where do you go? What errand of
    thrift or pride
Carries you on that memory of a corpse by the roadside?

You're a ghost to me, no, less than a ghost, the ghost of less
    than a man,
The ghost of a son, the son of a ghost, the son of a ghostly tribe
Who have done the things their father did until they are no
    more
Than ghosts of the ghosts of millions of men who sat on an
    earthen floor
And ate the food their fathers ate and wore what their fathers
    wore
And spoke to their women the ghosts of words that ghosts had
    spoken before.

There was a time when your fathers took new gods and built
    things new,
Their great ghosts stir the sands of time and make the hot winds
    roar;
They raised the tomb of Jehanghir and the avenues of Akbar
And carved the marble filigree in the gardens of Shalimar;
But these move past my vision with never a sense of loss,
Their turbans the same, their gods the same, until their passage
    across
From a waste of sand to a waste of air is light as a wind almost
A wind in concrete pillars that whines with the voice of a ghost.

South India

1 *Men and Gods*

The people grow as thick as paddy-stems   *Indian Landscape*
Out of wet mud; only the thinning hand   *Poetry Chicago* 1944
Of cholera or famine clears the ground;   R. N. Currey & R. V. Gibson: *Poems from*
In the hot humid climate each womb swims   *India* (Oxford University Press 1945)
With spawn like fishes' spawn; forgotten dreams
Paint symbols on men's foreheads and men's minds;
Cattle and naked children throng compounds
Of small square houses made for folded limbs.

Towers like ugly oblong pyramids
Are thick as festival streets with spawning gods,
Garish with colour, mad with fantasies
Of mighty lust where animals and men
And gods are one; from multilabial shrines
The gods peer out with little glittering eyes.

2 *Hindu Temple*

Gods overhang this soil like tropical trees;   *Indian Landscape*
Their numerous arms are branches, their hands hold   *Poetry Chicago* 1944
For jewelled flowers and fruit objects of gold,   R. N. Currey & R. V. Gibson: *Poems from*
Silver and stone; their metamorphoses   *India* (Oxford University Press 1945)
Are baffling as the dappled processes   *World Digest* 1946
Of cobras among aloes, pythons curled   British Council for
Round nameless animals, huge elephants hurled   Harvard Poetry Room 1972
Through mottled leaves by gold ferocities.   113

Indian Landscape

The walls are tiger-striped; the colonnades
Alive with parakeets are overgrown
With tropical luxuriance of carved stone;
The trails of individual deities,
Their incarnations and strange ecstasies
Are easily lost in jungle lights and shades.

3 *Shiva* I

Indian Landscape
Poetry Chicago 1944

Shiva the Destroyer, God of Death
And springing reproduction, Sundeswar
The Beautiful, the boy Bikshatanar,
Seducer of the chaste wives of the sages,
And Nataraja, dancer of the ages,
The dancer with a hundred thousand poses,
The Dancer on the Elephant, all these guises
Great Shiva's name and shape changed in a breath.

Vrishabavanamoorthi, on his Bull,
Parvati by his side, and he and she
Shiva himself, woman and man in one;
While from the lingam carved beside the throne
Bramah dives to the depths and Vishnu flies
To find the end of this infinity.

4 *Shiva* II

Indian Landscape

Now which of these is Shiva, the Lord Shiva:
The lingam growing from eternity,
The principle of birth in field and tree,
The ever-living faith of every lover,
God, man, and demon, the unfathomed River
Of Life, the hope of immortality
Through children or the sacred mystery
Of souls' reincarnation: is this Shiva?

Or is the triple crest of cobras his:
The Dance of Death, the high-step of destruction,
Fire, and flood, and earthquake, revolution;
And all iconoclastic energies
That burn, and stab, and strangle, and pour down
Strange shapes of death on village and on town?

Here in this shrieking place of parakeets
Menakshi lives, goddess with fish's eyes
That only have to glance to fertilize;
Rati (or is it Leda?) rides her swan,
Goddess of Love; her pretty handmaid sits
Behind her on its tail; huge lions prance
Around Drowpathi, wife of five at once—
Look down, Menakshi, on the sleeping spawn!

Indian Landscape

Shiva comes every evening to her shrine
On his high palanquin; his bearers run
Urgently through the colonnades; tall flares
Sweep past, and fans, and shelters from the sun
That never came in here; a curl'd conch blares—
Look down, Menakshi, on the thronging spawn.

6 *Kali* I

Offer up ghee and flowers before the throne
Of Kali, exquisite dancer of the ages,
Dancer of Shiva's hundred thousand poses,
Dancer defeated by that God alone,
And by a shabby trick. Smear ghee upon
Her vast and shining features, burn sweet oil
Beneath her nostrils, throw a woven coil
Of flowers round the neck of this divine
Untiring dancer.
                    After a sickness she
Will dance you back to joy; see how she stands
And sways for you; she dances with her hands,
Her wrists, her arms, her head, her neck, her eyes,
A hundred thousand steps; but not to please
Great Shiva will she dance immodestly.

Indian Landscape

7 *Kali* II

O Kali, exquisite dancer, once a year,
When ghee and flowers and the burnt oils fail,
Dance Shiva's dance of death; great goddess fill
Your wide, dilating pupils with austere
And bloodless images of death, and wear
For floral garlanding the smooth plain coil
Of seamless silken cloth that does not spill
A drop of blood...

Indian Landscape

Indian Landscape

This was a traveller
Who shuddered once and died without a groan,
His neck marked only by the sacred line,
The delicate symbol of eternity...
Oh hideous modesty that cannot bear
To show the lips of shame, and dare not see
The lips of wounds that murmur cruelty!

8 *Ganesh* I

Indian Landscape
Poetry Chicago 1944

Ganèsha, Ganopàthi, Gannanàta,
The Elephant-Head, the Ivory-Tusked, the Fat,
The Long-Nosed, and the Rider on the Rat;
When you are praying to this god remember
His hundred and eight names, his perfect number
Of godly attributes, God of the Gate,
The Patient Watcher for the Perfect Mate,
Ganèsha, Ganopàthi, Gannanàta.

If you should start a journey, choose a date
For some important enterprise remember
Ganèsha, Ganopàthi, Gannanàta;
The Wise, the Wonderful, the Fortunate,
Lord of Propitious days, Briber of Fate—
Preserve his holy Rat, plague-carrier.

9 *Ganesh* II

Indian Landscape

Ganèsha Ganopath has an elephant's face
In keeping with his lineage, gravely sits
Among the cowdung ash the suppliant puts
Upon his forehead in a holy place;
Or, huge on his high altar, looks benign
(As from a children's book) at boys who bend
Their skinny knees to him, and crones who spend
Their pice on ghee and flowers for his shrine.

Ganèsha Ganopàthi, bachelor,
Waits patiently above the entrance gate
Of countless temples for his longed-for mate;
Throughout the ages he has waited for
His perfect mother's equal—here you see
Him waiting with a virgin on his knee.

*Written soon after returning from India. Ganesh, the elephant-headed god, is
thought to give special favour to students, Lakshmi favours gamblers, and Saraswati
is the goddess of learning and the arts; she is usually shown holding a lute.*

What gods can these boys pray to for success?
Whom have their parents to propitiate?
What good-luck Ganesh here can mitigate
Initial fears, and smile out nervousness?

What open-handed Lakshmi gives excess
To those who staked all on a gambler's fate?
What gentle Saraswati gives sedate
Encouragement to past industriousness?

11 *Childlike Men*

Those nothing-if-not-ubiquitous Bruin Boys   *Indian Landscape*
Have turned up here; Hanuman in this shrine
Is Jacko to the life, but saturnine,
Powerful-looking, and with cruel eyes,
And carries with him toys that would surprise
The excellent Mrs. Bruin; the benign
Ganèsha is undoubtedly of the line
Of good old Jumbo—till somebody tries
His pachydermatous pride; a parrot-laugh
Is multiplied among the colonnades
Into a shrieking choir; a slight giraffe
And boyish tiger move among striped shades.
Are these naive blasphemies, or have we seen
Gods playing at animals with childlike men?

12 *Hindu Women*

Beneath these lusting gods what feminine grace!   *Indian Landscape*
Women with vessels held against full breasts,   *Poetry Chicago* 1944
Walking with queen-like carriage to the place
Where a whole street draws water, hands and wrists
Moved carelessly to touch the sleek black hair
Or raise a heavy vessel to the head;
Wearing their single garment with an air
Of swaying gracefulness I once thought dead.

117

Indian Landscape

They have not learned the rhythm of pointed heels,
Their sandalled feet are gravely innocent
Of time as measured by revolving wheels;
They touch their palms in greeting, lift cupped hands
And liquid eyes for gifts, not diffident
In raising both in prayer to these gross gods.

13 *South Indian Cattle*

Indian Landscape
Poetry Chicago 1944
World Digest
The Poetry Review 1959
BBC Far Eastern Service 1945
(Read by Dylan Thomas
for John Arlott)

The world moves at the pace of cattle here,
These beautiful white beasts whose masters sit
Between them on the shaft, whose painted carts,
Balanced with hay or sacks upon two wheels
Or carrying one squatting passenger,
Move gaily down the roads: they have small feet
And lift them lightly; some have bright green paint
Upon their tapering horns; all carry bells.

Here where they have been taken from the shaft
They stand among their masters in small groups.
They are not driven to graze, but eat cut grass
While he eats rice; their horizontal shape
Contrasts with his slim vertical brown stance—
At home they'll go with him into the house.

14 *Krishnarajsagar Dam*

Indian Landscape

Under the battleship shoulders of this dam
Are pleasances and gardens, terraces,
Cascades, and flower-beds, and flowering trees,
Such as a scientific Kublai Khan
Heir to the Moghuls and to-day might plan,
With channels where a thousand fountains' spray
Is leaping fire by night, white lawn by day
And tall perfection between cypresses.

The poised great lake above, the roar, the power
That lights whole provinces are held at bay
By routine maintenance from day to day,
And flower petals thrown from hour to hour
To Vishnu and to Ganesh at the foot,
And the Lord Krishna playing on his flute.

1 *Langurs*

Spending the day up here wired in by rain
I watch this fragment of a folk-migration,
A tiny tribe perhaps of the great nation
That roamed the country with green Hanuman
For centuries before earth-footed man
With his pedestrian conglomeration
Of bows and cooking-pots; in their own fashion
These langurs cross a landscape spiked with rain.

They have no sort of shelter from the rain;
It drives through the soft foliage of the trees
Down their black glistening trunks; from one of these
They drop down gracefully upon the grass,
Squat black-glancing round, and softly pass
With half a dozen bounds in twos and threes
To an assembly point between two trees,
And gravely sit and contemplate the rain.

They seem in their close discipline in the rain
A portion rather of some regiment
Of the great force that Hanuman once sent
(In those far ages when the Apes and Bears
Were Infantry and Indian Engineers!)
To bridge the narrow waters to Ceylon
And hurl the demon-head Ravanna down
Beneath the silver arrows of the rain;

When, through the first-recorded sun and rain
This Hanuman—the Monkey-God, the King
Of all who leave the ground and lightly swing
From living branch to branch, who, man and boy,
Wear side-whiskers and tumble for sheer joy—
With Shiva's symbol walked the waving trees
From Rameswaram to far Benares
In thirty strides through glittering sun and rain;

A portion of the force that braved the rain
Before stone temples thrust above the trees
Their crowns of writhing many-limbed deities:
Langurs and chimpanzees and huge baboons
Swinging across the creeper-hung lagoons,
Mandril and gibbon, ape and marmoset,
Some with the fighting colours that even yet
Shine out like firefly tails through monsoon rain.   119

Indian Landscape

They face in one direction through the rain,
Fawn-overcoated figures with black faces,
With cowls and monkish mows and quick grimaces
And circular scratchings; this stout veteran
Without a tail looks round him like a man;
He wrings his black-gloved hands quite humanly,
Scatters a shower of spray, then suddenly
Sets off with easy bounds into the rain.

They move across the open through the rain
Like race-horses in prints, but *chest*-à-terre,
Wasp-waisted, with a black-faced teddy-bear
At each camp-follower's breast; here on the ground
Their tails are strong black snakes curled out behind;
Now that they bound and swing among new trees
Their tails are ropes, their fawn agilities
Viewed through the vertical cage-bars of the rain.

2 *Family Station*

Spring seems perpetual beneath these banyans;
The moveless light is green against the leaves;
The brown straight-hanging roots are seaweed curtains
As still as stalactites beneath the waves;

So far beneath the waves there are no murmurs
Of storms that shake the naked world above;
Monkeys among the branches pass on rumours,
And unconvincing pigeons mourn and grieve

Among the leaves … no thud of fleets, of total
Assault upon a continental shore;
Among weed-carven pillars Neptune's cattle
Busily crop the grass of the sea-floor.

Rhythmically-scything heads are hung with gentle
Musical bells that emphasise the peace.
A sudden crunch of wheels: 'Platoon, pile cycles!'
Insidious war beneath the banyan trees.

This Other Planet
R. N. Currey & R. V. Gibson: *Poems from
India* (Oxford University Press 1945)
Roy Macnab with Charles Gulston:
South African Poetry (Collins 1948)
Jack Cope & Uys Krige:
Penguin Book of South African Verse (1968)

Like birds, when first light breaks,
One of them stirs, and speaks;
The other drowsily
Makes some reply.

I cannot where I lie
Make out their commentary,
But chuckling word on word
Tells their accord;

Their brittle flow of words
Echoes the chirp of birds;
Without proviso they
Accept the day;

While their half-chant has thrown
My thoughts back to my own
Two boys who laugh and play
War-years away;

Whose morning orisons
Used to awake me once,
Prelude to culmination
In invasion—

Their barefoot blitzkrieg! We
Were buried helplessly
Beneath the rosy flood
Of flesh and blood.

This one dive-bombed the sheet,
The other mined our feet,
While both drove clutching tanks
Across our flanks.

Checked at this point, they
Might for a moment stay
Quiet beneath some stale
Time-serving tale;

But their bridgehead was won,
And our resistance done;
We must accept, as they,
The fact of a new day.

Indian Landscape

Poetry Chicago 1944

4 *Hill Station*

This is my ivory tower. This ring of mountains
Raises me high above the tainted plain,
So that with lake, and trees, and silver fountains
Of light and water I am back again
In England, perhaps Grasmere, on a day
Of liquid birdsong, ignorant as heaven
Of gods spawned out of the hot interplay
Of sun and teeming earth, of millions driven
Like slaves through shortened lives ...
                                        Here roses grow

In small front gardens and pear-blossom falls
Across a net gate and a tidy path;
While in this bungalow these two know how
With flowers, and tolerant words, and logwood hearth
To raise brief England within brittle walls.

5 Dam

I feel uneasy living beneath this dam.
The walls reach up to hold the infinite sky,
The hidden weight of waters, the poised hills—
And all the unguessed future; fragile walls
Buttressed by relics of a feudal past
And some two centuries' power, a world propped up
By boards that curve and strain; through sizable cracks
The waters splash and spray along the rim.

O lovely world of morning-plumaged skies
And wide gun-metal waters; teal and snipe—
The whirring fighters and formation flights
Of poised out-reaching bombers; as I lie here,
Under the atlas-shoulders of this dam,
I hear the waters walk above my head!

Indian Landscapes
John Lehmann: *Penguin New Writing* no. 28
(1946)
Alan Ross: *Poetry 1945–50* (Longman 1951)
Ronald Blythe: *Components of the Scene*
(Penguin 1966)
Ian Hamilton: *Poetry of War 1939–45*
(Alan Ross 1965)
Ronald Blythe: *Writing in a War*
(Penguin 1982)
British Council for
Harvard Poetry Room 1972

6 Landscape

Many have planted
Individual kindnesses
But stones have stunted
Their tender growth;

Roots are twisted
By suspicion,
Humiliation
Eats the shoots.

In this hard land
In an hour
The sun can burn up
Root and flower

As men are burned, but ash
Of petal and skull
Fails to enrich
The bitter soil.

Indian Landscape
Guy Butler: *A Book of South African Verse*
(Oxford University Press 1959)
British Council for
Harvard Poetry Room 1972

Indian Landscape

Deccan

Indian Landscape
John Arlott: *First Time in America*
(Duell, Sloan and Pearce, 1948)

1 *Ajanta* I

O interlude of vast austerity
Carved out beneath the mountain's curving frown
And looking down
On green serenity.

Between the older demons and the younger gods—
Action and passion—
Renunciation
Is carved from stone,
Cave after cave,
Head, trunk and limb,
Through ecstasies of pillared time.

Huge Buddhas dreaming through the centuries
Sitting cross-leggéd under bodhi trees;
Vast contemplation
Rooted in stone
Through green eternity.

2 *Ajanta* II

Indian Landscape

Before the rabble of competing gods
Destruction, Reproduction, Good-Beginnings,
Blood-Sacrifice, Discretion, Gamblers' Winnings,
Boars' heads and lions', elephants' and birds'
Ran through men's minds with pictures and bright words
Threats, and deceits, conceits, and double meanings,
Disguises, dancing poses, ritual cleanings,
Ruthless and fatal as invading hordes—

Buddha the ruler made renunciation,
Buddha the man accepted the negation
Of love, ambition, and desire's fulfilment;
Here, in old stone, is ageless concentration;
Here, cut from time, is timeless contemplation,
An age-long instant of enlightenment.

124

What miracle formed these lovely matrices

Indian Landscape

Of stone-and-mortar buildings that had shape,
Colour and meaning under open skies?
What held men there through time and change of faith
Hollowing out a mountain—ecstasies
Of austere contemplation?—human hope
Of ruthless help from powerful deities?—
Or an artist's dream of half-outwitting death?

These vaults are far removed from warping sun,
Insinuating rain and normal danger
Of mankind's cruelty or the gods' anger;
How many masons, priests and gritty years
Carved out these saints, gods, demons, worshippers
Remote from love and light in the heart of stone?

4 *Kailasa Temple, Ellora*

After austere centuries monk-masons,

Indian Landscape

Carving their age's mind in disciplined rock,
Tapping and tapping while their chisels spoke
Of ever wordlier Buddhas, with musicians,
Dancers and patrons, animal decorations
About the dreaming heads, felt little shock
When under their chipping hammers the stone broke
Into a dancing riot of jungle visions.

Chisels carved through a stupa to a nandi,
A Buddha to a lingam: then stopped short
To find an elephant's head, a wild boar's snout—
Or figures locked in love along a frieze:
Ravanna, many-headed, shook Kailasa;
The temple broke its way through to the skies.

125

Rajputana

1 *Royal Tombs*

Indian Landscape

Among the galleried rubble of the dead
The proud competitive memorials
Of this Singh, that Singh, lions every one
And every one descended from the terrible sun;
Here where their bones were burned in insatiable flame
That swallowed, as an aside, the widowed shame
And gentle flesh of wives and concubines;
Where only a nandi or a lingam signs
Stone death certificates, writes elegies
Among the irregular-crowded canopies …
Dropping out of the trees, leaping from tomb to tomb,
The little agile black-faced monkeys come.

Among the fallen pillars, the heaps of stones—
Forgotten rulers and perfunctory sons—
With shrunken grey-bonneted faces, these grave well-bred
Old ladies peer up quizzically, ask to be fed:
Their worried myopic gaze moves round and round
While wrinkled black-velveted fingers take nuts from your hand.

When rajahs die they cheer the path of the stranger
By sending dancing girls, and ease his hunger
By feeding the sacred monkeys. Are these then priests
Familiar in both worlds—or the puzzled ghosts
Of queens who failed the fire, kings without sons
Waiting another death, a more fortunate chance?

2 *Elephant* I

Indian Landscape
Poetry Chicago 1947

Here elephants are a measure. Rajahs ride
Under tall arrogant gates that take the sway
Of towering howdahs, and still wear to-day
Their diadem of spikes against the pride
Of battering foreheads; palace yards are wide
For elephants to turn in; this stone stake,
This thick-set wall, this chain are made to take
The shock of fighting elephants, ankle-tied
And tugging at earth's centre.

                    Men admire
Their monstrous masculinity; gentle women
Affect through sandalled lives their swaying motion.
Here elephants are gods, and gods lead fashion;
They summarise achievement and desire;
A rajah rides his object of devotion.

3 *Elephant* II
'*Leviathan … is king over all the children of pride*'

The elephant is the microcosm of state:
Upon his workaday back he balances
The delicate-pillared silken palaces
Of his gold rulers; under eyelash valances
They stare across the carpeted hill terraces
Of his twin temples, born to contemplate
Thus distantly the gaudy fly-blown fate
Of bowing subjects.
                    To exaggerate
Leviathan is impossible; he can bear
The heavens, and never turn a small black hair,
Cruelty, sawn tusks, the spike behind his ear,
The mahout, like a vizier, on his head
Squatting, standing, dancing. Kind as God,
He overturns the world when he goes mad.

Indian Landscape
Poetry Chicago 1947

4 *Widow*

Don't mention widows; widows are accursed,
They have prayed vainly to be taken first;

Vainly joined hands to gods who favour men,
Moved, always moved, uncertainly since then;

Uncertainly, ash-pale, with shaven head
Grotesque among the living and the dead;

Grotesque as ghosts between the lives and life,
And inauspicious both to maid and wife;

As inauspicious at festivity
As a child's corpse at a nativity.

Indian Landscape

✧

Indian Landscape

Sister of suttee, thuggery and sad
Birth of girl-children, over-population,
The shrivelled dug; this country's salted wound;
She was handed gagged and bound
At twelve to dull indifferent
Fifteen, with death incipient
In his dry cheeks.
The long pole creaks
On hired shoulders;
Swimming in colours
The children in
The palanquin
Stare outward at the crowd,
The loud musicians and the puny dancers;
Loaded with flowers for the sacrifice,
Dull even to surprise...

✧

After his death she bore a boy, but she
May not attend her son's festivity;

May not attend—all widows who have been
Happy at children's parties will see what I mean.

5 *Jaipur* I

Indian Landscape

Young beside Petra, but a rose-red city
Caught in a dance that carries time away:
Each facing row of houses is a spray
Of single roses with no parallel wonder
In our own time; heads up, with measured splendour,
They hold before our eyes, like a bouquet,
Wide vistas of green hills—these everyday
Houses and shops that tread in dignity

Beside the jewelled Palace of the Winds,
Beneath the swaying palaces that bear
White blossom nodding nodding in the air,
Terrace on terrace, crowned by cupolas:
How gracefully they wrought, those agile minds,
On flower-like stems domes light as primulas.

Those Rajput rulers in their alien day
Surrounded by their silk nobility
Kept jewelled women in captivity,
Who played within these walls their formal play
Of robing, love, fruition and decay—
And sometimes even wept to speak a line
Or felt authentic shivers down the spine
Seeing a pointed slipper turn their way.

Indian Landscape

Were they quite happy in their limited pale
Between the bathing-pools, the orange-trees?
Or did they turn from laughter to the street
And stare through window-slits at dusty feet
And vivid turbans of a jostling, male
Far world, and wonder at its ribaldries?

The men had colour in their lives and movement.
Around the carpeted square durbar floor
That held the jewelled and enamelled hour
Flowered the rows on rows of intent turbans,
Ochre, and mauve, and scarlet; a disturbance
Of rumour like a breeze swept through the court;
And, in a gateway, swaying like their thought,
The howdah of an unknown elephant.

Indian Landscape

Outside was poverty. These roseate lives
Sucked blood from hungry men, but made a start
Between their gem-hilt wars upon the art
And building that are our inheritance:
Grant them aesthetic standards, positives
Yet to be made mankind's experience.

8 *Jaipur* IV

Here in Jaipur the old and new worlds meet;
The forts, the temples, and the palaces
Look out on legislative offices
And schools and hospitals. This wide grave street
Worn by three centuries of slippered feet
And tripping pads of camels branches out
In roads that go impartially to meet
Old pleasure-gardens and new factories.

Here is a future growing from past beauty
Owning past inspiration—and a duty
To all men of all trades to build a city
Known for the flourish of its industries;
Its roads made smooth for ordinary men
And knowledge climbing stairs to soar again.

9 *Amber*

This city, swung between the branching valleys,
The gateways to the plain, and the high fort
That crowns the hill behind, preserves a thought
And gesture from the past; in this high palace
Within stone walls, behind a marble trellis,
The mothers of the noblemen who sought
Honour and glory offered finely wrought
Enamelled lifetimes to their rulers' solace.

How exquisite this foil; these sunken baths
These salons water-cooled, cold passages,
Even the water-closets add a line
To this luxuriously drawn design—
The fiery melodrama of their deaths
Alone gave worth to these sad terraces.

10 *At Agra*

Here is the world's most hackneyed metaphor,
Hackneyed as love, or parenthood, or death
Until met face to face. Subtract the pomp:
Here lies a woman well loved by a man;
She died at forty of her fourteenth child,
The centre of his world. Subtract again.

Eyes raised above the pains of common men,
Heart introvert. But still admit he raised
A memory as firm in earth as she
Yet reaching towards heaven, an act of prayer
Compact of jewelled flowers, moonlight, air,
Fragile as ivory; a miniature
In terms of God; in; terms of man a sheer
Gasp of imagination. First destroy
The photographs, the cribs, the metaphors,
Even the very name—and then discover
This beauty for yourself, as in a lover.

11 *Roadside Shrine*

Who lives in this rock-temple?

Between Two Worlds
(BBC Third Programme 1948 & 1951)

Just the god
And his attendants; who else would be allowed?
Can one see round the temple?

If the god
Is not asleep, engaged, or taking food.

Whom do you worship here?

We worship God.

You seem to worship the small spotted deer,
And elephants, and horses,
The ugly-handed turtles of the water-courses,
The sun, the first forefather of your kings,
And some folk-memory
Of a fabulous jewelled tree,
Whose emerald leaves and ruby fruits were given
Each year in charity;
You worship Shiva, Ganesh, Kali still
And a local deity who guards your springs;
You seem to worship all these things?

That's true; we worship God.

Indian Landscape

Between Two Worlds
(BBC Third Programme 1948 & 1951)

12 *Death of a Sweeper*

The man who touched the Feet of God
Poor clumsy Gunner Padavattan
Once village servant, records say,
Now, serving London and Manhattan,
His home three thousand miles away,
Has died to-day of typhoid.

He lived once with his wife Ramaye
His three small sons and infant daughter
In a hovel in an outcast quarter:
He died in hospital to-day…
He had full rites of burial….
He left no property at all.

Indian Beggars

Indian Landscape

To serve this nation
A man's compassion
Must be the drinking-horn
That ends in ocean:
My limited ration
Gave out some time ago.

This trunk has wooden blocks
For his hands' crutches;
His independence knocks
But lifts no latches;
I drop the catches,
Turn up the radio.

This crab man lurches
On bleeding hands;
His lacerated flitches
Make their demands—
His misery touches
My sleeve, as in a crowd.

This dog-curled comatose creature
Islands the pavement;
Only his excrement
Ties him to nature;
Pity, and relaxed bladder
Leak slowly toward the gutter.

Parade of skeletons,
Stump feet, vestigial arms,
And mutilated little ones,
With upturned palms
Probe deep within each walking man
For oh that impossible, that good Samaritan.

Indian Landscape

The Road to Madura

The over-brilliant moon on the tiger-striped
Mud-level road is the appropriate landscape.
The off-note veena in among the banyan
Finds roots among the sharps and flats of tree-frogs,
The hand-thud drum among the pad of feet.

Between Two Worlds
(BBC Third Programme 1948 & 1951)
South African Poetry Prize 1959

This dancer, with his jewelled conceptual movements
Shows pilgrims on the road to Madura;
The closed palm with stretched fingers, peasants' cattle;
The curved extension of the hand, palm upwards,
The movement from the road – to Madura;
The quick half-turn of fingers right and left,
Meetings with friends and laughing conversation;
The gleaming peasant with his glossy children
And bright-horned cattle going to Madura.
With what drilled grace he does the lotus-movement.
Young love upon the road. The slow-uprising
Butterfly-fluttering of close-cupped hands.
Stardust centrifugal fingers. Flying brows
That lift the body from the earth like wings.

Well, that's my last small coin.
The people here are living skeletons—
That woman there, stretched out along the roadside,
White cloth over her face,
Perhaps not living.

Here on the road
The poor are always with us; the next famine
Is always round the corner—
The half-burned corpses jostling down the rivers
Like tolerant football crowds;
Men push them off the shores with bamboo poles.

133

Indian Landscape

See at dusk when the colours return,
The women fetching water from the fountain
Erect as corn, with pitchers on their heads,
Each with the swaying gait—in her own dream
Of the she-elephant; the resignation
Seen in the eyes of heifers and Grecian girls;
The rounded bloom of clustered watermelons—
Images brought as slips by Alexander
From Europe and the Levant, and growing still;
They pass the goddess Lakshmi, letting fall
From outstretched hands, pale palms turned upward.
Petals before her feet,

This untouchable
Sings before Shiva;
He may not enter the temple gate.
He raises his head toward the god.
Shiva is there at the top of the steps,
Six arms about his head
His right knee lifted
In the Dance of Destruction—
Natarajah.

He rises to his knees
And sings to Shiva;
His voice is vibrant
With an edge of strangeness;
His song is blown like smoke to Shiva;
Lord Shiva, hear my prayer;
Bless my patch of earth and water;
The rice in the mud-walled tanks beside the road
Grows as we watch it, ripens for harvest.
The radiance on it is the eye of Shiva.

The million tongues that pierce the water
Whisper of bulls and tiger-striped temples,
Of stones and cobras sacred to Shiva.
Beside a temple sacred to Vishnu,
Strident, strident voices chanting:
Rama Rama Rama Rama.
Sita Sita Sita Sita
Rama Sita Sita Rama.
Sita Rama Rama Sita.
Interlacing of god and lover,
A two-word trance that has no ending;
Vishnu came to earth as Rama,
Came in splendour, not in a manger;

Rama Rama, God Incarnate.
Sita Sita, Earth's perfection.
Rama Rama, Sita Sita.

Moving hooves and running water.
Axles, Axles, Axles grinding
Back through dateless time, and finding
A long improbable epic way;
Earthquakes, Monsters, Apes and Bears.
A seven-league booted bridge to Ceylon.

The gods of different dynasties are connected:
Jupiter's Leda; Rathi on her swan.
Krishna—Christ, but with a taste for milkmaids.
Then the Trinity—Shiva, Change—
Mutability of life and matter.
Take one away and destroy the balance.
Shiva is lightning and flood. Germ warfare.
Reproduction and regeneration.
Grass growing between twisted blades of steel
A man can make love last a lifetime.
Gods, like movie-stars, change with each picture—
Each incarnation another waitress
Translated to the sky.

Here are lovingly-tended cattle,
Exquisite as toys, enamelled and painted,
Their delicate feet and symmetrical horns
Moving towards Madura.

Some draw families, some pale towers
Of toppling hay
Towards the town where temple gopurams
Thrust their way above the clustered palms.

The Great Temple of Madura

South African Poetry Prize 1959

This cliff of statuary stifles thought.
How the huge gopuram swells from the doorway
Fruited with statues of painted plaster.
Globular goddesses hang out of heaven,
Dangle their fullness to meagre streets.

There are many sounds in a temple.
The shriek of parakeets in Shri Menakshi's
Fertile colonnades spills as you enter.
Leave your shoes with the stooping porter—
He gets his drama from the eyes of sandals;
Face the eye of the Elephant-headed
Ganesh, God of Good-Beginnings,
Heavenly porter, Protector of the rat.

(A laundryman, on the way to Madura,
Opened his basket to find my shirt.
The mice ran in and out of the pockets
And over his hands—he looked on kindly:
Ganesh, protector of mice and rats!)

Outside on the gopurams, cruder than jack-fruit,
Those rows and rows of many-limbed deities
Tell naive stories to the outcast streets:
Here in the corridors, gracefully moulded,
Carved out of stone, they whisper in silk

Shiva Bigshatanar, beautiful beggar-boy.
Testing the chastity of the wives of sages—
Proving his point. By way of answer
Vishnu Mohini, in feminine beauty
Seducing the sages. Anasuya,
Her saree slipping, uttering prayers
That turn the lascivious players to children.
Fish-eyed Menakshi, the triple-breasted.
Drowpathi, the faithful wife of five.

Populous colonnade of yawning lions
Subramanian, god of war
Riding a peacock. Here, where the parakeets
Scream in their cages, hymn Menakshi,
Mother of millions; worshippers lie prostrate
Peer past the joss-sticks, the smoke-lit jewels,
The multilabial curtains that half-hide
Half-show the mystery. I, the infidel,
Squint and pass by.

The lords of death are the lords of life:
Kali the strangler, Kali the healer,
Her head encircled by her arms, her nostrils
Sniffing the incense of convalescent wives,
Swinging her necklaces of skulls, and dancing
Them back to health, and into a future
Of civilisation and the rule of women—
The Age of Kali, when men shall be slave.

They're lighting the lamps. In the flickering glow
The gods take on movement. Kali is dancing.
Shiva Natarajah is dancing
His formally perfect dance of destruction:
The arrogant smile, the lifted knee,
The blown-back hair.
Shiva Gajaramurthy is dancing
On the head of the elephant—really a demon
Bribed by those sages. These stories are serials.
Results are the causes of further action—
Further permutations.

                                   It's getting dark.
Here Shiva's Ardhanari, hermaphrodite;
Here Harihara, half himself, half Vishnu;
Here in his chariot a god of action.
Here Dakshinamurthy, Contemplation
When Sati died, his young wife Sati,
Shiva renounced the world for yoga
For fifty thousand ages. Here,
After a million years, see him with Devi
Dead drunk and dancing in cremation grounds.
All knowledge, all experience are Shiva's.
These endless half-lit colonnades alarm me,
These jewelled bodies set in shadowed stone;
Under the branching arms, the living headdresses,
The bellies, thighs and knees in quavering light—
A sign would set them running.

'I lie under the seed, of all creatures the seed that is changeless.
I am the heat of the sun, the heat of the fire am I also,
Life eternal and death.'
Here is the holy of holies. You must not enter.
You must not look. Here Shiva is the lingam.
All life, all reproduction.

Indian Landscape

Form after form of Shiva carved in stone
With wives and mistresses, and every one
Leans towards movement, so men who run
Await the freedom or the starting-gun.
Menakshi and Parvati wait to pour
Rivers of life upon the dancing floor,
Pause on the brink of movement.
These hollow corridors confuse all sounds ...
The gods have left their pedestals! But no—
Not gods but men! They come this way—
Shrieking wind-instruments and hand-thud drums—
They're playing as they *run*! They're in a frenzy.
The flares shine on their faces. They are here,
All round. As though above the din
In swaying darkness is a palaquin.
The flares below. No pomp. No dignity
As we would think of it—but every night
Shiva is carried to Menakshi's shrine
In that high palaquin—let's say for vespers!—
And every morning carried back again.

Is this philosophy, or the negation
Of all but the stream of existence;
I'd like to know! I'd like to go
South with the pilgrims to Ramaswaram,
Where Rama's Sita, looking towards Ceylon
Set up the emblem of Shiva in the sand.

But the enamelled dancer under the light
Beckons with jewelled hands and flying fingers
And eloquent movements of the head and brows
Along the shadow-pooled mud-level road,
Between the cocoanut palms and terraced tanks,
Among the peasants and their peaceful cattle,
To Madura.

Hiroshima, Nagasaki
Let the long-dead Lady Murasaki
Tell how cherry-blossom flutters
Over waiting-woman shutters
Past the whispering, shy screens,
Wind-blown then by hermit mountains,
Floating down by formal waterfalls and fountains
Through those undiscovered islands.

Nagasaki, Hiroshima,
Let the sleeveless fishermen of Suma
Tell how Genji once appeared
From the Inner City, stared
At those desolate, wide scenes,
Of the willow songs he chanted
And of the exquisite sad sunsets that he painted
In those exiled fisher-islands.

Nagasaki, Hiroshima,
Lively Nijo-in and exiled Suma,
Princely cherry-blossom dancing
Over brushwork pages, glancing
At those slant-eyed, sing-song scenes,
Dropping pollen poems that carried
Such delicate form, and wistful aspiration married
Through those unawakened islands.

Hiroshima, Nagasaki,
Let the purple-flower Murasaki
Tell of National Visitation,
Plague, and Palace-Revolution,
Renunciation behind screens
By creatures so considerate
That they could fear to kill by telepathic hate
In those yet-undevastated islands.

The Tale of Genji
Japanese classic of 11th–12th century.
Translator Arthur Waley
Between Two Worlds
(BBC Third Programme 1948 & 1951)
South African Poetry Prize 1959

V

Between Two Worlds

A Dramatic Poem

Between Two Worlds
(BBC Third Programme
produced by James McFarlan 1948
& Terence Tiller 1951)

*The following series of poems originally formed a part
of* Between Two Worlds. *It arose from R. N.
Currey's experience of the week spent travelling home
from India in February 1946, in a converted American
Liberator bomber. In this dramatic poem for radio
twenty-four soldiers and airmen are being flown home
— from war to peace, from service life to civilian life,
from the exile that some made home to the home that
for some will be exile. Sometimes they get glimpses of
the world from the cockpit, but most of the time they
travel blind and packed knee to knee in the underbelly
that used to carry the bombs. They are between home
and exile, future and past, 'between two worlds'.*

Between Two Worlds was produced with help in India
and England from John Arlott, Lord Noel Buxton,
James McFarlan, Denys and Vivien Milburn, Terence
Tiller and John Grenfell Williams.

Jonah

Latter-day Jonah, see the world
In monster-matrix, embryo-curled
Blind and deaf to all but the gloom
Of the close-walled womb, and the thud of the blood
As we sway through space, between far places,
Fons et origo, lush Euphrates,
The Fertile Crescent, the livid Nile,
Tripoli, Malta, Pantellaria . . .

So Jonah sailed the world (this was his area
And whales sail far), perhaps to Sicily
To Tyre and Sidon, to the Southern Pole,
To the Golden Gate and the Great Dust Bowl . . .
Four and twenty soldiers jonahed in a whale
And which of you has business in the head or in the tail?
Today this is our temper; as men squeeze
From front to rear, crawling along our knees,
Prod them like schoolboys; embryo-blind pass over
Lyons and Paris (they tell us) and the cliffs of Dover.

Between Two Worlds
(BBC Third Programme 1948 & 1951)
New English Weekly 1947

Flight up the Persian Gulf

The mountains beside the sea are golden-barren
In the bright sunshine as Midas, and the sea
Luminous turquoise green with milky edges,
And tiny boats bird-seed specks along the shore,
And very occasional villages geometrical
Against towered Nature, groined, irregular.

Now the Oman peninsula, golden crocodiles
Splayed out into the sea, and all their miles
Their hundreds of miles of mountains unaware
Of mankind's pentagon as this bright air.

And suddenly ahead, high as a cloud,
The mouths of Tigris and Euphrates spreading
Their vivid, million-channelled man-made flats,
Green and triangular, with straight-edged orchards
Of lined space-even trees and match-box houses
Along the straight canals: here man began
To impose his conscious pattern, and to mix
Unaccidental colours. The flying carpet
Has settled, a level delta, on the water
As vulnerable as our world in all this sea.

Between Two Worlds
(BBC Third Programme 1948 & 1951)
Spectator 1947

143

Between Two Worlds

Between Two Worlds
(BBC Third Programme 1948 & 1951)

The World Beneath my Eyes

The world beneath my eyes a tilting map,
So little's seen at once, a torch's circle,
The jerky patch of earth a field-glass holds—
And always easier to read a book
Than crane one's neck to scan and understand:
All day, far far below, the dust of peoples,
The smoke of cooking fires and funeral pyres
No different at this height;
All these displaced by clumsy history,
The strident tommy-gun and quiet bundle
Both hidden in the clouds of dust that move
Like Huns or Ostrogoths in one direction;
Always in one direction, the illusion
Of sunlight in a garden blotted out
By the kicked-up dust of men—and our escape,
Air-borne an hour or two, not permanent.

The Nile

Between Two Worlds
(BBC Third Programme 1948 & 1951)
New English Weekly 1947

Between two deserts the delta, a wide green band
Of channel on channel of river and sharp canal,
Flat, flatter than a table, cut in strips
Such delicate little strips, all shades of green,
So intricate, neat, exact, an Eastern carpet
Patterned with so many houses. so many towns,
Palaces, villages, and wide flat feminine ships,
The eye is confused by complexity, seeing here
A world, the matrix of a world, contained
Within a single glance; on the horizon
The sharp-edged pyramids and doubtful Sphinx;
On either side the tawny emptiness.

Departure from Tripoli

The Africa We Knew

Tall feathery grass by our huts;
Blue gums that shook their grey leaves out in the sun.
We entered the plane's fish-belly, went away
As Empires do, took, left no memories.

Shrewd Moonlight

Better to sleep
when high straight walls
are bathed in dusty
light that falls
on doll's house tiles
and noah's ark trees,
facades that keep
their privacies—
blind rooms and misty
garden lawns—
till dawn's light fills
the high vague square,
and walking feet
are everywhere;
houses and trees
are solid then,
exchange urbanities
with men
in morning air.

Moonlight alone
recalls the frailty
of quarried stone,
the unreality
of flesh and bone.

I Was A Poet

I was a poet and I had to go
Into the trade I did not wish to learn;
I wanted a corner table from which to watch
Man's foolish courage, generous egotism.
I did not wish to cross the dangerous chasm
Between the eye and the heart
But now, in my own pain,
I've learned the misery of exiled man;
I've learned the language of another existence,
The ritual speech and blasphemy of guns.

Between Two Worlds
(BBC Third Programme 1948 & 1951)
Time & Tide 1948

Between Two Worlds
(BBC Third Programme 1948 & 1951)
G. M. Miller & Howard Sergeant: *Survey of
South African Poetry* (Balkema 1959)

Between Two Worlds

Between Two Worlds
(BBC Third Programme 1948 & 1951)

Ours the Illiterate Imagination

Ours the illiterate imagination,
Our love has learned its homely A.B.C.
And struggles bravely with the three times table:
Seventy times seven is still fantasy.

This general never dreamt a politician,
This airman never quite believed in land,
This farmer wouldn't recognise the ocean,
And every one of them would pledge his hand

That only a mile beyond his country's border
Women are harpies and the men climb trees;
That murder twice removed is no more murder,
That slavery went out with Pericles;

That men who plant his wheat and tea and cotton
Should suffer hunger, terror and disease
Outside his mind—and, while their limbs go rotten,
Thank him for lesser mercies on their knees;

And this young man who flies his huge machine,
A bomber, five miles up, why, save his heart
He's never followed down his bombs and been
In the same room with lives he's torn apart.

Remote Murder

Between Two Worlds
(BBC Third Programme 1948 & 1951)

Radar, bomb-sights, each device
That makes mass murder more precise
At longer ranges, adds its nice
Amendment to our cowardice.

Eyes cannot and minds dare not see
The detailed map of misery;
God-like, remote, we cannot be
Involved in each man's agony;

Above the floor of clouds we press
Our button, savour the release;
Use pride, and drill, and friendliness
To insulate us from distress.

146

Each of us has his insulation;
The ruler has his god-like vision,
The mathematician his equation,
The housewife has her routine prison;

Behind the perspex, the commotion,
The engine's roar, the Crossword passion,
Church, job, precarious self-possession,
Is unreality, evasion.

Between Two Worlds

I Saw the Men I Killed

I saw the men I killed. I saw them die,
Sorted out their pathetic photographs,
Made human promises, lit cigarettes,
Knew there but for the grace of God went I.

I took part in five landings,
Death luminous and ticking on my wrist;
Beyond the long Caesarian of a beach;
And always carrying from the floating darkness
A comradeship as natural as routine.

The man who feels an enemy's breath
Hot on his cheek must find some myth,
Beer, boasting, bloody scalp, wherewith
To lay the stubborn ghost of death.

The man who sends an intimate arrow
From a matter of yards can see the furrow,
Feel in his bones the transpierced marrow
Of a companionable sorrow.

Between Two Worlds
(BBC Third Programme 1948 & 1951)

Ex-Gunner

Escaped the exacting service of the guns
But not the exciting memory in the veins;
As seas sing in a shell, their violence
Remains with us as a strange turbulence.

For us, Faust's triangle and signature
But neither Helen, nor second youth, nor power;
Only apprenticeship to a mystery
And short illusory moments of mastery.

Between Two Worlds
(BBC Third Programme 1948 & 1951)
New Statesman 1949

Between Two Worlds

Those foul-mouthed, tyrannous, and bloody guns
That we have oiled and greased, washed free of mud,
Deployed, raised, lowered, loaded, dragged and fired
Are like a woman's memory in the blood.

We spoke our drills, our spells for remote murder,
Held needles steady in the throat of thunder,
Prayed backwards, served a sinister calculation
And the daily intimate needs of ammunition;

Swung up our polished years into the breech
And rammed them home, and felt it slam across
Shoving the hand away—the rough reproach
Lost in the shattering orgasm of the piece.

We shook our four-gun curses at the hooves
That rode the trackless sky in a lurching lens,
Small bursting puffs of hate about those lives
That were the engines' fuel, the bombs' fuze;

Kept vigils, yelled responses, paid devotion
To nice adjustment, exquisite calibration
Of life and death—ourselves the ammunition
Briefly dispersed in a far-off commotion.

Return

Between Two Worlds
(BBC Third Programme 1948 & 1951)

You are my nerviness on landing,
You are my silence and my speech,
The things I want to ask the pilot,
The frequent glances at my watch.

You are the continents I've travelled,
You are the hours to my return;
You are the end of writing letters,
The hearth where we can watch them burn.

148

VI

Christmas & Family Verses

The poems that appear in the next two parts of my collected works very often refer to my own children and their descendants, or to places I have visited in the company of my family. We paid regular visits to Timberscombe in Somerset after Stella's father J. P. Martin retired from the ministry and went to live there (continuing to work until the end of his life). We also stayed in France and visited Italy as well as travelling around the British Isles, at a time when travel could be economical and slow, with long enough stays to enable us to enjoy the company and hospitality of family and friends.

Although I was never part of a group of writers, I played active roles in the Public Library Literary Society of Colchester, the Suffolk Poetry Society and the Essex Poetry Society. Each of these organisations gave me invaluable help and encouragement.

I would like to thank the following: Laurence and Jane Best, Ronald Blythe, Lawrence Brander, Ray and Yvonne Burl, Joan Culver, Ian and Jean Currey, Catherine Dell, Patrick Dickinson, Jack and Joan Elam, Francis and Philomela Engleheart, Malcolm Ford, Pat Green, Norah Henshilwood, Martin Hutton, Peggy Kirkaldy, Jack Lindsay, Roy and Rachel Macnab, J. P. Martin, Francis and Dame Alix Meynell, Denys and Vivien Milburn, Mavis Orpen, Howard and Grace Perkins, Romilly Redfern, W. R. Rodgers, Eric Sandon, Margaret Sinclair, Bob Sauvan Smith, K. O. Stuart, Mary Treadgold, Angus Wilson, Henry and Ruth Wilson and Marguerite Wood.

Christmas Verses

Nursery Rhyme

St Nicholas, patron of Christmas festivities, discovered that an innkeeper had murdered three boys and put their bodies into a tub with pickled pork. He forced the man to confess and pray for the boys to be restored to life.

Rub a dub dub,
Three boys in a tub,
A butcher, a baker, a candlestick-maker—
How can you tell
Boys' futures at all?
But that's not the point,
You monstrous innkeeper;
Pray to St. Nicholas
To bring this thing to pass!

New English Weekly 1935

Rub a dub dub,
Three boys in a tub,
A liar, a bully, a heartless dictator?
Flesh on to bones,
Blood into veins;
Pray for the miracle
Wretched innkeeper;
Though *this* should come to pass
Pray to St. Nicholas.

Santa Claus

St Nicholas was the patron saint of children, and of the other groups named in this poem

Now to St. Nicholas
Merchants and children pray,
Lest the good saint should pass
And not rein in his sleigh.

Time & Tide 1940

Children and merchants know
His bounty year by year,
And sailors, when winds blow,
Raise hands to him in prayer.

Christmas Verses

Repenting thieves today
Upon their knees are seen,
And threadbare scholars pray,
And men of Aberdeen.

Christmas Siege

1953

Now the frequent posts begin
And festivities set in;
Fog and family routine
Smear window and wind-screen;
Food and drink and custom blow
Up against our doors like snow.

Now the wishes and the words
Settle along our shelves like birds;
While the myths and mysteries
March behind invading trees,
And by every hearth again
Raise Birnam Wood in Dunsinane.

Traffic Jam, Côte d'Azur

1974

On Christmas Eve
On the Côte d'Azur
A private car
Held up
By three running dogs.

On Christmas Eve
On the Côte d'Azur
A private car
And the Toulon bus
Held up
By three running dogs
And a bell-wether with a clunking bell.

On Christmas Eve
On the Côte d'Azur
A private car
The Toulon bus
And a cement-mixer
Held up
By three running dogs
A bell-wether with a clunking bell
And a thousand swirling sheep.

On Christmas Eve
On the Côte d'Azur
A private car
The Toulon bus
A cement-mixer
And a lorry full of bottles
Held up
By three running dogs
A bell-wether with a clunking bell
A thousand swirling sheep
And a saddled donkey.

On Christmas Eve
On the Côte d'Azur
A private car
The Toulon bus
A cement-mixer
A lorry full of bottles
And a car-transporter
Held up
By three running dogs
A bell-wether with a clunking bell
A thousand swirling sheep
And a saddled donkey
Carrying a shepherd
With long moustaches and his face burnt black
Swigging from a bottle
Singing Noël.

On Christmas Eve
On the Côte d'Azur.

Willy Lott's Cottage, Flatford, Suffolk

1976
*Written at the
end of the Constable
bi-centenary year*

Willy Lott
Spent four days away from his cottage
In a lifetime;
To Constable he was a symbol of continuity.
Willy Lott's cottage
Seen in as many patterns of perpetuity
As Chartres Cathedral or the Taj Mahal
Is in itself a symbol of continuity.
Was Willy Lott's cottage
To lots of little Lotts
Hooped with holly
Mazed with mistletoe
A place where a mess of pottage
And huge chimney glow
Spelt Christmas continuity
Two centuries ago?

Those Other Shepherds

1978

Held up by the autumn flow
Of opulent Exmoor fleeces
Brimming a valley road,
I wonder about those other shepherds:
Did they lead their sheep
Through Bethlehem's channelled streets?
Did three crowned camels
Taller than oil-rigs
Lapped round by the bumping tide
Glitter in starlight
Waiting their turn?

154

'Paid for bread and wine at Christide, 2/6.'
        Churchwardens' Accounts, 1726

The Church of the Rock at Brentor,   1980
The rock that crowns the tor
St Michael and All Angels
That wheel above Dartmoor
Know well what pagan shrine stood here
Before their Holy War.

To carry up a coffin,
A bell-rope, or oak floor,
Or bread and wine at Christide
When off-sea whirlwinds roar—
All these are celebrations
Of victory in that war.

And food and wine at Christmas
When families come from far
Shared in a sheltered moment poised
Above the turbulent year
Stand out as affirmations
In a continuing war.

Christmas Photograph

This photograph of a young cousin   *To Roy & Ginny* 1983
Stepping from the blue of the Indian Ocean
Perfect in form and feature, in expression
Enigmatic as the wind about her head
The water about her feet—it all suggests
A far too easy Classical comparison.

But when I remember that her father,
Who took this photograph, did his stint
With unsupported Spitfires on a Greek island
I enter Homeric cockpits, admire his escape
Across the wine-dark sea, share his delight
In Venus Anadyomene rising from the foam.

Christmas Verses

To Elspeth 1983

Candlelight

Fire and flame and candlelight!
Last Christmas, in a power-failure,
We cooked and carved by candlelight;
And I was haunted by an ancient chorus:
Fire and salt and candlelight!
Neighbours from lit doorways brought more candles
And stayed to drink a glass before the fire.
Our other guest with flickering fingers
Chiselled and shaped the bone-formations
That link those present with those absent;
A young face close enough to touch
Summoned a presence greatly missed.
Fire and fleet, fire and sleet,
Fire and flame and candlelight!

1984

John Adlard, *Poet's England, Essex*
(Brentham Press 1984)
Hospice Book of Poetry

Anticipating Snow

Last year, near Christmas,
When skies were gun-metal blue,
It snowed—or rather, as we say in Essex,
That sn-e-e-euw!
The 'e' of the East wind entered the snow
As it does in the Sneeubergen in the Cape,
As it does across the sea in Holland;
And the children who went out to make a snowman
Left him unfinished, a broken pillar,
His red scarf staining the snow.

This Christmas, if there's snow,
Let it be the sort that passing schoolgirls
Shake down from soft-feathered laurels
Over their hoods and robin-redbreast faces
As they stand there and giggle and glow;
Let it be the sort that's spelt with an 'o'.

I sit a hemisphere away—   1985
My eyes aren't what they were
The batsman's face is hard to see,
The scoreboard's my despair;
But all the ritual attitudes
Of cricket are still there.

The visored batsman pats the crease
And practises a hit;
The bowler reaches for the ball
And moistens it with spit;
He paces out his platitudes
And polishes his wit.

The television camera
Directs me to a patch
Where running fieldsmen cluster
And leap, and try to touch
And shower with beatitudes
The one who took the catch.

The surpliced umpire stands his ground,
Ignores the choric roar;
Six pebbles in his pocket
Mean six balls and no more,
But there are certain latitudes
In judging leg before.

The tactics of the changing field
Are anything but clear,
But platitudes, beatitudes
And latitudes declare
That all the ritual attitudes
Of cricket are still there.

Renewal

A little over a year ago   1988
A powerful South wind blew,
Laying great trees from end to end,
Clearing our morning view.   157

Christmas Verses

A friend's neat field of Christmas trees
Intended for that year,
Lay flat, all facing the same way,
Like Mussulmans at prayer.

Within a throw of our prone oak,
With chains and saws still grappling,
We came upon a neighbour
Planting a sturdy sapling.

His sapling oak has taken root;
Beyond it I can see
Between his window curtains
A sparkling Christmas tree.

Christmas

1989

At Christmas-time, when each year ends,
We think especially of our friends.
This is a year in which we've seen
The send-off of a waggon, neat,
With disselboom and span complete,
Over a mountain range to lands
Of our anxiety; and have been
Supported by so many friends
Who came to wish us well, or sent
Messages of encouragement,
Their homing letters, flight on flight,
Finding our door, to our delight,
From many a longitude and latitude;
For these winged words we send our gratitude.

Spes Bona

Stepping outside into the brilliant night
To trace the Pointers to the Southern Cross
I felt the wind-carved presence of the mountain,
Reminder that at first Bartholomew Diaz
Called his discovery the Cape of Storms.
Henry the Navigator soon renamed it
Cape of Good Hope, a bolder prophecy.
We pray now that this jewelled constellation,
The true Cross of the Southern hemisphere,
Will shine again on our storm-battered hope.

Family Verses

Dialogue

For James
Fortnightly 1946

If the earth stopped turning
Would the seas fall from their sockets?
Asked my son.

Would fires fly off like rockets,
And money drop from pockets,
And eyes from their eye-sockets?

And where do you think they'd fall to?
Asked my son.

Look how the dusk is piling
Up like snow, said my son.

Gently drifting, softly filling
Hollow valley and land, and piling
Over the trees to the skies' ceiling . . .

But of course that would be space,
Said my son.

Where are we going with all this turning?
Asked my son.

The snow snowing and sun burning,
Wind blowing and rain raining,
Tide flowing and trees leaning
Against the wind of the world's turning . . .

Would the seas fall from their sockets?
Asked my son.

Zodiac

For James & Andrew
1946

The Zodiac is a heavenly zoo
With animals, people and something else too.

It has a bull called Taurus,
A wild goat, Capricornus,
A lion known as Leo,
A scorpion called Scorpio,
An archer, Saggitarius,
A waterman, Aquarius,
Also a fish called Pisces,
And a fine ram called Aries,
A sharp-clawed crab called Cancer,
And a pair of scales called Libra,
Where the heavenly twins called Gemini
And the girl called Virgo can weigh themselves free.

These twelve signs of the zodiac
Were once our calendar and almanack;
But anyone *now* who thinks it matters
Which you were born under must be scatters!

Christmas Child

For Clare & Hal
1966

Double-glaze the windows,
Double-bank the grate,
Use whatever trick you know
To make the seasons wait;
For time is on the doorstep
And change is at the gate.

But here, among light and laughter,
An infant child, age-old,
With bright-eyed smiles of favour
And small neat hands can hold
Back the intruding ice-cap
And the gate-crashing cold.

In the Quaker Meeting, Tamsin,
Her head as high as the bench arm-rest,
Left her mother's side
And moved with purpose
Along the silent row of knees
To open her grandmother's handbag,
Look in, close it, and then return—
Satisfied that her chocolate easter egg
Left there in protective custody
Was still safe and sound.

For Tamsin
1972

Kind Offer

Tamsin is always
Good with her pony,
Brushing his coat,
Polishing his hooves,
Combing out his mane,
And cleaning out his stable.

For Tamsin
1976

Tamsin came to see us
One weekend
When we were taking care
Of our neighbour's canary,
In his shining
Gilded cage.

Tamsin talked to him,
Whistled to him, coaxed him
To climb up his ladder
Swing on his swing,
Frisk and flutter
In his bath, and sing.

Then she turned and asked us:
'Shall I muck him out for you?'

Hundreds-and-Thousands 1941

One Boxing Day
When your father and mother
Were not much taller
Than Christmas stockings
The snow fell through the smoke of factories
On to a parade-ground
White as sugar-icing.
Finding myself in a snowball battle
I noticed, as I moulded the snow,
That particles had stained it
Red, blue, green,
A kaleidoscope of colour;
And the snowball that thudded
On my khaki shoulder
Scattered the white icing
With hundreds-and-thousands.

Pomp and Circumstance

The child and I this morning
Emptied across my bed a trinket-box,
Tumbled through necklaces and rings and brooches;
Then 'Beads on Teddy' she demanded, and
Teddy, yellow, juvenile, acquired
A gilded string of semi-precious stones,
Became an instant Indian chieftain.

                                                Kate
Surveyed her handiwork and found it good:
'More beads on Teddy, rings on Teddy' she
Swagged round him golden chains and ropes of pearl,
Long loops of lapis lazuli and moonstone
An intricate gilt confectionery of coral,
A garnet swollen to a royal ruby—
Each stone enormous in its new perspective,
Upgrading Teddy from a glittering brave
Into a Rajput prince, a Tudor king;
The soft and furry baby-features turned
To golden consequence and blood-red power.

Oviedo, Northern Spain

Family Verses

For Ian & Jean
1985

Under the steep edge of the city
Swung between a saddleback mountain
And a green-plumaged terracotta foreground
To tableclothed peaks, at this window
I stand as a stranger, I cannot turn
Olive-stone vowels and ewe's-milk consonants
To ask the simplest questions. How can I learn
To what coincidence of sea and manufacture
We owe these tapestries of silver mist—
Or what celebration closed the shops today?
And nobody in any case could tell me
If the rounding girl by the toffee-apple haystacks,
Festival-dressed to travel to the capital
And standing, when we saw her,
By a young man with a saddled donkey,
Bore the lines of a blessed conception?

Under Siege, Mafeking

Upstream 7 (3), 1989

It's not for nothing that I was born
In the siege town of Mafeking
Safe years after those broad-brimmed
Echoing events, but in good time
For adults to pat me on the head and say,
'So you, my boy, were born in Mafeking!'

No longer the star of an imperial crown
Tilted towards Cairo, my native town
Has slurred its vowels and become
Part of an unpronounceable homeland;
Proud Mafeking and boisterous mafficking
Are both forgotten;

And I, after the years, find myself
In a suburb of siege where Long Tom
Drops death amongst us and exact mausers
Target our pain; yet daily, hourly,
We hear and pass on exciting dispatches
Of brilliant sortie, tactical withdrawal,
Miraculous recovery, desperate defence,
And rumours of ambiguous relief.

Verse-Speaking

'I had as lief the town crier spoke my lines'
Hamlet's advice to the Players, III ii 1–27

The Listener
(printed as a letter)

There is a spirit sits upon the tongues
Of those who read our poems; he seems to me
A tiresome charlatan who fastens wings
On poems which in the way of poetry
Should take off by themselves; for it was he
Who told some reader poetry was a rune,
An incantation, and that he was free
To read it like a dog that bays the moon.

He has taught actors how to curl their tongues
Round mud and blood, wriggle in ecstasy
Of borrowed grief, with sudden show of lungs
Tear passions into shreds remorselessly,
At every point o'erstep the modesty
Of nature, mouth, saw air, use the bassoon
For chamber music—so that they may be
Like noisy dogs that bark at the full moon.

I have heard Irish poets whose rich tongues
Covered the semitones as certainly
As saints and angels stepping on the rungs
Of airy ladders; but this mimicry
By English voices trying earnestly
To dance some sort of roof-top rigadoon
In solo or cat-chorus, sickens me—
I'd rather hear a dog that bays the moon.

Dear Sir, convey my full apology
To any who have found the secret tune
In written words and sung it—but save me
From dogs that bark or bay at the full moon.

Letter to Tamsin from Cavalière, South of France

The mistral began
When we were walking home along the beach;
It nearly blew
Granny away,
But I caught her by an ankle and held on—
Well, I'll admit that isn't quite true,
But, seen from the top of our climbing path,
The sea was blue
Black, the colour of ink;
And it looked as if an invisible giant
With an invisible broom
Was sweeping out from the shore
A long line of spray
Like dust and fluff along a linoleum floor.

I'm glad you saw the train they call 'Le Mistral'—
The mistral is very like a train.
As we hurried home
Over the road where the coast train used to run
(And where people say a ghost train goes
On moonlit nights and when the mistral blows)
The big cork oak that overhangs the track
Began to creak
Exactly like a train
Straightening
After a curve;
And now we're back
In the villa once again,
The windows rattle,
The doors bang,
The shutters squeak,
And clack, the passing sirens and shrill whistles blow;
And, as you walk along the passage,
You lean against a wall that seems to sway—

And then you suddenly feel you're in a ship.
Ask your Daddy
If he remembers how the mistral blew
When we set off to Morocco
From Marseilles years ago,
And it said,
'You—oo
Thought you were a good sailor,
Didn't you-oo?
Well, you're NOT!'

165

French Bread

French bread comes in three sizes,
baguette, pain restaurant
and pain gros campagne

I went down to the Boulanger's
All alone
Under the pepper-trees
And brought back
Up the little path
The unmade track
Red wine
Fresh milk
And a long *baguette* in my haversack.

I went down to the Boulanger's
With Hal and Tamsin
Across the phantom railway
And brought back
Up the little path
The climbing track
Red wine, white wine
Milk fresh and pasteurised
And a large *restaurant* in my haversack.

I went down to the Boulanger's
The day the French family came
And brought back
Up that little path
That precipitous track
Red wine, white and rosé
Milk fresh and pasteurisé
And a whole *gros campagne* in my haversack.

VII

People & Places

England, Scotland & Ireland

Demolition of a Great House,
Tendring Hall, Suffolk

Sir William Rowley, Admiral of the White,
Put Sally Rovers and the French to flight;
Court-martialled, brought ashore his seaman's lurch,
Grounded his keel in Stoke-by-Nayland church.

Sir Joshua Rowley, Admiral of the White,
Sailed many a sea, but seldom had to fight,
Called 'our friend Jos' by Hood, who loved his joke,
Brought back his gilded frame to lie in Stoke.

Bartholomew Samuel Rowley, admiral too,
And other Rowleys, Red, and White, and Blue,
Sailed under brilliant skies, dressed over all,
Came back to marble Stoke-by-Nayland wall;

Brought back prize money with the White and Blue,
Paid Soane to make their sailors' dream come true:
A huge three-decker craft that sailed a hill,
Then ran aground, as such a vessel will.

The admirals and their ladies walk the poop,
Ogle the view through glass and telescope;
On portholed lower decks the servants run
With coals and water, never see the sun.

Were these the admirals Jane Austen knew;
Their skins mahogany, their language blue,
Only their seamanship and canvas chaste,
Wallowing in grog in the wake of men of taste?

The River Stour flows by. In World War Two
The lower decks enclose an alien crew
Of flaxen prisoners-of-war, who mope
By Adam fireplaces, lost to hope.

Only that windowed poop is there today.
Among the shrubs, perhaps, red admirals play
But even the moon can find no corridor
Where servants jostle prisoners-of-war!

Poetry Review 1959
John Smith: *The Poet's Gift*
(The Suffolk Poetry Society 1986)
Marjorie Baker: *Poet's England: Suffolk*
(Brentham Press 1994)
Suffolk and Norfolk Life 2000

169

King's Lynn

Angus Wilson: *Writers of East Anglia* (Secker
& Warburg 1977)

Angus Wilson:
East Anglia in Verse & Prose
(Secker & Warburg 1982)

Angus Wilson:
King's Lynn Festival Handbook (1982)

John Smith: *The Poet's Gift*
(Suffolk Poetry Society 1986)

Paul Berry: *Poet's England: Norfolk*
(Brentham Press 1994)

Just opposite the elegant Custom House
So feasibly attributed to Wren
We watched the racketting pile‑driver
Man‑shouldered into place
By greasy caps and coats with pennant linings
Fluttering heraldic in the north‑east wind.

Beside it on the quay a square‑hewn stake
Extracted from the past—a broken tooth
Stained at the root—the crude support
Of civic splendour in the years of grace.

Explore now, as a freak tide might explore
This town that history could have made a city,
Swirl round the leaning pillars of this church
That could be a cathedral, then move on,
Inquisitive as water,
Over the docks, across the squares,
Into courtyards, under entrances.

Leave tides below, and climb
The winding centuries of a merchant's watchtower
To scan the wide way to the wider sea
For pennants fluttering in the north‑east wind.

Step down to what the tides have left behind:
In the marsh‑sunken chapel‑of‑ease
Two Dutch‑scrubbed likenesses,
A merchant and his wife, as shrewd
And thrifty as the north‑east wind,
Square‑hewn,
Embedded in the local mud—essential
Supporters of armorial elegance.

Joseph Hall made clocks at Alston in Cumberland in the eighteenth century, and he
and his wife worshipped at Alston Meeting House, which still survives. These
verses incorporate a family tradition which a great-great-grandson, R. L. Hall, of
Colchester, communicated to the author. The family clock, minus the chimes which
Joseph Hall removed, is still preserved.

Joseph and Elizabeth Hall   *The Friend* 1965
   Ticked out their lives,
   Chimed out their lives
Among brown, elegant, and tall
Grandfather clocks that he designed
   Time out of mind
To talk of time from the firelit wall
Of rectory, surgery, manor-hall.

The masterpiece of Joseph Hall
   Engraved the hours,
   The weeks, months, years,
The saint's day and the festival
From each man's starting-time until
   His heart stood still;
His public hours in street and hall,
His private hours by the firelit wall.

When Joseph became a Quaker, all
   That he could see
   Was eternity.
Returning from the Meeting Hall
He opened the clock, took out the chime,
   Ordered his time
To tick on quietly by the wall
But never, never chime at all.

Joseph and Elizabeth Hall
   Ticked out their lives,
   Their chime-less lives,
Among brown, elegant, and tall
Grandfather clocks that he designed
Time out of mind
To speak, talk, pray by the firelit wall
But never, never sing at all.

171

Bewitched

New Contrast 94 (24 (2), 1996

Tied down to a high bed
By plastic entanglements of drip and drain,
I saw them enter in a shaft of light
That showed their purposeful forms but not their faces
A coven of young witches, sisters three,
Not quite laughing, not quite singing,
Circling me.
> *Round about the cauldron go,*
> *In the poisoned entrails throw;*
> *Fillet of a fenny snake*
> *In the cauldron boil and bake.*
I am the bubbling cauldron. One
With lifted chin examines the tall apparatus
That feeds me through a needle in my wrist,
And murmurs her approval. The second,
Half-hidden by the edge of the bed, considers
Unspeakable auguries, but adds
Exact notes of approval. The third
Seizes a pulse and shoulder, and inserts
Magic silver beneath my tongue. She too joins in
The chorus of approval. I feel her spell.
I am, once more, the good little boy
Who does not know what he has done
To deserve such praise, but takes it all the same ...
> *Gall of goat, and slips of yew*
> *Silver'd in the moon's eclipse ...*
Moon's eclipse ... The shaft of light
Shines as they leave on pleasing youthful faces,
A coven of white witches,
Sisters three.

View over Timberscombe

1979

From the steep knoll they call Black Ball
The eye takes in five valleys and the high
Smooth line of Dunkery, so recently
Spot-lit with beacon fire. Below,
Within the radius of a cricketer's throw,
The compact village, population
Much as in Domesday Book, huddles around
The red-brown church and the white school
> and chapel,

So far down that the cars in circulation
On the strips of road outside it seem to crawl,
And yet so near that the echo of a hammer
Reaches us here, and the thin, shrill sound
Of children in the schoolroom chanting together
Their tables, perhaps—or, later in the year,
Through an opened door the wind-torn stave
    of a carol.

Walking Over Grabbist

When we, by the almost obsolete
Placing of foot before foot have raised
Our eyes to gorse and bracken, then we may
Look round a moment on a world that was.

This track once shouldered wagons from Minehead.
Two preachers with one horse would come this way,
One riding and one walking; country people
Carried their sweat to church and chapel then.

Below, in the easy prose of wheels,
We ride the metalled roads, but now, up here,
Breathing the heather and the distance, feel
The measured, springing feet of poetry stir.

Ronald Blythe: *Places: An Anthology of Britain*
(Oxford University Press 1981)

Cattle Grazing

Cows shamble on with clumsy motion
Through ruminating ecstasies,
Trailing splay feet and some old notion
Of lovely girls with heifers' eyes.

So uncontrollable a bundle
Swings from each length of bony pole,
Legs stagger as they try to handle
Their coolie-burden, while the soul

Looks out with such sublime devotion
From yearning Hindu-actress eyes
That half a teeming population
Thinks of this model as it dies;

Poetry Review 1959

173

The perfect soul of saint-like beauty
Looks out from eyes that do not scorn
To show their calm and docile duty
Beneath an armament of horn;

Behind a show of strength to shelter
Their quiet lives, behind the wall
Of limited privilege to nurture
Their young in grazing-rights for all.

Along the skyline of these hillocks
They inch their heads: the sunlight slips
Over their sweating angular buttocks
And now their tails, those restless whips,

Fall on their quivering flanks and bellies
Like laughter from irreverent fountains
On soft unyielding water-lilies;
Like heretic rains on steadfast mountains.

Christmas Apples

1978

The two trees, unpruned,
Their long stems loaded
With ripening fruit,
Leaned from their steep bank
Out towards Dunkery,
Where the sun, molten
Below a black entablature of cloud,
Blazed out his rays
To polish up their colour.

The apples in this bowl
Were picked in that glittering
Pause between showers;
And some that escaped
Our mountaineering fingers
Ran down the grass slope,
Skipped down the stone steps,
Thumped on the kitchen door
Like red-cheeked children
Dancing in ahead of us
To dodge the downpour.

These valleys are full of Empire memories,
And more than empire, Persia, Mexico.
An Indian dancer dances in a window
With delicate balance of hands and body and chin.
One whom I knew was reminded of Pilgrim's Rest,
Where men sieved gold by day in mountain streams
And fought each other by night for booze brought up
By waggons from Natal. Only, my friend would say
These valleys are more savage!
He instanced a gipsy woman who would place
A small stuffed leopard to overbear her neighbours,
And the man who told him that the wife he'd buried
Was the finest woman to wear a pair of boots.
This bungalow's called 'Egypt'—what crocodile,
What scarab or what deity from the Nile
Or reminiscence of Shepherd's
Lives in the dreams of those who live in it?
They say Egyptians settled long ago
At Washford and at Watchet, as they say
That Brutus slew a dragon down at Totnes;
But these are newer nostalgias. Here is Bahrain.
I've been, at Bahrain in the Persian Gulf,
To an army mess approached across bare sand
Between high hedges of dead-green camouflage netting.
These brought to Bahrain the lanes of dear old England;
And now we have Old Bahrain,
A suffocation of heat and Lancashire hot-pot
Planted in Somerset beside a village
Mentioned in Doomsday Book.
An Indian dancer dances in a window
With delicate movements of hands and body and chin.
I'm dying, Egypt, said Mark Antnony.

Saloon Bar

The sentimental wash of background music
Maintains us in suspension; the still hub
Of the turning day is here; we have our basic
Ration of freedom from preoccupation.

Under a plastic tulip, red as blood,
A man whose faded face grows quietly older
Beside the ebbing glass where rings of mud
Throw up no starfish moment as his portion.

Dripped sentiment, for lover or for mum.
In the public bar a sudden burst of shrill
Excessive laughter points our minimum.
The alcohol of half-communication

Maintains us in suspension; we tread water
Among the separate strangers whose laconic
Rations of speech is like our own, who barter
Long working lives for this slight exaltation.

King's Burial-Place, Iona

BBC Third Programme c.1952

Under a blue, gull-crested wind,
Wafers of stone where kings of Scotland,
With cousins of Norway, Ireland, France,
Lie close beneath a plaid of grass.

Through every royal whim of weather
What a procession of ritual prows
To the cell made holy by the dove-named hermit
Lover of sea-birds but not of women;

Bearing the bones in the beaks of long-ships
Along the sea-lochs reticent of coracles
Past empty islands lining the route
Catching their food on the wing, like sea-gulls.

Rulers were migrant then, tirelessly following
Food and war over land and water,
Leaving their bones in celibate places,
Hunting their food in funeral procession;

And their exceptional ghosts, close-jostled
Do they haunt the Church and the Street of the Dead?
—Or sway in the wind at will, like sea-gulls,
Crying for the past round the holiday steamers?

176

Thoor Ballylee

This untouched morning at Thoor Ballylee   *Contrast* 45 12 (1), 1978
(Birds in the trees, a moorhen on the stream)
And Yeats in there, beside his trestle table,
His changeless Samurai sword and gyreing stair
That spirals through his poems like curled smoke rising
Or worms through dead men's bones—
And I wonder if by some such ceremony
As blowing notes on a trumpet I can bring
Him out to face me from his castle walls.

I cannot ask that great and stately man
To meet me at his gate. His friends are chosen.
The casual contacts of a later age
Have no place in his scheme. And yet, perhaps
A signature tune on a trumpet, sixteen notes,
A sennet, not a sonnet, might just bring
That courteous man on to his battlements.

Horseman, Pass By!

Under bare Ben Bulben's head   *Contrast* 45 12 (1), 1978
In Drumcliffe churchyard Yeats is laid.
The skies are bare, the trees are bare,
Naked of leaves as rock and tower;
The moor around was not more bare
When Yeats's grandfather was here
Blessing in grave and marriage⁄bed
This throng of slanting⁄headstoned dead.
The blank church tower, the elms that crowd
About it and above are loud
With rooks in congregated choirs,
Hundreds of black parishioners
Noisily building as they fly
Between high nests, untidily
Dropping their mire and rage upon
Tumbled graves and Yeats' smooth stone.
Cast a cold eye
On life, on death,
Horseman pass by!

Coole Park

Contrast 45 12 (1), 1978

This avenue of introspective trees
Muffles the sounds of wheels and trotting hooves;
The long North wall that shoulders off the wind,
The untrimmed hedge that smells of box and fox
Shelter the knickerbocker ghosts who carved
Their names on this railed-in tree. It was John Synge
Who took a man and a loy, as God took clay,
And shaped a Western world; and Bernard Shaw
Who cut his confident signature and left
For John Bull's richer island. Ivied ruins
Hide the silk shade of Lady Gregory,
The midwife of a nation's arts, her fate
To hurl the little streets upon the great
As surely as Maud Gonne, whose small caged birds
Sang night and day of blood; and Willie Yeats—
For Yeats it was created Hanrahan
And drove him drunk or sober through the dawn
And specimen-pinned the gardener whose shears
Snipped off an insolent farmer's upstart ears;
Poor Yeats, who ruffled in a manly pose
Despite his timid heart. He did not care
To mingle with the mob, but warmed to see
The differing skills of horseman, soldier, poet;
His peacock eyes took in the family tree,
The silver sconces and steel sacrifice;
At Coole, between his pride and modesty torn,
His lasting love of ceremony was born.

Italy & France

Fearful Symmetry

Brunelleschi became a hero of mine   1973
When I first saw his cupola float above Florence,
Lifted by the mist, then dropped and balanced
With fearful symmetry on nave and transepts—
Almost as he once fitted it himself,
Linking through half-domes, which from below
Bore the proportion of Child to Virgin.

The other day a team of excavators
Uncovered the tomb and bones of Brunelleschi
Under his dome, just where Vasari
Had said they should be.
The Superintendant,
Leaning to touch them with a hand that trembled,
Said that his six years' search was justified.
One of the workmen, fifty-seven from Prato,
Pushed back his cyclist's beret to report
That as he looked into the marble bier
He felt a sense of joy. Another offered
To bet his own life, and his family's too,
They'd find Giotto next.

The bones were small.
'A small man, very spare,' Vasari said,
'But what a daemon!'

Yes, and what a climb!
From goldsmith to architect, pepper-pot to cupola—
When nobody else had built a cupola
Since Roman times, and then no doubt by magic!

In the Pazzi chapel, and at San Marco,
And under the Duomo itself,
I marvel that such tension
Created such repose.

Leonardo

1973

After a day spent at the Uffizi
In the incandescent glow of masterpieces,
We sit outside and watch the nimbuses
Conferring sainthood on the heads of street-lamps,
The intermittent tapestries of fireflies;
The steady fresco-fire of the stars.
The kindling sounds of a children's party
Rise into conflagration, then subside
To embers of mothers calling in their children.
The hard flint of a female voice calls out:
'Le-on-arrr-do!'
At once the flint-struck spark becomes a star.

Cypresses, Val di Pesa, Tuscany

1973

Vines and olives are the food and drink
Of this steep, manuscript landscape. Cypresses
Provide the something extra men require—
Sometimes a touch of dignity. The Corsini
Have thrust an arrogant avenue of cypresses
Straight as Uccello's lance from their great door
Across the middle foreground of this hill
To meet the glancing shaft from their great gate.

Farmers have built their dusty apricot houses
On every crest that catches the cool breeze,
Then planted cypresses for summer shade
And winter wind-break, lined and spaced
To some ancestral fancy now forgotten—
Perhaps some fierce need. On every spur
Towers and houses share the dignity
Of tufted cypresses—or the caprice:
For this has rabbit ears and windmill arms.

These cypresses are all things to all men:
A perruqued gentleman and short plump wife
Stand with their backs to me day after day
And look across the grey-green labouring fields
As they have done for confident centuries.

180

As fauns and dryads of these classical slopes
They seem unchangeable, but tall white oxen
Have faded into tractor-furrowed air, while vines
Climb between concrete posts; the motor-road
Has cut a parvenue passage through the grace
Of the Corsini colonnade—Uccello's
Tip-tilted lance is roughly hacked in two.

Campo Santo, Val di Pesa

Follow the road between the olive groves
Towards the football field. The *campo santo*
Under black cypresses as tall as churches
Is square and inward-looking. Leading families,
Gori, Frascati and a dozen more,
Are occupants of the boxes, evenly placed
Around three sides of a theatre; coffins thrust
Behind starched marble into slotted walls
Acknowledge and receive acknowledgment.
With no less sense of occasion the lesser sort
Take up their places in the numbered stalls
Behind their linen-white symmetrical fronts.

A girl steps over a grave and leans to kiss
The inset photograph of a dear departed,
A dated father in his Sunday best;
His and such other faces all look inwards,
Not to the road outside, the open stage
Of hurrying cars and vespas. Flowers shine
On many graves, and rented flames will glow
After the fall of night, when cypresses
Higher than steeples will be black as ogres.

For the people in this little Tuscan town
Who live their lives and die their deaths in public
Each eternity is a public performance.

Night at Volterra

1973

High under the roofs of Volterra
Battlemented against the plain,
Concentration of cars and people
Within towered walls
Besieged by wind like the sea round Ararat;
Rumore from crammed bars
Rumours of wars
Echo up between precipiced shutters,
Cease after midnight like an anodyne.
From pantiles overhanging sleep
Cassandra cats
Utter forebodings
To the worn heads on the Etruscan Gate
Accustomed for so long
To so many attacks ...
From furry darkneas
Bombardment comes,
Crash and flash
Trying to coincide,
The rainfall solid
The streets ravines ...
In the first light
A man bales out his car;
Women in aprons with umbrellas
Carry out baskets from a pastry shop.
Intimate pigeons
Near enough to touch
Exchange melodious
Throaty satisfaction
On having survived the night.

Afternoon Shopping, Val di Pesa

1973

The shops reopen at four;
But if there is no shade at four,
Why open at four?
And if there is still no shade at five,
Why open at five?
Nobody will come to buy until it gets cooler
Except our English visitors
Who, if they stayed longer,
Would soon learn.

Miracle at Pisa

The Square containing the Cathedral, Baptistry and Leaning Tower at Pisa
is called the Piazza dei Miracoli

As we stepped into the Baptistry   *Contrast 1973*
Out of the green square
Under the blue sky
A boy's voice rose to the dome, and at once
Returned as a disembodied echo;
The miracle, in that place of miracles,
Silenced the children around him;
He sang the phrase again
And the same ethereal echo turned it
Into a thing of air.
The children stood as still
As if a pope or a well-known footballer
Had come into their lives;
Then remembered that their singing cherub
Was wearing a T-shirt as they were,
And laughed a little, and tried
A phrase or two themselves.
The young priest in charge roused an urgent echo
As he hustled them outside
In sight of the leaning inquisitive campanile
In that green place of miracles
Under the blue sky.

The Streets of Siena

The streets of Siena   1973
Are twelve feet wide
Between high palaces,
With wall-to-wall carpeting
Of paving stones.
They climb like the radii
Of a spider-web
Out of the shell-shaped
Central piazza;
The people who fill them
Like flood water
Move aside for buses
Cars and vespas
As they once did
For slithering carriages
And, before that,
For those fantastic
Heaven sent, hell bent,
Palio horsemen.

Is This a Poem?

1973

* At San Casciano

From a plaque by a gate
In a cypress avenue
On a hill south of Florence *
These words came out to meet me:
On 25 July
1944
Here fell
Taddei Pasquale
Taddei Guido
Vermigli Donato
Fra Ruffino of Castel del Piano
Barbarously killed by German bullets.
May Humanity remember.

The right words
In the right order
And the extra depth of meaning—
Is this a poem?

Lakeside Villages, Lugano

1973

Under the austere outline of these mountains
The ruthless overhang of rock and forest,
The Latin villages that edge the water
Reach out perhaps with over-compensation
Towards the passing boats. Along the front
They stand knee-deep in water, loggia
Holding up flowers, waving flags of welcome,
Sending out notes of welcome. A second row
Leans on the first row's shoulders, trailing creepers
That promise scented shade to anyone
Who treads the narrow pier. Behind again
A row of hooded windows winks a welcome
Over a longer stay. A belfry tower
Above a hidden facade, balustrades
With urns and cypresses are indications
Of continuity. From gilt pavilions
In Gothic galleries the terraced dead
Look out, as from long habit, at the boats.

I remember a village—visited rarely
By Gabriel the lake-steamer, promising blessing—
For a curved terrace under scented shade
And a singing family of three, in pleasant peasant
Bobble and sash and dancing zoccoli,
A father with a guitar and easy skill
In touching untried strings,
A pretty daughter with a naked voice
That played upon those strings,
A mother whose tambouring rhythm and velvet contralto
Lowered a flowered curtain. I heard their story
Of mortgage and music and illness
And all but touched the daughter's hand.

Today we pour across a postcard pier
Past purple drinks and paintings, up paved lanes
With steps, romantic, but as soon explored
As any casual pick-up. Restaurants
That line the waterside sell crowded space
To wait for the next steamer.
                              Take this lane
To the opposite end of the village, the cemetery
Where villagers are stowed away as neatly
As bottles in the caves behind the bars.

I look for their name on those neat stones,
And picture that curved terrace.
                              Perhaps it wasn't
In Gandria at all, but in some other
Of these too often visited villages.

Isola Bella, Lake Maggiore

1973

The high cool palace takes the crest
And two-fifths of this Borromean island—
A family with an embalmed cardinal,
As good as new, in a Cellini crown;
The shaded garden takes some three-fifths more,
Only, along one ledge,
Where servitors once clung,
The caterers cluster now,
A hanging hive of junk-shop lanes
And pressing terrace tables
Where tourists balance, and buzz, and wait for entry.

At three they swarm into the high cool rooms
And cloud the lovely vistas; in curious grottos
Confuse reflections and the sound of water,
Sway past irrelevant works of art
Of mediocre patronage, but pause
By shabby memories of Mussolini, swirl
Out of the palace doors into the garden—
Where sneering peacocks dodge the cameras
And bend white necks, and scream
At gross irrelevant statues on the steps
Of a vast platform blatant to the sun.

Male Chauvinism, Lake Maggiore

1973

A party from one nation, once the steamer
Had left the pier and settled to a blood-beat,
Began to eat and drink; big men, stout women,
With shouted words and spattered sausages
And bow-wave slops of beer. It was the women
Who hogged the conversation, elbowing
Forward across the trough.

                              Then the men
Carried their beer to another table
And sang, in practiced sentimental voices,
Of love, and family, and philandering,
And fighting for the homeland, drank and sang,
While their now-silent women, with no beer,
Sausage or conversation left, looked on
Resentfully, at something that had foiled
Them often, and would foil them again.

No Fable

Contrast 1976

Held up on our way South
Beside the sand⁄swirling Marne
At Chateau Thierry in October rain
We got them to open up the classieal villa
Where La Fontaine was born.
Under his portrait's calculating eyes
I walked the tight⁄rope
Esopian verses
Balancing line⁄and⁄colour dog and donkey
And fox and chanticleer
Wondering what reproof those animals
Would howl or bray or shout at a traveller
Held up by a broken axle—
Or impotent clutch—
Beside the Marne that has held up armies
At Chateau Thierry in October rain.

Sunset,
Villa de Bonne Espérance, Cavalière

For Roy & Rachel Macnab
Contrast 39 10 (3), 1976

Tonight, beyond encircling capes and islands
That make this bowl a wider Kommetjie,
Lie the snow peaks of a cloud⁄Corsica
Outlines softened by distance
Shading marks too fine
For the most feathery pencil
A range of hardened vapour here set down
In silhouette against an orange sky.

Now lighthouses begin to pirouette
Along the capes and islands; St Benat's church
Blurs into centaur shape; the sea blue⁄greys;
Yet, minute after minute, an hour almost
This accident of colour and light endures.

Darkness flows over it. I turn to see
Warm lamps glow out on near mimosa foothills
That hide those other Alps of snow and stone.

Pavane for a Provencal Fireplace

Contrast 39 10 (3), 1976

The mimosa which burns too fast
And the cork-oak which burns too slow
Make an accord of three
With the mica-tinselled driftwood
That holds the colours of the sea
The blue
Green
Peacock flame
Of waves advancing
Retreating
Spreading a fan of feathers
Flickering a cape
Of liquid gold
In the eyes of a man and a woman
And a solemnly dancing
Child.

VIII
Flashback to America

I would like to express my thanks to my sister Joan and her husband Harold Culver, Margaret Sinclair and Marguerite Wood; to Jack Cope of *Contrast*, and to Lawrence Brander of the British Council for passing a selection of the verses to the Harvard Library.

America, Far West

This country has no history
To bore the tourist through and through;
But she sure has a load of rocks,
And with geology she makes do.

Flashback to America

Contrast 1971
British Council for
Harvard Poetry Room 1972

Mount Olympus, Washington State

The gods live here,
But their red Homer nods—
Or they're less garrulous
Than Grecian gods.

Hurricane Ridge, Washington State

This arrogant platform
Close to the sky;
The Olympic Mountains
Around us lie.

Stupendous parapet
And cafeteria
Command fine views
Of this wide area.

The Olympic mountains
Capped with snow—
And no sign of life
On the slopes below.

The gods live here
With so little fuss—
Do we worship them?
Or they us?

Flashback to America

'You Are Now Entering Sappho'

Road sign—Washington State

The Queen of Song, whom poets praise,
Has fallen upon unhappy days!—
But no, this legend: DRINK ROOT BEER
Confirms that she was never here.

Bella Vista

In Europe, where the view is fine,
They put up a booth for beer or wine;
While here, where hygiene is the rage,
A rest-room cheers your pilgrimage.

Scenic Indigestion

Contrast 1971
British Council for
Harvard Poetry Room 1972

Wordsworth and Coleridge wrote with rapture
Of their small English world of Nature.
If they had seen the U.S.A.
They would have flung their pens away!

Crater Lake

Contrast 1971
British Council for
Harvard Poetry Room 1972

That gold prospector
Who stumbled over a mountain rim
And saw far below him in a cosmic cup
This blue, untouchable floor of water,
Called it the Deep Blue Lake;
Geologists improved on this—
They should have let it stand.
This is a vessel filled with the snows
Of primitive centuries, held up above the world
For tiresome gods of the Titan era,
Those muscle-bound heroes Llao and Skel,
To throw each other into, one thick skull
Making a useless island: the local Indians
Were right to leave it alone. Deep Blue,
Lunar, cold and hostile, royal blue,
Sapphire harder than stone, a jewelled pool
Fit for that pitiless prude of prudes
Diana herself to bathe in.

                              Only here
Above the hemlocks on this sunlit slope,
Above the soft fall-away of fir-branches,
Where Clark's nutcrackers, grey and black,
Dart between broken and blasted shadows,
And where warm families carry their lives
In bubbles of talk along this parapet,
Only here
Do I find the intense blue almost tolerable.

San Francisco

Take a clay model of a hilly peninsula   *New Coin Poetry* 9 (1/2), 1973
With sides squeezed in to make the rises steeper,
And you have the basis of San Francisco.
The planner who superimposed the grid
Of streets at right angles was artist or madman.
The streets climb up, steep as ladders,
Over humped spines that run at all angles.
Through Chinatown or Latin Quarter,
Past shops and skyscrapers, then, just as steeply
Fall to the sea. The sea is always
At the end of the street, either blue and sparkling,
Or hidden behind a curtain with the Golden Gate
And Alcatraz.
                    Once, near Fisherman's Wharf,
The mist lifted a corner, and showed for a moment
Four-masted barques clustered at the quays
With horsedrawn vans and handtrucks at their gangways,
And aboard, the adventurers with splendid moustaches,
Taking this city in their stride
En route for California or Alaska.
                              It fell again, then lifted
On a sudden canyon cut across buildings
And the debris and confusion of falling walls.

Contrast 1971
New Coin Poetry 9 (1/2), 1973

Firefall—Yosemite Valley

Nosing after nightfall
Under the mile-high walls of this valley
Among the firelit bases of giant trees
Into a sudden city of parked cars,
I watched the dark swirl
Of men, women and hand-held children
Stiffen as the resonant muezzin chanted:
'Let the fire fall.'
Far up from a point of light beside a star
A voice too faint for an echo fluttered an answer,
A thin ribbon of sound.
A ribbon of flame,
A floating
Bridal
Veil
Of flame,
A comet flaunting a peacock's tail
With a thousand eyes to catch and hold
The thousand eyes below.

The men, women and children,
Come from their slogan-blasted main streets
To see a miracle outside their lives,
Strain upwards for a sign.

Death Valley

Visit Death Valley if you harbour
Whimsy thoughts of the macabre—
In the summer, out of season
If you wish to lose your reason;
At evening, shrivelled to a toast,
Find a motel kept by a ghost.

In the winter crystal fountains
Bubble out of the Funeral Mountains;
The Devil's Golf Course is a joke
Frequented by hippies and flower-folk
Who show their sense of the mac-abor
By bumping off a loving neighbor.

Eat, Gas, Cold Beer

En yver, du feu, du feu,
Et en este, boire, boire!
C'est de quoy on fait memoire
Quand on vient en aucun lieu.

In winter, a fire, a fire;
In summer, a cold drink—
Wherever we arrive
It is of these we think.

So said Charles d'Orleans
Long centuries ago—
And hay to feed our horses—
We think of that also.

Such years, such miles away!—
What we say here,
Far more succinctly, is
Eat, Gas, Cold Beer.

Painted Desert, Arizona

Between horizons this wide vat boiling:
Chocolate, orange, apricot, mocca,
Vermilion rock and cinnamon sands,
Corn-cob yellow, scented with sage-brush—
A sweet to feed to Indian children;
For me, a taste for one travelling day.

Indians brave in borrowed feathers
Stand by their squat and secret adobes;
Women under pitiful shelters
Must learn to weave the vivid colours
Of this most beautiful, frugal land;
Castellated walls at the end of the valley
High as their impotence hold them in.

Flashback to America

Indian Reservation

'The Indians are no problem.'

As we cross the desert
On millionaire roads
Cut and tailored
To gulch or canyon,
The barren face
Of a red-streaked mountain
Seems stained with poverty
And Indian blood.

Marble Canyon, Arizona

Nature outdoes man: the walls of Avila,
Marrakech, Fez, Meknes—or Jerusalem;
Dravidian temples in rose-red limestone;
Pyramids; sphinxes, their paws in sand;
And now, beneath a twin-towered gateway
Guarding the end of the valley, a boy
Kicking up the Indian dust, demanding
The missing noise and stink of history.

Covered Viewpoint, Grand Canyon

Contrast 1973

The sunset gilds this splendour of rock formation,
Sets its red roses in the earth laid open—
Lest we go short on awe and inspiration
An amplifier serves us with Beethoven.

Grand Canyon, South Rim

New Coin Poetry 9 (1/2), 1973

The sheer surgery of the Colorado
And the red ligatures of geologists' time
Lay open this portion of the earth's surface.

196

And yet the pattern of these promontories
Of rock repeating rock is not organic
But architectural: the recurrent motif
An Indian temple, pillared, corniced, square,
A monolith of limestone, ochre-red,
Like those once carved at Ajanta and Ellora
By flesh-and-blood monk-masons. Just above
The pyramidal Dravidian root,
Two tiers of limestone cliff; below
A pedestal base that falls away
In oriental folds, like a Burmese fan,
To yet another cliff, minutely perched
Above the black-and-granite Himalayan
Precipice which falls
Down to the dead-pan muddy Colorado—
Dead-pan through distance hiding the glint of speed.

This is the pattern: the temples below us
Garish and roughly hewn; those opposite
Soft with the texture of distance, hiding
Exquisite carvings of countless gods
In numberless incarnations—there are as many
Temples here as Hindu incarnations.

As one stares down a mile of vertigo
Homely details appear, a string of mules
Smaller than ants, a speck-line half-way down
To that green smear they christen Phantom Ranch—
Deciphered through a glass as trees and cabins.

Jules Verne's journey to earth's centre
Suddenly made possible?
                    Even the Colorado's
Ambitious surgery only cuts the skin.

North Rim, Grand Canyon

Below, from here, no temples but choir stalls
New Coin Poetry 9 (1/2), 1973
In gnarled red stone for oak, with misereres
Carved on their upturned seats above,
A bas-relief frieze, out of proportion,
With saints and martyrs, patrons, kings—
Prophetic Nature pre-copying art
With a fine disregard for human dimension;
Far down, the size of a single stall,
A buttressed, impregnable mediaeval wall.

We see the earth in sections: heavy mountains
Lie like a dough upon thin layers of plain—
A table, double-boarded, set on trestles
With feet in darkness, lost in future time.

Brimming Over, Grand Canyon

Wide as the Bosphorus from rim to rim;
Deep enough to swallow up Manhattan;
But not, it seems, these mountainous suburban
Moms in Bermuda shorts that throng the brim.

Zion Canyon, Utah

Zion for whom? This red-rock valley
Of valleys walled off from valleys
Each isolated from isolation
Is presided over by the Three Patriarchs
Whose peculiar perversions of perversion
Led them to wander in this wilderness.
They are tall and hooded, like the Klu Klux Klan,
And they hold court in this valley of valleys,
Each sheer on three sides, the fourth a curtain
Of unassailable rock.

High, flat-topped masses
Of red or white sandstone
Are called Angels Landing or the Great White Throne.
This monstrous block, white stained with red,
Is the Altar of Sacrifice where Abraham took Isaac.
The Eastern Temple has walls that run with blood
While others are the Organ, the Pulpit, the Cathedral;
But these are names of a later dispensation.
What I shall remember are the Three Patriarchs,
Cloaked and hooded, the beard hidden;
They preach a rugged doctrine, twisted
Outside the tolerance of toleration.

Two sentrymen, the Watchman and the Sentinel,
Guard the Three Patriarchs who rule the valley.
When I entered first a trick of light
Gave one of the Patriarchs a gaping mouth,
A contorted face, warning me away
From that red-rock isolation from isolation.

Salt Lake City

The Mormons who have made their way
To preach in England seem outré;
But here in Utah, as you see,
Mormons are really C. of E.

Comparative Religion, Salt Lake City

If Jonah-in-the-Whale is a lot of boloney,
What do you say to the Angel Moroni?

Nature Trail

The asphalted Nature Trail,
Which starts at the slot-machine,
Is hand-railed at dangerous places,
And marked with numbered pegs
From one to twenty-eight
For Points of Instruction and Interest.

Alas, I must decline
To put my coin in the slot:
Those twenty-eight lectures
In the bright emphatic tones
Of the Self-Instructing Leaflet
Might make me forget to use the handrail.

View-points, Yellowstone Park

If you want the perfect view
LOOKOUT POINT is the place for you.

If you're an artist guy, the joint
Just made for you is ARTIST POINT.

If you still can't get creation,
Then come to POINT INSPIRATION—

But boy, if that should fail you too,
Then SUICIDE POINT is the point for you!

Contrast 1973

'Molesting Bears Prohibited'

No doubt it's perfectly right and fair
To discourage me from molesting a bear;
But there's another notice I should like to see
Discouraging the bear from molesting me!

Old Faithful, Yellowstone Park

The Ranger's speech is an appetiser
To the high belchings of this geyser.

He says he's always proud to blaze a
Trail to the side of this fine geyser.

In fact, you could not meet a nicer,
More regular guy, sir, than this geyser,

Who sneezes hourly—what a sneezer!
What an unspeakable old geyser!

Written in Yellowstone Park, USA, where,
for reasons unconnected with the church calendar,
Christmas is celebrated on 25th of August.

Christmas comes but once a year—
Enough for most of us, I fear—
But here at Yellowstone, where price
Does not deter, they have it twice.

Here, where the fragile earth sets free
The sulphurs of eternity,
Under the mistletoe and holly,
We do our damndest to be jolly.

While geysers belch at summer stars
And bears mooch round to watch the cars,
And Rangers range and salmon rise,
We feast on turkey and mince-pies—

Or so we might, but turkey's off;
It seems they didn't kill enough;
So let us wish you better cheer
Where Christmas comes but *once* a year!

The Tetons

Half way down the long cattle valley
That leads to the rustlers' town of Jackson,
With its bars and its brothels
And its high-heel brothers quick on the draw,
Three French trappers, heavy for the joys of Jackson,
First saw these mountains, rounded, feminine
And cruelly unattainable, and shouted:
'Voilá les Tetons!' and launched, and then:
'Grand Teton!" and spoke of a woman in Jackson.

A later observer saw in these mountains
Peaks like church spires, fir-trees like worshippers;
He named them the Cathedral Group—
I prefer the name given by the trappers.

Les Tetons, Rainier, Nez Percé

REN-NEAR, TEETONS, which is worse?
I think the winner is NEZ PERSE!

Cowboy's Love Song

O mistress mine, where are you? Wyoming?

Saloon Bar, Jackson, Wyoming
It is illegal in Wyoming to carry a concealed weapon

Contrast 1973

It comforts me to know they're law-abiding,
These citizens drinking shorts before my eyes—
Men in ten-gallon hats, and not one hiding
The pistol holsters gleaming on his thighs.

Buffalo Bill Museum, Cody

Contrast 1973

Buffalo Bill's original feat
Was filling men's bellies with buffalo meat;
Then, when their empty bellies were full,
He filled their heads with a load of old bull.

Mississippi, near Hannibal

Contrast 1971
British Council for
Harvard Library Poetry Room 1972

On this wide river Huck and Tom and Jim
Lived through those golden days that last for ever,
Days that were mine as well, in another time,
On another continent with no such river.

IX

Formal Spring

French Renaissance Poems
French & Spanish Romantic
& Nineteenth Century Poems
in translation

To my Mother

Formal Spring
(Oxford University Press 1950)
(Reprinted by Books for Libraries Press,
New York 1969)
The first edition
included the French originals

Formal Spring, though first published in 1950, consists mainly of verse translations written before the Second World War.

I should like to thank the following: Lord David Cecil, D. B. Wyndham Lewis and Vernon Watkins for valuable encouragement and criticism; Professor A. Ewert for expert criticism at the proof stage; Frances Ambery-Smith, E. H. Cunningham, Dr G. S. Purkis and Hal Martin for specialist advice over a period of years; and Philip Mairet and Seumas O'Sullivan for taking a personal as well as an editorial interest in so many of these versions. I should like to record my debt to Edward Thompson for many generous and outspoken comments. A. C. Ward gave me very useful advice in the preparation of the manuscript. I also had generous help from Ronald Blythe and Paul Hulton.

Acknowledgements show poems as having appeared in translation before 1950 in
The Adelphi
The Dublin Magazine
John O'London's Weekly
The Listener
Modern Languages
The New English Weekly
The Observer
Translation
and *Time and Tide*.
Several of the translations
were broadcast on the BBC.

French Renaissance Poems

GUILLAUME DE MACHAULT

(c. 1300–1377) had great influence on the poetic forms of this period. In 80,000 lines of elaborate verse-forms and intricate rhyme-schemes he said very little of importance, but it was within this formal framework that French poetry developed and such individual masterpieces as Villon's greatest ballades were written. Had he managed to infuse any genuine feeling into his exquisitely fashioned forms he might have been as well known as Petrarch—like whom, incidentally, he spun out endless verses to a lady who married somebody else. Secretary to the King of Bohemia; canon of Rheims; he was also a musician: he set some of his own work to music and composed a mass for Charles V's coronation.

Rondeau

White as a lily, redder than a rose,
Bright as a ruby from the Orient,
I stare and stare while your rare beauty glows
White as a lily, redder than a rose;
So overcome, that I keep watch with those
Who serve for ever by love's precedent:
White as a lily, redder than a rose;
Bright as a ruby from the Orient.

Formal Spring

EUSTACHE DESCHAMPS

(c.1340–c.1410) held various feudal offices at the courts of Charles V and VI, and his voluminous writings give many details of the life of his time. The girl in his 'Virelay' belongs against a background of castles like those painted by the Limburg brothers for the Duke of Berry's 'Book of Hours', which was begun in 1409. He did much to establish the rondel and ballade forms, giving them a more realistic content than most poets who came before and many who came after. His ballade to Chaucer gives an interesting commentary on a man whose outstanding claim to fame in the eyes of French contemporaries was that he had translated the Roman de la Rose *for the barbaric inhabitants of England.*

Ballade

To Geoffrey Chaucer

The first stanza refers to Geoffrey of Monmouth's
Historia, which describes the (entirely mythical)
conquest of Britain by Brutus, or Brut,
great-grandson of Aeneas of Troy; he began by
killing some giants at Totnes. Pendrasus was a
legendary Greek king from the same work.
The second stanza traces the name England back to
an equally legendary Saxon girl called Angela.
Lewis de Clifford, however, in the third stanza,
was a real person, Ambassador to France in 1391
and 1395, and a friend of both Chaucer amd
Deschamps. Deschamps, one of the creators of
the Ballade form, was huissier d'armes *to the*
French king. The 'rose' references are to the
Roman de la Rose, the 13th century French classic
which Chaucer translated as The
Romaunt of the Rose.

A Socrates in your philosophy,
A moral Seneca in English guise,
A second Ovid in your poetry,
Concise in speech, in rhetoric most wise.
A brilliant eagle, lighting from the skies
Your country, where Aeneas once held sway,
Brutus's Isle of Giants. In this way
Planting out flowers and our Rose-tree there,
For those Pandrasus cannot reach today,
O great translator, noble Geoffrey Chaucer.

You are of courtly love the deity,
And of 'The Book of the Rose' in Albion eyes;
In Saxon Angela's land, which now must be
Called Angel's Land, or England—this applies
In all the latest etymologies.
You have translated 'The Rose'; and now you pray
For other flowers and seedlings that you may
Pick out for planting in that garden where
You have been growing them for many a day,
O great translator, noble Geoffrey Chaucer.

For you an authentic draught must always be
One that the fount of Helicon supplies
And that stream runs in your authority
My agonising thirst it satisfies.
Streams out of Gaul could only paralyse
My throat before these waters came my way;
I'm Eustace; take this plant. I hope you may
Approve such scholarship as you find there,
And Clifford will be bringing you today,
O great translator, noble Geoffrey Chaucer.

O lofty poet, beyond praise from me,
A nettle in your garden I must be,
What I have sent to you, I pray, consider
Your noble plant and your sweet melody,
And let me hear from you, write back, I pray,
O great translator, noble Geoffrey Chaucer.

Eustache Deschamps

Virelay

Am I, am I beautiful?

Formal Spring

It seems to me that I possess
A good brow and a pretty face
And a rosy mouth as well:
Tell me, am I beautiful?

Shining eyes with dainty brows,
Blond hair and a well-shaped nose,
Rounded cheeks, throat white and small:
Do these make me beautiful?

High firm breasts, as they ought to be,
Fingers and hands made slenderly,
And such a slender figure: Tell
Me please, if I am beautiful.

Good back, good waist—would you agree?—
Trim bottom, and such pleasantly
Rounded legs and thighs, and—well,
Would you call me beautiful?

Small plump feet in stylish shoes,
And plenty of expensive clothes—
And always gay and cheerful:
Tell me, am I beautiful?

Coats furred tastefully with grey,
Lots of hats and trimmings gay,
With many a silver pin as well;
Do you think I'm beautiful?

207

Silk and taffeta draperies
In whites and golds and brownish-greys—
Too many pretty things to tell:
Am I really beautiful?

Only just fifteen, and see
What a treasure belongs to me—
And so I keep the key! . . . Oh tell,
Tell me, am I beautiful?

Any man who hopes to be
The lover of a girl like me
Must be brave and masterful:
Am I, am I beautiful?

But I swear that I will be
True while he unwaveringly
Shows me he is dutiful:
Do you think I'm beautiful?

If he has poise and courtesy,
Courage and breeding too, then he
Shall win what he desires in full:
Am I really beautiful?

Earthly paradise to win
And keep for ever such a one,
So fresh, so new.... And now please tell,
Tell me if I'm beautiful?

All you timid ones, agree;
Consider what you've heard from me;
For here ends my canticle:
Am I, am I beautiful?

CHRISTINE DE PISAN

(c. 1363–c. 1430), 'bourgeois poetess at a bourgeois court'—that of Charles V—wrote poems to make money to bring up her family when left a widow at 25. Daughter of Thomas de Pisan, the King's astrologer, she was born in Italy, but came to France as a child. She wrote in defence of women, in particular against the description of feminine character given in the later part of the Roman de la Rose, *and used Joan of Arc as an example of feminine excellence in her* Dittie de Jeanne d'Arc.

Rondel

If I'm at church these days
It's just to see her there,
Fresh as new roses are.

Why gossip, then, and raise
Interest in the affair,
If I'm at church these days?

Whatever paths or ways
I follow lead to her;
Fool, to say fool, and stare
If I'm at church these days.

Formal Spring
Review of Reviews 1934
Observer 1936
Thomas E. Saunders: *Discovery of Poetry*
(Scott, Foresman 1966)

CHARLES D'ORLÉANS

(c. 1394–1465), head of the House of Orléans, nephew of one French King and father of another, is the archetype of the court poet of the waning Middle Ages; his life has the colours of an illuminated manuscript—in all its contemporary splendour. Eldest son of Louis I of Orléans, who was assassinated in 1407 by men in the pay of the Duke of Burgundy, the years in which he grew up were occupied with the consequent vendetta.

His rank made him, at just under 21, titular commander of the 'flower of European chivalry' overwhelmed by the English bowmen at Agincourt, and he was chief among those captured and held to ransom after the battle. It was twenty-five years before he was able to return to his native country—during which time Joan of Arc saved his ducal city of Orléans, and the affairs of his house were looked after by the Bastard, Dunois, his much abler half-brother. On returning to France he lived in colourful, disillusioned retirement at Blois, surrounded by artists, jongleurs and poets—among whom for a short time was Villon—and wrote a large number of chansons, rondeaux, and ballades. His poems lack depth, and most are frankly escapist, but every now and then, as in the 'Ballade for Peace' and some of the spring rondeaux, sincere feeling shines through the formal outline.

He had a further connection with England, in that his first marriage, in 1406, was to the child-widow of the deposed Richard II. During his captivity, too, he wrote nearly 7,000 lines of poetry in English, about half of them with analogues among his French poems. Holinshed says he was more at home speaking English than French at the time of his return. There is now no reasonable doubt that the English poems were his; and it also seems likely that many of them were written in the household of Chaucer's granddaughter, the Countess of Suffolk.

Ballade for Peace   LXXVI

Formal Spring
Review of Reviews 1933
Adelphi c. 1938
Synopsis 1938

O pray for our peace, sweet Virgin Mary,
Queen of the heavens and the earth's mistress,
And bid the saints pray too, for courtesy,
Women as well as men; in gentleness
Approach your Son, in his exaltedness,
To take thought for his people in this day,
Whose ransom he once gave his life to pay,
By ending war that must all things destroy;
And do not tire of praying when you pray—
But pray for peace, the very heart of joy.

Pray prelates, and all men of sanctity,
Friars and monks, who sleep in idleness,
And scholars, and all learned company,
For war must always mean that studies cease,
And churches are destroyed that none redress,
And services neglected in that day;
Now that your peace and quiet have gone their way
Pray so that God hear soon, not shy or coy,
But as the Church has ordered you to pray;
And pray for peace, the very heart of joy.

Pray kings, and princes, and nobility,
Barons, and counts, and men of courtliness,
And gentle knights brought up in chivalry,
For evil men are killing gentleness;
Your wealth is spoil for their wickedness;
By violence and strife they force their way
To rank and power—you see it every day!—
Using the money you could well employ
To be your people's comfort and their stay;
So pray for peace, the very heart of joy.

Pray, people who are suffering tyranny;
The lords you serve are now so powerless
They can no longer use their mastery
To guard and save you in your great distress;
And loyal merchants, whom all men oppress,
The yoke is heavy on your backs to-day
When there is no safe-conduct and no way
Is free from gravest danger and annoy
To men who carry merchandise. O pray—
And pray for peace, the very heart of joy.

God in his power comfort us to-day;
Let heaven and earth and sea unite to pray
That He may soon provide all we enjoy—
For He alone can turn our ills away:
O pray for peace, the very heart of joy!

Charles d'Orléans

Rondel   XXXI

The year has put his cloak away
His cloak of cold, and wind, and rain,
To wear the embroidery again
Of radiant sunlight, clear and gay.

No bird or beast but joins to-day
His song or jargon in this strain:
The year has put his cloak away,
His cloak of cold, and wind, and rain.

Rivulet, stream, and spring to-day
Wear as splendid livery
Spangles of silver filigree,
All of them in new clothes to-day;
The year has put his cloak away.

Formal Spring
Independent c.1934

211

Rondel XXX

Formal Spring
Independent 1934

Summer has sent his stewards on
To put his house in readiness,
To hang up woven tapestries
Of flowers and foliage, and put down

Rough carpets of green grass to run
Across the country's emptiness;
Summer has sent his stewards on
To put his house in readiness.

Those who've been gloomy and cast down,
Thank God, have health and happiness.
Be off, then, to some other place;
Winter, you *shall not* linger on!
Summer has sent his stewards on.

Rondel XXXIV

Formal Spring

As we look at these gay flowers
Love's new season has on show
Let each put on new beauty now
And paint in her most pleasing colours;

They are so drenched in freshest odours
That every heart feels younger now
As we look at these gay flowers....

While the birds becoming dancers
Over many a flowering bough,
Make such a joyful singing now
With their airs descants and counters:
As we look at these gay flowers.

Rondel XXXIX

Formal Spring
Time and Tide 1940

The first day of the month of May
Of tawny, winter-soiled green,
And my poor heart, God knows, is seen
In very shabby clothes to-day.

Tell me, I asked my heart to-day,
What does this style of dressing mean,
The first day of the month of May?

My heart replied, I shall not say,
But know too well why I have been
Engaged to sadness and to spleen
I wear their livery, take their pay,
This first day of the month of May.

Charles d'Orléans

Ballade XCVII

One day I asked my heart,
In confidence, if he
Had put by any part
Out of our property
When serving Love? Freely
He promised me a true
Account as soon as he
Had looked his papers through.

Formal Spring
Dublin Magazine c.1936
John O'London's Weekly c.1936

He promised this, my heart,
And took his leave of me;
And soon I saw him start
To rummage busily
Among the note-books he
Keeps in his desk. I knew
He'd speak immediately
He'd looked his papers through.

I waited, and my heart,
Returning presently,
Showed me the books he'd brought,
And I was glad to see
That he had carefully
Entered the facts—so now
I'd know as soon as he
Had looked his papers through.

I asked if I should start
On them myself, but he
Politely begged me not
To trouble; expertly
Began to add for me
Profits and losses too—
Bade me come back when he
Had looked his papers through.

I said: 'I never thought,
And no-one would, to see
Love, in which all take part,
Show such small gains. Thus he
Cheats us, but won't cheat me
Again ! My heart might do
Some rubbing out—when he
Has looked his papers through!'

Love should not censure me
For blaming him—he'll know
How small my gains . . . when he
Has looked his papers through!

Song LXXIV

Formal Spring

Lovers, avoid the shafts that fly
Out of the windows of a street;
Arrows and bolts cannot compete
In swiftness and in certainty;

Turn right nor left, but keep your eye
Upon the ground before your feet;
Lovers, avoid the shafts that fly
Out of the windows of a street.

Unless there is a doctor by,
A good one, right there in the street,
Send for a priest at once, entreat
God's mercy and prepare to die:
Lovers, avoid the shafts that fly . . .

Rondel XIX

Formal Spring
British Council for
Harvard Poetry Room 1972

Stephen le Gout, in the nominative,
Quite recently tried in the optative
Mood to proceed to the copulative,
But failed when it came to the genitive.

Six ducats he placed in the dative
To bring him his love in the vocative—
Stephen Le Gout, in the nominative.

He came up against an accusative
Who made of his robe a mere ablative;
From a window whose height was superlative
He jumped, taking blows in the passive:
Stephen Le Gout, in the nominative.

Rondel *CCCXXXIII*

Winter, you're nothing but a lout.
Summer is polite and gentle;
Only look how May and April
Accompany him day in, day out.

See how fields and woods and flowers
Wear his livery of verdure
And of many other colours
According to the rule of Nature;

But, Winter, you are all filled out
With snow and sleet and wind and drizzle;
It's time we sent you into exile;
I never flatter, but speak out;
Winter, you're nothing but a lout.

Formal Spring
John O'London's Weekly 1937

Rondel *CCCCXXXV*

Greet all the company for me
Where you are met so pleasantly,
And say that I'd give all I have
To be with you, but I am slave
Of age, who has control of me.

Not long ago youth used to be
My master, but that's gone from me,
And now I only ask to be
Excused—greet all the company
And say that I'd give all I have....

I loved once, but that's gone from me;
In Paris I lived gallantly.
Good-bye to those days and the brave
Trim figure that I used to have;
My belt's let out now, as you see.
Greet all the company for me.

Formal Spring
Modern Languages 1937

215

FRANÇOIS VILLON

(1431–?) One of the very few poets of this period who were not court-poets; popular and realistic in an age of well-bred poetry of escape. His real name seems to have been Montcorbier, but he took the name of a chaplain of Saint Benoît who brought him up. He studied at Paris, where he was a member of the University, and took his MA degree in 1452, but led a disorderly life and in 1455 killed a priest in a brawl. He left Paris, and wandered in different parts of France, usually in criminal company. For a time he was one of the literary company at Charles d'Orléans's court at Blois, but this did not last; the 'Ballade Villon' which he wrote there mentions a pension which for some reason or other had been taken away from him. Later we hear of him being freed from the prison of the Bishop of Orléans, a lucky chance, since he happened to be there when the doors were opened in celebration of the reigning monarch! In 1462 he was condemned to death at the Châtelet for a second murder, and it was then that he wrote his 'Epitaph in Ballade Form', a poignant personal complaint that was something new in European literature. In his two 'Testaments' we move in the cruel medieval Paris, whose streets were infested on winter nights by the 'wolves that live on wind'; among bawds, prostitutes, housebreakers, and pickpockets; yet to an extent that makes him outstanding, not only in his own but in every age, he found all experience a subject for poetry. The 'Ballade of the Women of the Past' has a lyrical quality that defies translation. Villon wrote ballades, a few rondeaux, and eight-lined verses with a regular rhyme-scheme: verse of an ordered, formal pattern that perhaps satisfied him as a complement to his disorderly life.

Villon's Epitaph in Ballade Form
Written while waiting with his companions to be hanged

New English Weekly, c. 1936
Formal Spring
British Council
for Harvard Poetry Room 1972

O brother men, who live on after us,
You should not in your hearts be too severe,
For if you pity wretches such as us
Then God shall pity you the readier;
Some five or six of us are strung up here,
The flesh we nourished all too lavishly
Has rotted and been devoured utterly,
While we, the bones, in dust and ashes fall;
Let no man laugh at our extremity
But pray to God that He forgive us all.

Why should you think it so presumptuous
Of those who suffered death by law to dare
To call you brothers still; not all of us,
As you know well, have common sense to spare:
Now that we're dead, forgive, and offer prayer
Before the Virgin Mary's Son, that He
Spare mercy even for us, and graciously
Preserve us from Hell's lightnings when they fall.
We're dead. Let none torment our misery,
But pray to God that He forgive us all.

The rain has thoroughly washed and whitened us

And the sun dried and blackened us up here;
The crows and magpies have gouged out our eyes,
Ripped out our beards and plucked our eyebrows bare;
At no time may we rest, but always veer
This way and that way, turning helplessly,
At the wind's pleasure carried endlessly,
So pecked we're pitted like thimbles; do not fall
As we did into this fraternity,
But pray to God that He forgive us all.

Prince Jesus, having all authority,
Let us not fall beneath Hell's sovereignty;
Grant that we have no dealings there at all.
Men, there is no excuse for mockery,
But pray to God that He forgive us all.

Lines on Death, and Ballade

I'm sure I make no claim to be

An angel's son, in diadem
Of single stars or galaxy;
My father's dead, God pity him!
His body lies beneath his tomb,
And my poor mother must prepare,
As well she knows, to follow him,
And soon her son must follow her.

I only know that poor and rich,
Wise men and foolish, generous, mean,
Great men and humble, lay and church,
Nobles and peasants, handsome, plain,
Ladies with turned-back collars, none,
Whatever her degree or station,
What tire or common headdress on,
None but must die, without exception.

Though Paris die, and Helen too,
Whoever dies, must die in pain,
Feeling his power of breathing go;
Over his heart his gall bursts then;

217

God, how the cold sweats from him drain;
And none relieves his agony,
Child, brother, sister, there's no one
Who at that time his pledge would be.

Death makes him shudder and turn white,
His flesh grow soft, his neck distend,
His nose grow hooked, his veins stretch tight,
His joints and sinews swell, extend.
O, woman's body, so smooth-skinned,
Tender, soft, precious, must *you* even
Be brought by fate to such an end?
Yes, or else go alive to heaven.

Ballade
Of the Women of the Past

Formal Spring
Dublin Magazine 1938

O tell me where and to what land
Has lovely Roman Flora gone,
Where is Archipiada, and
Thaïs, who was her kinswoman,
Echo, whose voice answers one
Over rivers and over meres—
Whose beauty more than human shone:
But where are the snows of other years?

Where learnèd Heloïse, ordained
To bring poor Peter Abelard down
To be made monk, but first unmanned—
This was the judgement his love won!—
And, tell me, where has that Queen gone
Who had that Buridan of hers
Thrown in a sack into the Seine:
But where are the snows of other years?

And Queen Blanche, of the lily hand
And siren's voice, where is she gone?
Big-footed Bertha, Beatrice, and
Alice, Arembour, who alone
Ruled all the Maine, and Lorraine Joan,
Burned at Rouen in English fires:
O Virgin Queen, where are they gone;
But where are the snows of other years?

Prince, do not ask where they are gone
This week, this year, for all your prayers
Can win back one refrain alone:
But where are the snows of other years?

François Villon

Ballade

I die of thirst beside the fountain's brim,

Formal Spring
New English Weekly 1936

As hot as fire, with my teeth chattering,
In my own land a stranger, a pilgrim;
Beside a brazier I stand shivering,
Bare as a worm, in rich appareling;
I laugh in tears, while waiting hopeless here
And taking comfort of my sad despair;
Rejoicing, although pleasure I have none,
Powerful, with nothing that I can or dare—
Welcomed by all, and he whom all men shun.

Nothing is sure to me except a whim,
Obscure, except the clear and obvious thing,
Only in certainties my faith is dim,
And knowledge has an adventitious ring;
I am the loser, gaining everything;
At dawn I bid good evening, and I fear,
While lying prone, lest I should fall from there;
I'm rich, and have no coin beneath the sun,
Expect a legacy, though no man's heir,
Welcomed by all, and he whom all men shun.

I care for nothing; taking care to trim
My course for profit, claim no single thing;
The man who flatters most, I'm vexed with him;
Who speaks most true is most dissembling;
He is my friend who has me crediting
Of each white swan that it's a raven here;
Who thinks to help me brings disaster near;
Jesting and truth, to me they are all one.
Remembering all, I yet see nothing clear—
Welcomed by all, and he whom all men shun.

Kind prince, I pray you that it please you hear
That I know much, yet have no sense to spare,
Am partisan, yet all laws bear me down.
What then? Make me once more your pensioner—
Welcomed by all, and he whom all men shun.

Lament of the Old Woman
Remembering her Youth

I hear the former beauty, she
Who used to be the *beaulmière*, sigh
For her lost youth, regretfully
Speaking thus of days gone by:
'Proud, pitiless old age, oh why
Should you have brought me down so soon;
And what's to stop me violently
Taking my life now, to be done?

'You have deprived me of the power
My beauty gave me over men;
Merchants, and churchmen, men of law,
For no man born but would have given
His every penny to me then,
However repentance changed his views,
Provided only he could gain
What even beggars now refuse;

'What to so many I did deny—
It wasn't very wise of me!—
And all for one ungrateful, sly
Boy that I loved too generously;
Whoever else I cheated, he
Was never one; I gave him love
And he returned me cruelty,
Loved me for what I had to give.

However much he bullied me
And wore me down, I loved him so
That though he dragged me brutally
Round by the hair, a kiss or two
Would make me quite forget my woe;
And then that crooked scoundrel came
And took me in his arms—and now
What have I gained but sin and shame?

'Well, he's been dead for thirty years
And I, grown old and grey-haired too,
Remember those good days with tears,
What once I was, what I am now:
And when I'm naked, then I know
How utterly changed I am by age,
Poor, skinny, shrivelled through and through—
I think of it, and shake with rage!

'Where's the smooth forehead I had once,
The arching eyebrows, the light hair,
The wide-set eyes whose pretty glance
Could take in even the connoisseur,
The dimpled chin, the small neat ear,
And straight nose, neither large nor small,
The beautiful red mouth, the clear
Good-looking face—where are they all?

'Forehead lined, and hair gone grey,
Hairless eyebrows, eyes quite dull,
That were smiling once and gay,
The cause of many a merchant's fall;
Hooked nose, far from beautiful,
Hairy ears with folds of skin,
Face all lifeless now and pale,
Flabby lips, nut-cracker chin.

'Lamenting thus the days gone by,
We sit together, poor foolish hags
On skinny haunches, wretchedly
Huddled like bundles of old rags
Around a fire of hempen tags,
Soon kindled and soon burnt away,
So dainty once, and now such hags!
But many and many end this way!'

Epitaph

Here lies, in this small chamber,
One that love's arbalest* brought down,
A very poor and humble scholar
By the name of François Villon known,
Who never a yard of land did own
Yet gave you all he had, remember,
Basket, and board, and bread thereon;
Over him then let his friends murmur:

RONDEL
Grant, O Lord, eternal rest
And lasting glory to this soul
Who never was, with dish or bowl,
Or even a sprig of parsley blessed
But bald as a scraped turnip, dressed
For cooking—eyebrows, head and jowl:
Grant rest!

Formal Spring
** Crossbow with mechanism
for drawing the string.*

221

Harsh justice exiled him, addressed
His backside with a spade, poor soul;
Although he called out: 'I appeal!' —
Not an ambiguous request!
Grant rest!

OLIVIER BASSELIN & JEAN LE HOUX

Olivier Basselin was a fifteenth century Norman poet of whom little is known for certain but who seems to have done no more than inspire, at the distance of more than a century, the poems by which he has been chiefly remembered. The legend we have of him is, however, solid and circumstantial. According to this we are indebted to him for the many songs of wine, cider, love, and war that bear his name, and also for the word 'vaudeville'. He was born at Vire, where he owned a mill beside the bridge of Vaux, so that the songs he wrote came to be known as the 'vau de vire', from which the modern word has come. He is said to have suffered both as a result of his good living and of the English invasions in the Hundred Years War, and to have died fighting against the English— though the word Engloys *in the popular ballad about him could mean 'moneylenders'!*

'Alas! good Oliver Basselin,
Are we to hear no more of you?
Have the English put an end to you ?...'

So much for the legend. The presence, in the verses attributed to Basselin, of many marks of later origin, was accounted for by their having been edited, in 1610, by the Virois lawyer JEAN LE HOUX *(c. 1550– 1616); but it now appears that Jean le Houx was not editor but author (or all but author) of the best known of these verses, including the two poems printed here. It is known that he made a journey to Rome to get absolution from the sin of merely editing them, so it is not surprising if he did not admit to full authorship! Those 'vau de vire' which definitely date back to Basselin's time are naïve and often patriotic. Perhaps the real Basselin did not prefer his glass to his warlike helmet, and 'Engloys' meant 'English' after all!*

As Brave as Caesar

I am as brave as Caesar in this war
Armed to the very teeth with jug and glass;
Better a charge of wine that leaves no scar
Than bullets spilling life that soon must pass.

Give me the bottle's for the battle's clash,
Barrels and casks of rich vermilion wine
For my artillery with which to smash
This thirst that I invest and undermine.

As far as I can see a man's a clown
Who would not rather get his broken head
By drinking than by fighting for renown;
What use will his renown be when he's dead?

War and Wine

I am as brave as Caesar in this war
Armed to the very teeth with jug and glass;
Better a charge of wine that leaves no scar
Than bullets spilling life that soon must pass.

Give me the bottle's for the battle's clash,
Barrels and casks of rich vermilion wine
For my artillery with which to smash
This thirst that I invest and undermine.

As far as I can see the man's a clown
Who would not rather get his broken head
By drinking than by fighting for renown;
What use will his renown be when he's dead?

The head brought down by drinking can recover;
When the wind buffets it you feel some pain,
Then after a short sleep the trouble's over;
On battlefields all remedy is vain.

Better to hide your nose in a tall glass
Than in a casque-of-war, more safe, I think,
Than following horn and ensign, just to pass
Beneath the yew and ivy to a drink.

Better beside the fire drinking muscatel,
Here inside the tavern and never in default,
Than outside on the ramparts playing the sentinel
Or following a captain to the breach, to the assault!

But I dislike and do not seek excess.
Good drinker, not born drunkard, is my due.
Good wine, that makes for laughter and friendliness,
I've promised more than I can keep to you.

*Olivier Basselin
& Jean le Houx*

Better to hide your nose in a tall glass
Than in a soldier's helmet, better far
Let drum and ensign call in vain, and pass
Beneath an inn-sign to this other war.

Tiresias (shorter version in margin)
Formal Spring (full version)
Dublin Magazine 1938
Thomas Moult:
Best Poems of 1938 (Cape 1938)
O'Sullivan: *Editor's Choice* (Dublin 1944)
Argosy 1948
Roy Campbell (Editor):
Tate and Lyle Magazine (c. 1948)

To His Nose

Brave nose, whose rubies cost such casks of rare
White wine and claret,
Whose splendid colour has so rich a share
Of red and violet,

Formal Spring

Huge nose! The man who sees you through a glass
Thinks you a snorter,
In no way like the nose of the poor ass
Whose drink is water.

More scarlet than a turkey cockerel's throat,
Rich men have prayed for
A nose as rich; a work of so great note
Long years have paid for,

Long years of painting with a brush of glass
And vintage wine,
Until not even cherries can surpass
This nose of mine.

They say wine harms the eyes, but who is master?
Wine is the cure
Of all my ills—though windows meet disaster
The house stands sure.

CLÉMENT MAROT

(1495–1544). Had connections with the fifteenth as well as the sixteenth century, with the Reformation as well as the Renaissance. Editor of Villon and translator of the psalms, he was also one of the first translators of Ovid, Virgil and Lucan. His interest in the Huguenot movement drove him as an exile first to Bordeaux, and then successively to Béarn, Ferrara, Venice and, after a return to France, to Geneva; here he displeased Calvin—a thing the rich sensuousness of a poem like the 'Vineyard Knife' would seem to make inevitable!— and was expelled, to die at Turin.

Song of the Vineyard Knife

Enough of love; let's leave for something new
All that to-do, and sing the vineyard knife;
No grower of vines but has recourse to you,
Makes use of you to prune his vines; O knife,
My vineyard knife, my little vineyard knife,
Renewing life, you make my good vines grow,
From which year after year the rich wines flow!

Vulcan, the high gods' blacksmith, did design
This shape divine, in heaven hammered out
The white-hot steel, and dipped it in old wine
To give the fine edge temper; and the shout
Bacchus gave out proclaimed beyond a doubt
That even devout old Noah could not find
A knife for pruning vines more to his mind.

With vine leaves crowned, young Bacchus brings his slim
Curved blade to trim and bless the fruitful vine;
With flagons old Silenus follows him,
And from each rim, in one unbroken line,
Pours down the wine, tries dancing, lies supine;
And for a sign his nose is cherry-red;
Of his great family many men are bred.

Carol

A shepherd and a shepherdess
In an orchard where they played
At ball one day, and, briefly, this
Is what one to the other said:
    Lithe
    Shepherd lad,
    Blithe
    Shepherd maid,
We've played enough at ball, they said,
Let's sing Noël, Noël, instead.

Remember what the prophet said
In telling of the great things done
In heaven, how the perfect maid
Would bring to birth the perfect son;
> The thing
> Is done,
> We sing
> The son
Of the perfect maid on heaven's throne;
Sing Noël, Noël, everyone.

Clément Marot

MELLIN DE SAINT-GELAIS

(c. 1490–1558). Student of philosophy, mathematics and astrology. Poet at the brilliant court of Francis I, he was made almoner to the Dauphin and subsequently librarian at Fontainebleau palace. His neat, witty rhyming made him acceptable to the court—until the appearance of Ronsard, after which his popularity waned. Perhaps some of the bitterness he felt at this is expressed in 'On a Detractor'.

On a Detractor

I pray for poverty for you,
With fireless winter, roofless age,
No grain in store, no cellarage
Of cooling wine the summer through.

Formal Spring

I pray to God, in equity
To see that all you have displease
So gravely that for greater ease
You'll search for prison sanctuary.

I pray to God, the King of Heaven,
That you may have to beg your bread
Exiled, alone, uncomforted
By any words or gestures even.

I pray that you may have to wait
Outside a door a whole night through,
While a slow gutter drips on you,
And she cares nothing for your state.

PIERRE DE RONSARD

(c. 1524–85). *Born of a noble family, he grew up in court life, travelling as a page to Scotland, Flanders, Germany, and Piedmont. Returning to France at 19, he became deaf, and turned to a literary life. He met du Bellay in 1548, and formed with him, Baïf, Belleau and others the group which became famous as the 'Pléiade'. He shared to the full the interest of his age in the Classics, and introduced classical forms, notably the ode, into French writing; attaining in his shorter odes and his sonnets a rich but subtle perfection that marked him out in his own time, as since, as one of the greatest of French poets. He and his friends, as Mr Belloc has said, 'fixed the literary renaissance of France at its highest point'. His 'Sonnets for Hélène', again to quote the same writer, 'are*

Roses

Tiresias
Listener 1938

Scatter by this jar of wine
Roses, in the scent of roses
Pledge one to the other, sign
That all griefs the heart encloses
May be drowned in roseate wine.

Alternative version
as in *Formal Spring:*
The rose's beauty enters in
Everything by which she lingers;

The rose is beauty's origin,
Adorning all by which she lingers;
Venus has a rosebud skin
And the dawn has rosy fingers;
The young sun has a ruddy mien.

Rosy hips and rosy thighs;
The rosy glow of health suffuses
Hebe's hands; the Charities
Are pale, but richly crowned with roses.

The nymphs, they say, have breasts like roses,
Elbows, and hips, and thighs of rose;
Hebe's hands are made of roses,
And the Graces bind their brows,
Pale though they are, with crowns of roses.

Over Bacchus this complete
Conquest have red roses made;
Without them he will not sit
In shirt-sleeves in the leafy shade
Drinking through the summer heat.

To Remi Belleau

Formal Spring

To think, Belleau, that such a man
As you translates Anacreon—
You drink so little! Did you see
The comet which not long since burst
And lit the sky? It foretold thirst,
Or I'm no use at prophecy!

226

These hot stars that in heaven blaze
Usher in parched and thirsty days
In order to make all men drink;
So drink, for after death we go
With other shades to drink below
At God knows what dark river's brink!

But no! On second thoughts, Belleau,
If you have set your mind to go
With the nine Muses on their mountain,
Keep on avoiding, as you do,
Bacchus and his unseemly crew,
Staying instead by learning's fountain.

And those who set out to combine
Venus with the God of Wine,
Say goodbye to sober sense.
Bacchus needs a pedagogue
To correct his fault and flog
Him well, as did Silenus once;

Or else the young girls who were there
To care for him, when Jupiter
From his burned mother took him up;
That these were Water-Nymphs is plain:
'For Bacchus damages the brain,
Unless the Nymph is in the cup.'

Sonnet

As on a branch, in May, we see the rose
In her most lovely youth, in her first flower
Making the red sky jealous at the hour
When washed in dews of dawn her colour glows;

Her petals grace and sleeping love enclose,
And freshest scents on trees and garden shower;
But, beaten down by rain or the sun's power,
Drooping and dead, they one by one unclose.

So you, in your first glowing youth, with duty
Paid by both earth and heaven to your beauty,
Fate has cut off; in ashes you repose.

Now at your funeral accept my tears,
This vase of milk, this basket full of flowers,
Whose body, dead or living, is a rose.

Formal Spring

To Cassandra

Formal Spring

My love, let us see if the rose
That we watched this morning unclose
Her crimson dress to the sun,
Has not lost, now evening is here,
Those tight crimson folds, or that clear
Fresh colour, so near to your own.

Alas! In how little a time
The petals of her lovely prime
Lie strewn on the ground in our sight;
How utterly harsh Nature is
To let such a flower as this
Last only from morning till night.

Believe me, my Love! in this hour
Before the first exquisite flower
And green tender freshness has past,
Gather in, gather in your first youth;
For, as with this flower, in truth
Your beauty will wither at last.

Sonnet

Formal Spring
Western Literature in a World Context
(St Martin's Press 1995)

O, I could wish, most richly yellowing
To drops of golden rain, from heaven to shower
Into Cassandra's lap about the hour
When clouds of sleep her eyes are shadowing;

Or, made a bull by some such lavishing
Of dazzling whiteness, take and carry her
Gently through April fields, where like a flower
She walks, a thousand flowers ravishing;

And I could wish, my burning pain to cool,
I were Narcissus, she my fountain pool,
That in her waters I might plunge, and stay

The whole night through—and I could wish night drawn
Out to eternity, so that no dawn
Might ever light me to a coming day.

Epitaph on Rabelais

Pierre de Ronsard

Formal Spring
Western Literature in a World Context
(St Martin's Press 1995)

If it's true that Nature can
Raise new life from a dead man,
And if generation
Springs out of corruption,
Then a vine should issue forth
From the stomach and huge girth
Of our Rabelais who contrived
To keep on drinking while he lived,
Who, with his mighty throat sucked down
Far more wine, all on his own,
Through nose and mouth, in a gulp or two
Than a porker drinking milk can do,
Than Iris from the rivers, or
From the waves of the African shore.

   Nobody in morning sun
Ever saw him sober; none
From sunset until late at night
Saw him anything but tight;
Without pause our Rabelais
Kept on drinking night and day.

   When the fiery dog-days brought
Round the season of the drought,
Half-dressed, with his sleeves rolled up,
He'd lie down flat beside his cup
Among the glasses on the rushes
Among the richly-loaded dishes,
Sprawling there quite shamelessly
Floundering as messily
As a frog does in the mud;
Then, when drunk, he'd sing aloud,
The praises of his good friend Bacchus,
How he came to be victorious
Over the Thebans, how his mother
With such warmth received his father,
That, instead of making love,
He just burned her up alive!

   Sing of Gargantua and his mare
And the huge staff he used to bear;
Splendid Panurge; and the domains
Of those gaping Papimanes,
Their houses, customs and strange laws;
Of Friar John of Antoumeures;

229

And of the battles of Epistème;
But Death, who never drinks, took him,
The drinker, to the world below,
Where no other waters flow
Than the turbid streams that run
Down into wide Acheron.

Whoever happens to pass this way
Empty here a glass, I pray;
Pour out flagons, scatter cheese,
Legs of ham and sausages;
For if any feeling now
Animates that soul below,
These to lilies would be preferred
However freshly they were gathered!

To a Fountain

O lovely Bellerie
Fountain as dear to me
As to the Nymphs, your daughters,
Who run away to hide
In your cool depths from satyrs,
Chased to the very side
Of your protecting waters,

Still your eternal hands
Bless my paternal lands;
And I, your poet, this mead
And fresh green bank adorn
With a young suckling kid,
Each firstling of a horn
Just showing on his head.

In summer-time I doze
On your green banks, compose
On willow-shaded grass
These lines to send your fame
Out through the universe,
So that your gentle name
May live on in my verse.

The heat of the dog-star   *Pierre de Ronsard*
May not burn up your shore;
Always your region yields
Close shade beneath the boughs
To shepherds from the folds.
Tired oxen from the ploughs,
And parched beasts from the fields.

For ever the princess
Of fountains, I address
Your hoarsely-murmuring
Rock-conduit as it jets
Endlessly-following
Water that foams and frets,
Babbling and chattering.

JOACHIM DU BELLAY

(1525–60) Lieutenant of the 'Pléiade', and author of its formal manifesto, 'Deffense et Illustration de la langue françoyse'. Like Ronsard, of noble birth, he accompanied his cousin, Cardinal du Bellay, on a diplomatic mission to Rome, and on his return was made a canon of Notre-Dame by a du Bellay who was Bishop of Paris. His sonnets show very clearly the effect of the decayed splendour of Roman civilization on a man of his time; and the most delicate of his shorter poems, 'A Winnower of Wheat to the Winds', is a translation from the Latin of Navagero. His 'Epitaphs' on his pet dog and pet cat suggest a whimsical tenderness; despite their slightness, it seems worthwhile printing these two poems in full for the informal details they give of the life of a nobleman of studious habits in a formal age. He was of a melancholy temperament, being sickly from childhood and dying at the early age of 35.

Epitaph on a Pet Dog

Beneath this turfy mound   *Formal Spring*
With rose and lily crowned,   *The Lady* 1936
Lies little Peloton
Whose silky coat once shone
So white, fleece-like, and curly
On side, and back, and belly.
   His snub-nose and large size
Perfectly clear eyes,
His long soft silky ears
Matted with crinkly hairs,
His tail that wagged a gay
Tassel like a bouquet,
His slender leg, his paw,
As light upon the floor   231

As a cat's among its kittens,
His dugs like four neat buttons,
His little ivory teeth,
The smart black beard beneath
The dainty muzzle; stance,
And absurd countenance,
In fact each single feature
Of this deserving creature
Earned him the pleasantest
Of graves in which to rest.

  He used to spend his day—
In the ordinary way—
Barking and growling, chase
Himself from place to place;
With fierce outlandish cries
Levy his war on flies;
These teased him cruelly,
But he, most dexterously,
Gave what he got, would lie
On one ear, patiently
Watching the traitor light,
Letting him start to bite,
Then, with a loose, quick snap
Hold him there in the trap,
Immured as close as death;
And all the while his teeth
Kept time with his small bell
Like a spinet manual.

  He did not leap to greet
Strangers, and he would eat
From his master's hand alone,
Always stayed round about
His heels when they went out,
Except when he ran on,
Keeping some secret, gay
Head-tossing holiday.

  Peloton always kept
Watch while his master slept;
And did not soil his bed
In any way; instead
Would fuss and scratch about
Till someone let him out;
He was, as may be seen,
Exemplarily clean.

  Even the worst crimes done
By little Peloton
Were neither here nor there;

But sometimes he would hear
Noises and bark at night,
Breaking his master's sleep;
Or, seeing him start to write,
With one fantastic leap
He'd land right on the table,
And wildly scratch and scrabble,
Knocking over his pen;
A few such crimes, but then
Has nature ever yet
Made anything perfect?
Beauty that has no small
Blemish in it at all?

    At meals he did not eat
Much in the way of meat,
But much preferred to wait
While many a dainty crumb
Softened by finger and thumb
Came from his master's plate;
And right up to his death
He always had sweet breath.

    What fun it was to watch
The little fellow scratch,
His silly head shaking
And making his bell ring;
What fun when Peloton
Along a pole would run,
Or sit up in a white
Cloth cap, just like a monkey,
Holding himself upright
Like a squireling of the gentry!

    Oh, I can see him now,
On two legs, with firm brow
And shouldered pike, march by,
Stepping so soldierly;
Or, when upon his spine,
He'd lie, and with quaint mien,
Pretend that he was dead;
Or suddenly run, and bowl
Head over heels, and roll
Along, a ball indeed!

    In short, my Peloton
Was such a lamb, no one
Could find another creature
Of so benign a nature.

    But Death was envious
Of our brief happiness,

My joy was cruelly
Taken away from me;
Poor Peloton had to go
Away to old Pluto,
And roam the shadowy plain
Whence none returns again.
My curses on the dread
Sisters who spin the thread
Of fate, thus enviously
To take my dog from me.
They sent him down below
To live with old Pluto
Though he deserved translation
To a new constellation,
The Dog-Star tempering
With his perpetual spring.

Epitaph on a Pet Cat

Formal Spring
John O'London's Weekly 1937
John O'London's Anthology 1938
Dublin Magazine 1940
Mona Gooden: *The Poet's Cat*
(Harrap 1946)
Marmaduke Skidmore: *The Triumphant Cat*
(Robinson Publishing 1993)

My life seems dull and flat,
And, as you'll wonder what,
Magny, has made this so,
I want you first to know
It's not for rings or purse
But something so much worse:
Three days ago I lost
All that I value most,
My treasure, my delight;
I cannot speak, or write,
Or even think of what
Belaud, my small grey cat
Meant to me, tiny creature,
Masterpiece of nature
In the whole world of cats—
And certain death to rats!—
Whose beauty was worthy
Of immortality.

Belaud, first let me say,
Was not entirely grey
Like cats bred here at home,
But more like those in Rome,
His fur being silver-grey
And fine and smooth as satin,
While, lying back, he'd display
A white expanse of ermine.

Small muzzle, tiny teeth;
Eyes of a tempered warmth,
Whose pupils of dark-green
Showed every colour seen
In the bow which splendidly
Arches the rainy sky.

Plump neck, short ears, height
To his head proportionate;
Beneath his ebony nostrils
His little leonine muzzle's
Prim beauty, which appeared
Fringed by the silvery beard
Which gave such waggish grace
To his young dandy's face.

His slender leg, small foot—
No lambswool scarf could be
More soft, except when he
Unsheathed and scratched with it!
His neat and downy throat,
Long monkey's tail, and coat
Diversely flecked and freckled
In natural motley speckled;
His flank and round stomach
Under control, his back
Of medium length—you see
A mouser, obviously!

This was Belaud, a gentle
Animal, whose title
To beauty was so sure
He'd no competitor!
A sad and bitter cross!
Irreparable loss!
It almost seems to me
That Death, though he must be
More ruthless than a bear,
Would if he'd known my rare
Belaud have felt his heart
Soften—and for my part
I would not wince and shrink
So from life's joys, I think.

Joachim du Bellay

But Death has never watched
Him as he jumped, or scratched,
Laughed at his nimble tricks,
His many wild frolics,
Admired the sprightly grace
With which he'd turn, or race,
Or, with one whirl of cat,
Tumble, or seize a rat
And play with it—and then
Would make me laugh again
By rubbing at his jaw
With such a frisky paw
And such a dashing manner!—
Or when the little monster
Leapt quietly on my bed,
Or when he took his bread
Or meat most daintily
Straight from my lips—for he
Showed in such various ways
His quaint engaging traits!

What fun to watch him dance,
Scamper, and skate, and prance
After a ball of thread;
To see his silly head
Whirl like a spinning-wheel
After his velvet tail;
Or, when he made of it
A girdle, and would sit
Solemnly on the ground
Showing his fluffy round
Of paunch, seeming to be
Learned in theology,
The spit of some well-known
Doctor at the Sorbonne!
And how, when he was teased,
He used to fence with us—
Yet if we stopped to fuss
Was very soon appeased!

O Magny, now you see
How he diverted me,
You'll realize why I mourn—
And surely no cat born
Has ever had so nice
A style with rats and mice!

He would come unawares
Upon them in their lairs,
And not one could escape
Unless he'd thought to scrape
A second hole—no rat
Ever outran that cat!
And let me add at once
My Belaud was no dunce,
But very teachable,
Knowing how to eat at table—
When offered food, that is:
That eager paw you'd see
Held out so flirtingly
Might scratch you otherwise!

Belaud was well-behaved
And in no way depraved;
His only ravages
Were on an ancient cheese,
A finch and a young linnet,
Whose trillings seemed to get
On Belaud's nerves—but then
How perfect are we men?

He wasn't the sort to be
Out everlastingly
After more food to eat,
But was content to wait
Until his meals, when he
Ate without gluttony.

And he would never spread
His traces far and wide
Like many cats, who do
Havoc wherever they go.
If Belaud, dear creature,
Fell short in any feature
Of sheer propriety,
He had the modesty
To cover under cinder
What he was forced to render.

He was my favourite plaything;
And not for ever purring
A long and tunelessly
Grumbling litany,
But kept in his complainings
To kitten-like miaowings.

My only memory
Of him annoying me
Is that, sometimes at night
When rats began to gnaw
And rustle in my straw
Mattress, he'd waken me
Seizing most dextrously
Upon them in their flight.

Now that the cruel right hand
Of death comes to demand
My body-guard from me,
My sweet security
Gives way to hideous fears:
Rats come and gnaw my ears,
And mice and rats at night
Chew up the lines I write!

The gods have sympathy
For poor humanity;
An animal's death foretells
Some evil that befalls,
For heaven can speak by these
And other presages.

The day fate cruelly
Took my small dog from me—
My Peloton—the sense
Of evil influence
Filled me with utter dread;
And then I lost my cat:
What crueller storm than that
Could break upon my head?

He was my very dear
Companion everywhere,
My room, my bed, my table,
Even more companionable
Than a little dog: for he
Was never one of those
Monsters that hideously
Fill night with their miaows;
And now he can't become,
Poor little puss, a tom—
Sad loss, by which his splendid
Line is abruptly ended.

God grant to me, Belaud,
Command of speech to show
Your gentle nature forth
In words of fitting worth,
Your qualities to state
In verse as delicate,
That you may live while cats
Wage mortal war on rats.

Joachim du Bellay

Sonnet

Newcomer, you who look in Rome for Rome
And not a sign of Rome in Rome can see,
These palaces, this ruined masonry
Of wall and arch still bear the name of Rome:

But what huge pride and what a fall! Her fame,
Her laws once held the world in sovereignty;
Seeking to conquer all, she bent the knee,
And now time has consumed all but her name.

This Rome is but Rome's monument and tomb,
All-conquering Rome has only conquered Rome.
The Tiber, ever-moving towards the sea,

Is all that stands of Rome—O fickle world,
Where firm, enduring things to ruin are hurled
And passing things resist eternally!

Formal Spring

Sonnet

He who would like to see what art and nature
And heaven can achieve should visit Rome,
That is, if he knows how to guess the sum
Of greatness from his glimpse of a dead picture.

Rome is no more; and if her architecture
Can throw before us shadows of old Rome
It is as if some corpse should leave his tomb
And walk at night by a magician's order.

The bones of Rome in dust and ashes fall;
The soul of Rome has gone to make its home
With the great spirit of this earthly ball;

Formal Spring

239

But her great writings, snatching from the tomb,
Despite of time, the praise of her past worth,
Have sent her image wandering through the earth.

Sonnet

I hate the money-lending avarice
Of Florentines, the violent Siennese,
The very rarely truthful Genoese,
The sly Venetian's subtle artifice,

The Neapolitan's vanity, some vice
That I've forgotten in the Ferrarese;
I hate all Lombards and their treacheries,
The cowardly Roman's unpreparedness;

I hate the surly Englishman, swaggering Scot,
The talkative Frenchman, false Burgundian,
The arrogant Spaniard and the German sot;

I hate some vice or other in every nation,
And in myself a hundred vices find—
But none I hate like a pedantic mind.

Sonnet

Happy as Ulysses, his voyage done,
Or he who went to get the Golden Fleece,
The traveller who returns to live in peace
In his own place, rich in experience grown!

When shall I see my village, and my own
Fireside with warm smoke rising, find my ease
Within my own small house, on lands that please
Me better than a province or a throne?

Better the walls of my ancestral home
Than the proud-fronted palaces of Rome,
Fine slate than all their glittering marble too;

For me, French Loire surpasses Tiber still,
Better my Lyré than the Palatine Hill,
Than ocean winds the soft air of Anjou.

Formal Spring
Modern Languages 1938

To you, light throng,
On aery wing,
Through the world blowing;
The shady verdure
To whispering murmur
Stirred by your going:

I offer roses,
Lilies, and posies
Of violets to you,
The little red roses
This moment uncloses,
And these new pinks too.

With your sweet breath blow
Across this plain now;
Fan cool, I pray,
This place where I sweat
As I winnow my wheat
In the heat of the day.

LOUISE LABÉ

(1526–66) *'La Belle Cordière' of Lyons, comes fittingly at the end of a period Christine de Pisan all but began. She has been called the greatest woman poet since Sappho, and indeed both her life and achievement incite to extravagance. Strikingly beautiful, an expert rider and fencer, she is said to have worn armour and fought as a man—le Capitaine Loys—at the siege of Perpignan. She was a leader, with Maurice Scève, of the Lyons school at a time when Italy, Germany, Switzerland and France met at Lyons, and literature flourished on a basis of industrial wealth outside the limiting influence of the Sorbonne in Paris and the Inquisition in Toulouse. Her love-poems have a fire and subtlety that mark her out, with Ronsard and du Bellay, as belonging to the end of this formal era. In France, owing to Malherbe and the French Academy, the succeeding era was formal, too; it was in England that the first free flowering of Post-Renaissance poetry took place.*

From 'Elegy'

Time makes an ending of the Pyramids,
Time dries up the fountains in their beds,
On splendid Coliseums has no pity,
And makes an ending of our dearest city;
It has a way of ending, in their turn,
Our fires of love, however well they burn;

Formal Spring

But these in my case grow more violent
As time goes by, and cause me more torment.
Although the love of Paris was so strong,
Oenone did not keep it very long;
Medea, loved so short a while before,
Was turned away by Jason from his door.
These loved their loves so well they surely proved
That they deserved in their turn to be loved;
And if by those loved love is so neglected
Then those who are *not* loved might be expected
To tire of love, and you, love, should allow
The pains I suffer to be ended now.
Do not, I beg you, make me try to prove
That even death is kindlier than love;
And if you wish me to love steadfastly
See that the one who means the world to me,
With power to make me laugh and make me cry
And at all hours of the day to sigh;
Feels in his very soul, his blood, his bone,
A love at least the equal of my own.
I'd bear my burden far more easily
With someone else to share its weight with me.

Sonnet

As soon as I begin to overtake
On my soft bed the sleep I'm longing for,
I seem to feel my lonely soul withdraw
And without waiting for your presence make;

And then, at last, my aching arms can take
And hold, it seems, the joy I've waited for,
That I have sighed so long and deeply for,
And sobbed for till I thought my heart would break.

O gentle sleep, most happy, happy night,
Delightful rest, full of tranquillity,
May I, night after night, know this illusion;

And if for ever you withhold delight,
Never allow me the reality,
At least may I preserve this dear delusion.

JACQUES LE MOYNE DE MORGUES

(c. 1533–88) Le Moyne was a native of Dieppe. The first thirty years of his life are entirely undocumented, but it is probable that he received his artistic training locally, for Dieppe was a renowned centre for fine cartography and illumination. In 1564 he was commissioned to accompany a Huguenot expedition to Florida in order to carry out essential mapping duties and to make a graphic record of all he saw, notably the native Indians and the flora. In September 1565, the strongpoint established by the French, called Fort Caroline (near present-day Jacksonville), was attacked by the Spaniards, and most of the colonists were massacred. Le Moyne was one of the few who escaped, returning to France after enduring great privations. He later wrote his own account of the French expedition, and some of his illustrations of Indian life were posthumously published by Theodor de Bry in 1591.

Le Moyne, a Huguenot, finally settled in England 'for religion', probably around 1580. In London his most important patron was Sir Walter Raleigh, and he also knew the artist John White (fl.' 1585-93), who was to accompany Raleigh's 1585 expedition to Virginia.

Both before and after the expedition to Florida, Le Moyne seems to have been occupied in making studies of plants. The watercolours illustrated in this diary must have been painted within about three years of his death, since the prefatory sonnet bears his name and the date 1585. They are mostly familiar garden flowers and fruits, studied with a delicacy and distinction remarkable for the period. In 1586 Le Moyne published a series of woodcuts of plants (many of which were simplified versions of the watercolours now in the British Museum) and animals, dedicated to his patroness Lady Mary Sidney. Part bestiary, part florilegium—the earliest printed work of this kind to be produced in England—La Clef des Champs was intended as a pattern book for the embroiderer, jeweller or painter, and was Le Moyne's last traceable work.

Sonnet

Discordant harmony and balanced movement,
Winter and Summer, Autumn, reborn Spring,
Renewing her sweet scents and colouring,
Join in the praise of God's unfailing judgment.

This loving God gives every argument
To look for zeal from each created thing,
O bless His Name eternally and sing
All He has made in earth and firmament.

Above all He made man with head held high
To watch each morning as new light arrives
And decorates earth's breast with varied flowers

There is no fruit, or grain, or grub, or fly
That does not preach one God, the least flower gives
Pledge of a Spring with everlasting colours.

Paul Hulton:
The Work of Jacques Le Moyne de Morgues
(British Museum 1977)

Sonnet

Though pale and nervous, threatened by my fear,
Though in my breast my heart beats painfully,
I'm not quite stripped of hope: tongue-tied and shy,
I find a new importunate boldness here.

Down then, my knee, eyes lowered. Kneeling there
Upheld by confidence, beneath your eye,
Trembling with happiness, I hopefully
Offer my Book, the humble gift I bear.

My Lady, I have banished fear and shame
To offer now to your exalted Name
My love, my humble duty, my vocation;

And since your Virtue, holy ornament,
Lifts you from earth to scale the firmament,
I pray that you accept this dedication.

MARIE STUART

(1542–87) The career and tragic death of Mary Queen of Scots are too well known to require comment. These lines, said to have been written when she left behind the familiar, civilized life of her adopted France for the inhospitable kingdom of Scotland, have also been attributed to an eighteenth-century journalist, but there is no final reason to suppose that she could not have written them, as she is known to have been the author of the 'triste et doux chant' on the death of her husband, Francis II. She was Queen of France from 1559 to 1560, and was not yet 19 when she made the five-day voyage from Calais to Leith in August 1561.

Farewell to France

Lines attributed to Mary Stuart,
and said to have been written on board the ship
which took her to Scotland

Formal Spring
Independent 1936

Good-bye to pleasant France,
    To my own land,
    Beloved land,
My childhood's land, my France;
Good-bye to my best days!
The ship which parts our ways
Leaves half of me behind,
Half of my love to be
Your own, and call to mind
The half which comes with me.

French & Spanish Romantic & Nineteenth Century Poems

in translation

LOPE DE VEGA 1562–1635

Little Song of the Virgin

As you sweep over, *New English Weekly 1937*
Good Angels, keep
From rustling the fronds;
My baby's asleep!

Palm-trees of Bethlehem
That the winds beat
Angrily, noisily,
Please, I entreat,
Do not disturb him;
Move softly, and keep
From rustling the fronds;
My baby's asleep!

The heavenly child
Is tired of crying
Down here on earth
And longs to be lying
Asleep in my arms,
So, Angels, please keep
From rustling the fronds;
My baby's asleep!

The cruel ice and snow
Around him so deep,
And there's no way I know
Of guarding his sleep;
So, as you fly over,
Good Angels, keep
From rustling the fronds;
My baby's asleep!

The Horn

I

I love the sound of the horn at the end of day
As it sings in the depths of the woods; of hounds at bay,
Or the faint farewells of huntsmen, echoing brief,
And blown by the cold north wind from leaf to leaf.

How often, alone in the dark while others slept,
I've smiled to hear it—but more often wept
To think that these were the sounds that once foretold
The approach of death to paladins of old.

Mountains of azure, region that I love,
Crags of Erazona, Marboré ringed above,
Cascades that fall from Pyrenean snow
Where fountains, streams and furious torrents flow,

Mountains that throne two seasons, Winter, Spring;
Ice for your crown, your foothills flowering—
There on your grassy slopes I sit and ponder
The far-off sound of the horn, so sad and tender.

Often a traveller, when the air is quiet,
Will make the night reverberate with this riot
Of brazen sounds, whose singing cadence swells
The harmony of bleatings and lambs' bells.

A hind, instead of hiding, stays to hear,
High on a crag, unmoving, poised there,
While the huge cataract, in leap headlong,
Blends its eternal dirge with this brief song.

Spirits of long-dead knights, do you return?
And are you speaking in the voice of this horn?
O Ronçeval, has not great Roland's ghost
In your dark valley found his peace at last?

II

His knights lay dead, for none had run away.
He alone stood—Oliver near him lay.
The Africans surround him, nervous still;
'Yield, Roland.' cried the Moor, 'or we kill!'

'Your knights are lying dead in the mountain streams!'
Roland roared back, like a tiger: 'No man tames
Me, African, until the Pyrenees
Roll down their streams and corpses to my knees!'

'Then, here they come!" the Moor replied, "So yield!'
And from the highest peak a boulder rolled.
It bounded and then rolled down the ravine,
The pine-tops by the water snapped off clean.

'Thank you,' called Roland, 'you have cut a route!'
He rolled the boulder to the mountain's foot,
Sprang like a giant upon it. At this sight
The Moors wavered on the edge of flight.

III
Charlemagne and his knights ride easily
Down from the mountains, talking cheerfully;
Before them now the far horizon gleams,
With Argelès and Luz marked out by streams.

The soldiers start to cheer. The troubadour
Sings of the willows down by the Adour;
The wines of France the foreign goblets bless;
The laughing soldier chaffs the shepherdess.

Roland guards the mountains at their back.
Archbishop Turpin calmly sits his black
Palfrey caparisoned in violet.
Then speaks—his fingers on his amulet.

'Sire, those flaming clouds are signs of danger!
Hold up your march. We must not tempt God's anger!
The souls of men, by great St. Denis's name,
Are passing through the air on wings of flame!

'Two flashes. And two more. The skies are torn!'
And now, far off, they hear the sound of the horn
The astonished Charlemagne jerks back in fear,
Checking his mettlesome steed in mid-career.

'Did you hear that?'—'Yes, shepherds on some rise
Calling their scattered flocks.' Turpin replies:
'Or even, perhaps, the green dwarf Oberon
Calling his fairy queen in muted tone!'

Alfred de Vigny

247

The Emporor rides on, his anxious brow
As dark and terrible as a stormcloud now.
'Treason!' he thinks, and lets his wild thoughts run;
The horn sounds briefly, dies, and then sounds on.

'Alas, my nephew Roland's latest breath!
He'd only call if on the point of death!
Back, knights, across the mountains! Treacherous Spain
Must shake beneath our horses' hooves again!

The horses paused on a high mountain's brow,
Foam-flecked, with Ronçeval beneath them now
Just coloured by the dying fires of day—
The Moor's standard flying far away.

'Turpin, what do you see in the torrent lying?'

'I see two knights, one dead, the other dying;
By one black rock they both lie crushed and torn.
The stronger still holds up an ivory horn.
His spirit called us twice as it fled away!'

✧

How sad it sounds in the woods at the end of the day!

THÉOPHILE GAUTIER   1811–72

Symphony in White Major

Swanwomen of the ancient Rhine
Out of old Northern legends wing;
With white necks curved in graceful line,
They swim inshore and, swimming, sing:

Or, hanging on some branch the light
Garment of plumage they put on,
Make their white skins shine more white
Than the snow of their swansdown.

One of them at times flies down
Among us, close before our eyes,
White as a gleam of moonlight on
A glacier beneath cold skies;

Inviting the inebriate whirl
In eyes that face her boreal freshness
To banquetings of flesh-of-pearl,
Debaucheries of utter whiteness'

Her breasts, snow moulded into globes,
Rise in white insolence to fight
The satin whiteness of her robes
And her camellias' floral white.

These fierce white engagements rage
Till flowers and silks, which cannot be
Hopeful of victory or revenge,
Turn yellow out of jealousy.

Upon her sculptured shoulders, white
As glossy-textured Parian stone,
As in a brilliant polar night
Invisibly the frost comes down.

Out of what mica heart of snow,
What white-pulped centre of a reed,
What host, what taper's waxen glow,
Was the white of her skin made?

Did they pick out the milky drop
That clouds the blue of winter skies,
The lily's silver-tinted pulp,
Or the white foam of the seas;

Alabaster, the cold, pale
Flesh of gods and goddesses;
Dulled silver, or the milky opal
Bestreaked with blue of irises;

Ivory, where her white hands hover
Above the keyboard, butterflies
Letting their fluttering kisses cover
The delicate notes that fall and rise;

Ermine, unsoiled, virgin-clear,
Which, to lessen shiverings,
Softly pads, with fleecy fur,
Their shoulders and emblazonings;

Quicksilver of fantastic flowers
Like those that stained-glass windows wear,
White lace of fountain-bowls, the tears
Of undines in the frozen air;

The hawthorn branch in May that bends
Beneath the white frost of its flowers;
Marble, where Melancholy finds
Renewal of her longed-for pallors;

Upon some manor roof the white
Snowfall from the breasts of doves;
Or the falling stalactite,
The white tear of the winter caves?

Did she come from Greenland's floes,
Or Norway's, with the Seraphita?
Is she Madonna of the Snows,
Or the white Sphinx carved by winter,
Sphinx that an avalanche holds fast,
Guardian of glaciers, starry-bright,
Who, deep within her frozen breast
Holds icy secrets, frosted, white?

That heart, so calm beneath such snows,
Oh! who can rouse it to delight!
And who can bring a hint of rose
To that indomitable white!

Old China

It is not you on whom my heart is set,
Nor you, my gentle Juliet, that I prize,
Ophelia, nor Beatrice, nor yet
Blonde Laura with big appealing eyes.

She whom I love, now I'm in love again,
Lives with her aged parents in old China,
In a high tower of delicate porcelain,
With cormorants, beside the Yellow River.

Her slant eyes curve into a graceful up-turn;
Her small foot fits into my hand; her skin
Shines like the burnish of a copper lantern;
Her nails are long and reddened with carmine.

She looks out through her lattice at close wings
Her forehead lightly touched by the passing swallow,
And every evening, like a poet, sings
Of frail peach-blossom and the weeping willow.

Théophile Gautier

Noël

The earth is white, the sky is black.
Ring out, O gay carillion!
Jesus is born. The Virgin bends
Her lovely face towards her son.

No curtains to festoon him round
And guard from cold his infant dreams,
Only the dusty spider-webs
That hang down from the rafter-beams.

The dear little infant Christ
Shivers upon the straw, new-spread;
The ox and ass, to keep him warm,
Breathe round about his manger-bed.

The snow hangs fringes from the wall.
The heavens open—scriptures tell—
And, clothed in white, the angel choirs
To shepherds sing Noël! Noël!

JOSE ZORRILLA

1817–93

Bull and Picador

Rasping and panting, with hot, scalding breath
That steams upon and moistens the baked sand,
The bull looks at the horseman with his bland
And lofty gaze, and peers for the red cloth;

New English Weekly 1946

The picador, impatience pricked to wrath,
His dark face pale and set, and in his tanned
Forehead a strong vein working, takes his stand,
Braced for the violent impetus of death.

251

The wild beast hesitates. The Spaniard calls.
The huge bull stands and tosses his horned head
Then snorting, scours the ground, blows sand about;
Starts suddenly forward as the man compels;
Then bellowing, flees, while from his neck the red
Blood bursts, and from the crowd an immense shout.

CHARLES BAUDELAIRE   1812–67

A Voyage to Cytherea

As free as a bird, my heart took off in flight;
Happy among high cordages it flew;
The rolling ship, beneath a sky of blue,
An angel tipsy in the brilliant light.

And that dark island?—That is Cytherea,
They tell us, famed in song, its banal shores
The El Dorado of old bachelors—
And, when you come to it; so poor and bare.

—Island of troths and secret promises,
The splendid ghost of Aphrodite hovers
Over it like a perfume, filling lovers
With warm desires and languorous fantasies.

A lovely island of myrtles bright with flowers,
Revered through time by men of every nation,
Where the long sighs of lovers' adoration
Roll like rich incense over rosy bowers,

Or like a turtle-dove's unending coo!
—This Cytherea was a desert land,
Where harsh cries echoed on a stony strand,
And an unthinkable object met the view.

This was no temple under shady trees,
Where a young votaress, in love with flowers,
Might walk, her body warmed with secret fires,
Her robe half-open to the passing breeze;

But, as we hugged the shore-line, passing by
So close that our white sails disturbed the birds,
We saw it was a gibbet with three yards,
Black as a cypress seen against the sky.

252

Charles Baudelaire

Ferocious birds, that perch upon their prey,
Tear at a hanging body in their rage,
Thrusting in beaks like instruments to gouge
His blood-clot cavities of foul decay.

His eyes two holes; and from the caved-in frame
The entrails floated over thighs and knees;
His torturers, gorged on hideous delicacies,
With beaks like daggers had castrated him.

Below the dangling feet, with upturned jaws
Four-footed creatures roughly crammed and swirled;
A larger beast among the others prowled—
A hangman with his under-officers.

Native of Cytherea, of skies so blue,
You've borne in silence these indignities
To expiate the infamous practices
And blasphemies that closed the tomb to you.

Poor hanging fool, your sufferings were my own,
I saw you hang so helplessly in death,
And tasted, in the vomit round my teeth,
The drawn-out flow of agonies I'd known.

In watching you, poor devil, I've felt afresh.
Dear memory, all those tearing beaks and claws
Of carrion crows, the eager crunch of jaws
Of those black panthers revelling in my flesh.

—The sky so exquisite, so calm the sea,
Yet all I saw was dark and steeped in blood;
My heart since then, as in a heavy shroud,
Is buried for ever in this allegory.

Upon your island, Aphrodite, just
One thing is standing, a symbolic gibbet,
With my own heart and body stretched upon it:
—Lord, strengthen me to see it without disgust.

Mad Boat

After 'Bâteau Ivre'
Tiresias

As I was carried down impassive Rivers
I missed my haulers' guidance through the shoals;
They were a mark for yelling Redskins' quivers,
Nailed up stark naked to their gaudy poles.

I ceased to care if I held English cotton
Or Flemish wheat, or where my crew had gone;
My haulers and their uproar were forgotten;
The Rivers let me travel freely on.

That winter, through the waters' furious whirlings
Deaf as a baby's brain, ecstatically,
I raced! Peninsulas torn from their moorings
Have never known such glorious anarchy.

The tempests blessed my wakenings at sea.
Light as a cork, for ten nights did I dance
O'er waves that roll their dead on endlessly,
And never looked for a lantern's vacant glance.

Green water, sweet as flesh of unripe apples
In children's mouths, poured through my hull of pine,
Bearing away the rudder-lines and grapples,
Washing out stains of retchings and spilt wine.

And, after that, I floated in the poem
Of seas reflecting stars and milky grown,
Driving through azure-green, where, livid flotsam,
Thoughtful and rapt, a drowned man may sway down,

Where, suddenly staining bluishnesses, slow
Rhythms and frenzies fierce beneath day's fires,
Red tints of bitter love seethe up and show
More flame than alcohol, more range than lyres.

I know skies torn by lightning; sea that heaves
Up waterspouts, surf, currents; evening; dawn
Uprisen like a multitude of doves;
And things that men have only dimly known.

Seen the low sun, with mystic horrors flecked,
Illumine with long, violet curdlings,
Like actors in old plays with wine-lees streaked,
Waves rolling far their shutter-flickerings.

I have dreamed on emerald nights of dazzling snow,
Long kisses mounting to the eyes of seas,
Unheard-of springs of sap, the singing glow
Of blue and yellow phosphorescences.

For months on end have watched the long swell beat,
Wild as stampeded cattle, on the rock;
Not dreaming that the Virgins' shining feet
Could hold the monstrous panting seas in check.

In unthought Floridas have seen the glow
Of panthers' eyes among the flower-stems,
Men's skins, and rainbows stretched like reins below
The sea's horizon to its glaucous teams.

I have seen the marshes boil, giant traps where forms
Of dead Leviathans rot among the rushes;
The curve and fall of breakers in dead calms,
The distances that cataract down abysses;

Glaciers; silver suns; pearled seas; burnt skies;
In deep brown gulfs the hideous wreckages
Of giant serpents eaten through by lice
That fall among black odours from warped trees.

Children would love the dolphins, golden fishes,
And singing fishes of those halcyon
Blue seas, where foaming flowers were sailing-wishes,
And airs ineffable would wing me on.

Sometimes, a martyr tired of poles and zones,
The sea, whose gentle sobs rocked me at ease,
Would raise up shadowy flowers with yellow cones;
I'd stay there, like a woman on her knees.

A loud peninsula on my decks tossing
Droppings of clamorous, white-eyed birds; then keep
To my free course again, my frail ropes passing
By drowned men moving backwards down to sleep.

So I, boat lost in some luxuriant creek,
Hurricane-flung into the birdless ether,
Whose sodden carcass none would stop to take,
Warship or Hansa schooner, from the water,

Loose, steaming, hung with mists of violet,
I, who once pierced the sky, a reddening wall,
On which, exquisite jam for a good poet,
Blue clots of mould and sunny lichens sprawl,

Who ran, mad plank, with flickering lights aglow,
Escorted by black hippocamps through the foam,
When the Julys, with sudden cudgel-blow,
Shattered the bright-blue heavens' blazing dome,

Who shuddered, feeling fifty miles from me,
In groaning rut Maelstroms and Behemoths,
Roving through moveless blue unendingly,
I long for Europe's ancient parapets.

I have seen star-archipelagos and isles
Of whose delirious skies a ship is free;
Is it in these deep nights you sleep as exiles,
O million golden birds, Life Energy?

But I have wept too much. All dawns are bitter,
All moons a horror, and suns cruelty.
Harsh love has swelled me out with drunken torpor;
Break free, my keel, now! Let me put to sea !

If I wish for a water in Europe, it's the dull
Cold pool, by which a child kneels miserably
In scented twilight, and lets go his small
Boat that's as frail as a May butterfly.

I can no longer, bathed in the waves' languors,
Sail in the wake of cotton merchandise,
Or brave the pride of flags and warlike angers,
Or float beneath a pier's horrible eyes.

The Sleeper in the Valley　　　　　　　　　　　　　　　*Arthur Rimbaud*

John O'London's Weekly 1938

A leafy hollow where a stream sings loud,
Hanging with silver tatters in its flight
The grasses, sun-lit from the mountain proud,
A little valley bubbling with light.

A soldier, young, with open mouth, bare-browed,
Bathing his nape in the blue cress, asleep,
Stretched out upon the grass, beneath a cloud,
Pale on his bed of green where sunbeams weep.

Smiling a sick child's smile, he takes his nap,
His feet among the sword-grass; in your lap,
Cradle him warmly, Nature, he is cold.

Scents in his nostrils waken no unrest;
He sleeps there in the sun, hand on his chest,
Quite calm, his side by two red bullets holed.

Tramp

I wandered, hands in my torn pockets thrust,
My thin coat losing all reality,
But, Muse, with you for friend beneath the sky,
What splendid loves I conjured from the dust.

A hole in my one pair of trousers, I,
Tom Thumb the dreamer, plucked rhymes by the way;
My inn was the Great Bear, and where I lay
Stars made a silken rustle in the sky.

I listened, sitting by the roads, on fine
September evenings, with the vivid smart
Of dew upon my forehead, like dry wine;

Or, rhyming while fantastic shadows grew,
Plucked at my torn elastic-sided shoe,
Held like a lyre, a foot against my heart.

The Hungry Children

Black against the fog and snow
In the lighted grating's glow,
   Small bottoms rounded,

Five little figures kneel and stare
At the baker baking bread down there,
   The blond loaves pounded,

The strong white arm that works the dough,
Heavy and grey, and hides it through
   The vivid door;

They hear the sizzle of baking bread;
The smiling baker nods his head
   To some old air.

Huddled together, and not a move,
In the breath of the rosy space they love,
   Warm as a breast;

And when the new bread's taken out,
Made in this crescent shape, no doubt,
   For a midnight feast;

When, underneath the smoky beams,
The fragrant crust sings as it steams
   To the crickets' buzz;

And such life breathes from that warm hole
As to transport each tiny soul
   Beneath his rags,

They feel so strong a sense of life,
These little creatures, frozen stiff,
   Only to be

Leaning against these bars and pressing
Their reddened muzzles there, and blessing
   All that they see

In song so quiet it's like a prayer;
They bend right down towards the glare,
   And heaven find.

Thin trousers rip as they stretch there,
And white rags flutter in the air
   Of the winter wind.

FRANCIS JAMMES

Il y avait des Carafes

Carafes of clear water were
Set out in the pastor's little garden
At the house that seems so austere,
And, on the cloth, large glasses where
Leaves on the shutters formed a pattern.

The month of June. And in the alley
A sliver of fishing rod was thrown,
Split like a reed. The day was cloudy
And overcast—we'd call it heavy
With great drops ready to fall down.

A dark, sad gap of window. Glossy
Laurels below. The notes of a piano.
The little panes so green. O surely
A place for being truly happy
As in those books of Rousseau, long ago.

Return to Vaaldorp

Impressions of a Return Journey to South Africa 1960

A verse drama in several voices,
broadcast by the BBC Home Service on
29 August 1961
and rendered into prose by Jack Cope (1970)
and Andrew Currey (1998)
Jack Cope *Seismograph* (Reiger 1970)
Contrast 21 6 (1), 1969

Arrival: Late Night/Early Morning

Vaaldorp. Yes, Vaaldorp. Too late last night to pick out landmarks. Why can't I sleep? I'll try opening the window.

Crickets. So many years in England, and I still find the night insipid without them. Brr — it's cold.

What are these iron lattices across the window? Ornamental, but still iron bars. Like jewellers' shop lattices. What are they here to protect? Gold life? Diamond chastity? Or are they to protect the stars from my smash-and-grab? Two Cullinan diamond pointers to the Southern Cross. Set in black velvet. Over corrugated iron. The homely provincial Southern Cross.

Too late last night to pick out landmarks. All the way up from Zululand in other people's dust. Road a red assegai pointing at the sun. Plumes of dust. Each car a running warrior of dust. Forty years of eroded dust. Distance. Altitude. Isolation. No recognizable landmarks. But our radius then was that of a horse and trap.

No landmarks till I saw the location. A rabble of shacks across the shallow valley. The African location. Now half surrounding Vaaldorp. Across the shadowy, reedy pale of the vlei. Fires in the grudging highveld twilight. The curving fires of a besieging army. Looking in on confident, electric Vaaldorp. Smooth, macadamized.

But without the gum-trees. Those graceful avenues of gum-trees gone. The whole perspective altered, even in the half-light. And nobody misses them. Nobody cares a damn. Stompie. Piet van der Merwe. The frightful Hennie. *Predikant* now, and Mayor, and Principal. Nobody misses them. Not even kind Miss Bland.

'He wants to know, Mr May-or, if we remember the blue-gums.'

'Ach, Miss Bland, it was my job, as may-or to have them down. They took the good from the soil.'

'They undermined the walls of my kerk.'

'Always I tell my pupils the blue-gums are Australian, not South African at all.'

How Miss Bland stared at me in the lighted doorway. My face a mask of ochre dust, super-imposed on the mask of forty years. Nice of her to give that party, though all I wanted was a bath and bed.

All the families I really knew have gone away. The Gibsons, the Duncans, the Petries, the Greys — a tartan of families, the flowers of the forest. Stompie, and Piet, and Hennie hold the field. *Predikant*, Mayor and Principal. Proud of their slick, remote suburbia. Why should they regret *my* Vaaldorp, my eucalyptus-scented Vaaldorp abandoned forty years ago.

'Vaaldorp is modernized since you was yere. We have fine macadam roads, man. Up-to-date buildings. New suburbs.'

'We have fine new school buildings.'

'I want you to see my new *kerk*.'

261

Return to Vaaldorp

'As May-or of Vaaldorp I'm proud to say that Vaaldorp has no slums.'

'No slums? But I came in tonight by the African location.'

Piet van der Merwe. 'The may-or', they call him. I still can't place him. Says he was in my year at school. Took my hand in a fist the size of a ham. A genial giant — till I mentioned the location.

The Old Manse

Sunshine and the coo of pigeons. Did we live on this eventful *erf* of ground for a century or under two years? The white catherine wheel of pigeons' wings. Th twinkling green-and-black spokes of the trap. Over there on a circular brick well-top under the highest of the fir-trees Theo and Betsy sat over their unending voluble meals. One day, from above, I threw down fir-cones and a lovely new term of abuse.

'Hlekabafazi! Hlekabafazi!'

Theo grabbed a branch, threatened to come up after me. Successive green cart-wheels of resiny spokes whirled me like a helicopter up, up, to the slim, swaying dark-green plume at the top. I looked down at the house, verandaed fore-and-aft like a parson's hat, and gloatingly added the height of the tree to the stone-plop depth of the well.

When I came down Betsy scolded me, then hugged me against her acrid smell.

The white wheel of pigeons' wings. The green-stencilled wings of Red-Eye, the Black Leghorn rooster. Over there by the stables Red-Eye stalked up and down behind the wire-netting, plotting to attack man, woman and child.

His red comb flopped over to one side. His eyes were bloodshot. When he attacked me first I was knocking a tent-peg into the ground. His spurs were ten feet long and his wings filled the sky. Scratched and screaming, I held out the mallet.

'That's right. Hold him off!'

The sole of a black clerical boot received the force of the next air-borne charge. A laced clerical instep took Red Eye under the breast-bone and lifted him backwards over the wire-netting into his pen. Why did we keep him? He attacked the family, the Petrie children who came to play with us through the gaping barbed-wire fence, the black boy fetching hymn books, the coloured boy stealing peaches — and who stuck most vulnerably in the fence. On this occasion Red-Eye was the sword of the Lord, the angel at the gate of the Garden of Eden.

We in the family learned to meet him with a twiggy branch, pushing him back until he tired. My father relied on his lifted leather sole — I think he enjoyed these substitute encounters with the Evil One.

The Vlei

This is the edge of the dorp. Here in the dust alongside the macadam strip of the road hundreds of bare Man-Friday footprints. Pointing in one direction. A river of footprints flowing across the vlei to the location beyond. Here on the barbed wire a butcher's shop. The butcherbird's board.

262

Flies. Beetles. A small snake. Spiked on the wire. Drying in the sun. Best quality biltong. He had to use a thorn-tree in the days before barbed-wire!

Here's a piece of *ouklip*. Old-stone, wrinkled and furrowed. Like a piece of prehistoric anthill. A large snake, a rinkhals, emerged from among the aloes. We threw lumps of *ouklip*, crushed in its head. We ran home to report.

'Mommy. Mommy. We've killed a big snake. A rinkhals!'

To my mother the only good snake was a dead snake. She lived in fear for us of snakes, scorpions, hail and lightning.

'If you have to tackle a snake a stick is safer, but be sure you bring it down flat against the ground.'

We took the dead rinkhals and spiked it on to the barbed wire — just as the butcherbird would. Why? it was the usual practice. Traitor's Gate? A warning to snakes not to be snakes?

'Now if ever you're bitten by a snake, are you sure you remember what to do?'

No-man's Land

From this point you can see the full curve round of the vlei. Willows vivid as poster-paints mark the line of the watercourses. A no-man's land between dorp and location. There's a *sakabula*! Long black plume of a tail. We believed you could run a *sakabula* down in a rainstorrn, catch it by its waterlogged tail. We never succeeded. Here are the brickfields. The birth-battered matrix of the town. Yellow clay-water like lentil soup drew us day after day in hot weather. The brick-fields were deep, unhygienic, utterly forbidden. Only when our parents found how long we'd been swimming there did they give up trying to stop us. We swam *kaalgat*, as the phrase went. A homely language, Afrikaans! No costume, no tell-tale towel. We rarely went on a Sunday, but one hot Sunday we did. Three of us. We lay relaxed in the sun, comparing physical changes. We were on the point of going in again when we heard a distant singing. Hallelujah! Again and again — Hallelujah!

A huge procession of Africans was moving towards us along the shallow reedy vlei from the direction of the location. As they came nearer we saw that they were led by a white parson in long robes and with a crozier in his hand. Women in long white robes followed immediately behind him, and then the ant-like crowd of worshippers. Every one of them singing Hallelujah.

The parson moved forward down the slope into the yellow muddy water of the brickfields. He moved with a dignity that included prudence, feeling the depth with the crozier that was staff as well as symbol. What were they doing? What were they going to do? My friends were as baffled as I was. When the parson was waist-deep he turned towards the now-silent congrega-tion. The women in white — black, shiny-faced young women — came down the slope and slithered and balanced out to him one by one.

'Baptists. American Baptists.'

My little sister. In the name of the Father, and of the Son — and of the Holy Ghost.

'He calls each one his sister. Did you hear that? He counts five for the Father, five for the Son, and *ten* for the Holy Ghost. D'you see them spluttering when they come up?'

The service over, they moved off in their wet robes back to the location, still singing. A great force, with a God not unlike our God, had taken over a place we thought of as our own. By tacit consent, we picked up our clothes and made for a smaller pool further up the vlei.

The Church

I suppose I've remembered this from other angles. Now the variant clicks into place. The tin-roofed church, the wooden framework that holds the bell — and beyond, the Edwardian bone-and-lace roof-line of the house, the functional straight ridge of the barn. Here's the bell. For a time it used to be my job to ring it. Half an hour before service, and then when service was ready to begin.

'Why can't Kleinbooi ring it?'

'I'm not going to have you growing up to rely on the labour of others.'

The rope's still coiled round the cleats in exactly the same way. Uncoil it? Pull?

The doors stand open. The sun shines in along the aisle. Town Clerk Fraser with his Afrikaans wife. Two little daughters. Mr Denis, General Stores. His wife, who sings. Miss Bland, her brother, her parents — the Gibsons, Petries, Duncans, Robinsons, Greys. Fanny Grey, an emanation of golden light among five blonde ordinary sisters. Rawden, at the Government farm, Croft the stationmaster. Poor gentle Spencer, with his large insubstantial shabby family, Randall the policeman, the lawyer, Du Toit. Wives. Sons. Daughters. Major Buxton, the mayor, who sometimes took the service.

'My text is from St Matthew, Chapter 6. For I am a man under authority. Will somebody take that damned dog out!'

The New Manse

There's still a quince hedge between the church and the house. One day we cut switches six feet long and used them in a clay battle. You could throw a gobbet of clay a hundred yards. Wheep! Wheep!

Ow! The battle stopped when someone was hit — it was unexpectedly painful. The crying victim was despised but the war ground down to a stop.

Yes, there's the house — Edwardian from the guttering upwards, the dainty, spiky, lacy line of the roof. The oaks are taller. The peach and the apricot trees are gone. And the little low strad-dling vine, with clusters of grapes like udders. You could sit under it out of sight and eat as many as you liked. And here opposite the quince hedge stood the windpump. The windmill, we called it. No doubt that went out when the reservoir was finished. The iron ladder cut the arches of your feet. It was terrifying up there on the narrow platform.

Stand on the ground, and watch it smoothly turning, slightly swaying with the wind. In a land without running water watch a windpump turning, watch wind run smoothly along the hard leaves of a tree, over its ever-changing folds of a flag. Hyponotic as running water ... And what a splendid clanking noise it made!

And then the reservoir's other casualty. The outside closet, with buckets emptied at night by men whose faces merged in darkness. It stood in humble isolation, half way between the house and the stables. I was marooned there once in a freak hailstorm. Hailstones big as glass marbles, some as big as pigeons' eggs, fell onto the corrugated iron roof. The noise was like that of the surf at Durban.

'If you're caught in a hailstorm when riding in the veld, take off the saddle and put it over your head. The horse will turn his back to the storm. Kneel down and draw him towards you by the reins.'

Family Pony

How the road's altered with the blue-gums gone. Here are two in somebody's garden. They *are* as tall as I remembered — tall and feathery against the sky. With round, smooth silver-barked trunks. Here's where Father — frock coat and parson's collar — ran out to tackle the runaway horse.

'Sit on his head. Sit on his head.'

He had the horse on the ground, but kept on shouting.

'Sit on his head.'

My regular job was catching and inspanning the family pony when my father had to meet or catch a train. The pony was allowed to graze — loosely knee-haltered — on the veld around the dorp. You unfastened the *riem* from his knee, looped it through his mouth and rode him home barebacked. My father always rang up to find what time the train had left the next station. He never expected it to make up time, so we often took the last half-mile to the station in a canter.

'Woa, there, woa ... Take him home slowly, mind. And don't forget to give him a good rub down.'

Father prided himself on 'knowing something about horses' and on 'bringing up boys to be useful'. One full moon I drove with him to a 'moonlight service' at a farm. We came to a wide spruit with a narrow railless bridge. I tried to pass him the reins. 'I'm leaving this to you. Give him his head and he'll take us over nicely.' My mother was curiously angry when I told her.

'Dad's always so sure he knows how to deal with horses. I sometimes think he bears a charmed life.'

Going to School

This is the way to the School. The Junior School. A mile and a half, but we didn't go in the trap. It wouldn't have been good for us! We soon picked up the Gibsons — the Petries were with us already. By the time we got to the spruit the numbers would begin to build up. Boys on one side of the road. Dawdling. Stripping bark off the gum trees, dragging satchels — we called them schoolbags — very aware of the girls on the side opposite. The girls, better behaved, but no less aware of us. I was constant in my awareness of Fanny Grey, but to cross the road and talk to her would have been taboo.

She's your *vryer*.

She's your *vryer*.

Circus

The lemonade factory was over there; it made a cheerful stamping noise like that of a roundabout at a fair. We used to buy the glass marbles out of the broken bottles from a man at the back door.

Yes, and here the circuses used to come.

'Five golden sovereigns — *vyf pond* — to the first man to sit for one minute on the bucking zebra.'

The ring was a bowl of electrified water. The zebra a coiled electric shock. Thick-haired young farmers, bandy-legged black boys, lined up to snatch and hold onto the living gold. As breeches made contact a sprawl met space. Again and again. Then one of our school-fellows, Piet van der Merwe, dug his knees for fifty seconds into the sizzling, sparkling dazzle of stripes.

Fifty seconds only, but the showman gave him the five pounds. Piet van der Merwe! Piet van der Merwe! His shirt was covered with Boy Scout badges. He was chosen to go to England, to the World Jamboree — a leopard-skin band about his Boy Scout hat. Instead he went riding in another direction.

'Ja, it's terrible man. Sannie du Toit in Standard Seven. He can't go now to the Jamboree. He'll have to marry her, man.'

The Voice of Vaaldorp

'This hotel? It used to be called *The Gum Tree*. A Middle-West establishment with wooden veranda and a rail to tie up horses. But I never saw cowboys, legs like parentheses, walk back-wards shooting each other in the road. And here was the bioscope. Was it arrogance or aspiration to call it the Coliseum? A narrow barn-like hall with a two-tier trestle at the back for boys. It creaked and swayed and threatened to collapse at a showing of *Tarzan of the Apes*.

Yes, and just opposite is the newspaper office. *Die Vaaldorper*. The *Voice of Vaaldorp*. Under the proud title, the proud motto: 'The pen is mightier than the sword'. I used to bring notices here for my father. They never failed to make mistakes. They never failed to arouse his wrath.

'Listen to this! Listen to this! "At the World Jamboree, the South African contingent of Boy Scouts will wear special hatbands of leper-skin!" Leper-skin, I ask you.'

Schools

The Junior School. The same Edwardian line of roof. This was Miss Bland's classroom. Or was this? How small they were — but so were the classes. I'd forgotten we sat in double desks. But not boy-and-girl. Girls on this side, nearest the courtyard. Boys on that, staring out at the veld. This, I am sure, was Mr van Niekerk's. He wore corsets and taught arithmetic. Stood upright by your desk and creaked. You had to get the sums right! Mr Uys, in the woodwork shed, over there. He walked up and down with his metal ruler.

'Put the mark on the face-side of the wood, if anyone marks the back-side, I'll mark his back-side.'

And this classroom. Pince-nez, spinsterish Miss Lowther.

'Ralph, why haven't you done your homework? What *were* you doing yesterday afternoon?'

What was I doing? We used to go home at half-past-one and turned up again next morning at a quarter-to-eight. Time and veld enough to forget the existence of school in. What was I doing? Walking. Riding. Swimming. Pouring melted lead into pumpkin stalks for catapult ammunition? Forcing screws into hard wood, carving it slowly into a peg-top, filing the screw down to a point? Then throwing it, spinning, to split another top in two? Playing leapfrog? Any one of ten varieties! Kennetjie? Knifey? Marbles? Reading the *Children's Newspaper* or the *Captain*, or yet another of the novels of Walter Scott?

'Please, Miss Lowther, I forgot.'

'Hold out your hand.'

It was a token action. I bore her no ill-will. It made very little difference to my work. The standards were not high. To leave you had to pass an exam in Standard Seven, or reach the age of sixteen. Many preferred to reach sixteen. I, at twelve, was regarded as '*slim*', as was the lovely fragile-looking Fanny Grey. When did I first start noting Fanny Grey? Always, across the classroom. Always across the road.

'We're doing a move to Jo'burg. Why don't you colonise my girl?'

I don't suppose he'd made any more progress than I had. On elaborate excuses we exchanged remarks—at birthday or Christmas parties, never at school. The taboo was too strong.

She's your *vryer*,

She's your *vryer!*

Fanny Grey—a focus for romantic fancies. Sexual curiosity: stories and rhymes and older boys' boastings. The two were only partly connected. Love was a mystery, subject to social sanctions. Just as fighting was. Fighting with bare fists. It started here – outside this window. They came up this slope. Pushing Piet van der Merwe before them.

'I challenge you. Bloody *rooinek*. I fight you after school!'

This was the first of a series of fights. Standard Seven English *versus* Standard Seven 'dutch'. In this plantation with bare fists after school. Few chose to fight. The herd chose for them. First the herd paired champions who gave the excitement and violence demanded. Then it amused them to pair the two parsons' sons — the youngest in each form.

'Ralph is fighting Stompie van Zyl. They don't want to fight. It'll be a washout.'

'Man, I remember it. We started cold but we satisfied honour. You blacked my eye and I blooded your nose.'

There's the Junior School.

Added to, but not much. Must have been quite up-to-date in those days.

This is new. The group of statuary over the main entrance to the school. Of course. The inevitable Voortrekker. Gaunt muscular figure. Close-set dedicated eyes. Jutting beard. Right hand pointed forwards with musket — to some imagined range of mountains. Left hand with finger on open Bible — held up for him by kneeling Bantu slave! It's open very near the beginning. The Old Testament. I can guess just where:

' ... out of the hand of the Egyptian and ... unto a good land and a large, unto a land flowing with milk and honey....'

With his Bible and his sword. The Cromwell myth has a lot to answer for!

Here's the school hall. The roof line's the same as I remember. No doubt we had prayers here — all I remember are the hymns: 'All things bright and beautiful'. But now –

'The Hall is the focus of our School Community. We are proud of our Christian National Education. We turn out pupils as patriotic South Africans. Not slaves of an outworn connection. South Africans.'

Now there are pictures round the walls of the school hall. Great moments of South African history. More Voortrekkers. Waggons in laager. Waggons on the Drakensberg at forty-five degrees. Great South Africans Jan van Riebeeck, Simon van der Stel. Piet Retief. Kruger. Malan. Strydom. Verwoerd. Not an English name anywhere.

'There's no English Medium any more in the Junior School. I am the last *English* English teacher there. When I'm gone there won't be one. There's not a single English South African on the staff of the High School.'

I spent a term or two at the high school as well. These *are* new buildings. Steel. Concrete. Glass.

'Our High School is a fine contemporary establishment. The sloping lecture-rooms are a new design. We can be sure that the books in the library are reliably chosen. They came from a central list approved by the Transvaal Department of Education.'

'In fact a model of what you now, I believe, call, Christian National Education.'

'It is a help to have guidance; but come and see our rugby pitches. There was nothing like this when you were here. Look how green they are — worthy of the great South African game of Rugby.'

'I always thought that William Webb Ellis, at Rugby in England — '

'Recent research has shown that ten years earlier, on the banks of the Modder River, a young Voortrekker –'

'Picked up a ball and ran with it, no doubt?'

'There's a book about it in the High School Library.'

When I hear the word Voortrekker, I want to reach for my gun. But they're more single-minded, quicker on the draw! Here it is, the old classroom block. Concrete veranda and corrugated roof. I remember a woman, Mrs De Wet — a voice like Clara Butt's — who taught us history here with histrionic skill.

'The British artillery rode up *with their guns thundering*. And the poor son of a Boer mother *lay weltering in his crimson blood*.'

It was a very rudimentary classroom — a crude stage for a performance like that. It seems to be used as a store-room now. For Boy Scouts?

'You won't see the Scout badge — the fleur-de-lys. Those are their symbols, waggon-wheels and yoke-skeys. Do you know what they call their Boy Scouts?'

'Not Voortrekkers?'

'Why not? The Predikant Mynheer Smith has waggon-wheels on his front gate. I think they look dreadful. His house is near the *Kerk*.'

Nagmaal

I must go back by the *Kerk*. In the main square. I remember the covered waggons camped round the *Kerk* at *Nagmaal* (quarterly communion) — how the whole place took on extra life! Black servants cooking at the camp fires. Heavy-bearded men and women in old-fashioned clothes in the streets, in the shops. Buying coffee, nails and bullets. Here's the *Kerk*. A new one. Contemporary Afrikaans clerical. A tall pencil spire. With all this space round it for cars. A part of confident electric Vaaldorp. Smooth macadamized but without the gum-trees. Those graceful avenues of gum-trees gone. No barefoot boys returning from the brickfields, carrying their boots by the laces, feeling the red dust between their toes. No dawdling in the two-miles colonnades. No stripping of the bark. No children's voices under the tinkling eucalyptus-scented trees, remembered from over forty years ago.

Conversation Outside the Kerk: *Early Morning*

A black servant scrubbing the church floor seen through open doors.

'He served my father when he was *Predikant* before me. He takes great pride in keeping the *Kerk* clean. There is nothing he likes better than to be on his knees in the House of God.'

'Is he allowed to pray?'

'You're joking, of course. Let me tell you about the Church. It's bare inside at present — as with your Scottish Presbyterian churches. I respect that tradition. Nevertheless, I am collecting money for a frieze — a bas-relief — commemorating the moments of history when God has helped the South African people.'

'You're not thinking, by any chance, of a frieze of waggons in laager? With scenes of the Voortrekkers leaving the Cape, crossing the mountains, fighting the savage Zulu and Matabele?'

'I am, as a matter of fact. How did you know? What have you arranged to do this morning?'

'Miss Bland is taking me out to see the Duncan Dam.'

'We now call it the Oosthuizen Dam. Duncan's assistant Oosthuizen did the main part of the work. Descended from the Voortrekker, Oosthuizen. As you are an old friend I don't mind admitting — between ourselves — that some features of our political problem are very worrying. You may not have noticed it, but the real problem of the future is the race problem — and here we have to stand together not only against the Bantu and Indians and Coloureds but against the unfair opinion of the rest of the world. I went north with the troops, and I've been to Holland as well as Scotland. I know the strength of that feeling. I know it is our duty at all times and in all places to build up a spirit of combined resistance — like that shown by our ancestors, the Voortrekkers.'

'You mean — a laager attitude of mind?'

'Our opponents laugh at the laager mentality — but it's the only possible answer. We are up against it, every bit as much as our ancestors were.'

'Do you hear singing?'

'Kaffirs in the location. The wind's blowing this way. This is the location smog, man. It's the fires they light before they come to work. It gets on my nerves. It's here at the same time every morning. The prevailing wind blows this way.

And every morning, like an army following a smoke barrage, the Bantu workers come streaming into the town. I say we should do without them. Learn to do without them altogether.'

Yes, here they come, behind the solid moving wall of the smog. Crossing the muddy, reedy vlei, in the rear of the *sakabula*-plumaged smog, in ten columns, each column dividing to advance up separate roads. Bare feet feeling the earth between their toes.

I thought when I came in last night that the location fires were like those of a besieging army.

'I assure you, my friend, that our western civilization is in danger. We must stand together now against the barbarian hordes. Come to the manse, and let me show you the plans for the frieze.'

Index of First Lines

Index of First Lines